DAUGHTERS
of
MAEVE

DAUGHTERS
of
MAEVE

50 Irish Women Who Changed the World

GINA SIGILLITO

CITADEL PRESS
Kensington Publishing Corp.
www.kensingtonbooks.com

CITADEL PRESS BOOKS are published by

Kensington Publishing Corp.
850 Third Avenue
New York, NY 10022

All Kensington titles, imprints, and distributed lines are available at special quantity discounts for bulk purchases for sales promotions, premiums, fund-raising, educational, or institutional use. Special book excerpts or customized printings can also be created to fit specific needs. For details, write or phone the office of the Kensington special sales manager: Kensington Publishing Corp., 850 Third Avenue, New York, NY 10022, attn: Special Sales Department; phone 1-800-221-2647.

CITADEL PRESS and the Citadel logo are Reg. U.S. Pat. & TM Off.

First printing: April 2007

10 9 8 7 6 5 4 3 2 1

Printed in the United States of America

Library of Congress Control Number: 2006935128

ISBN-13: 978-0-8065-2705-5
ISBN-10: 0-8065-2705-6

This book is dedicated to great Irish women everywhere,
especially my mother, Beverly Colombo,
and the incredible women of the Cavanaugh family,
Mary Beth, Mary Virginia, Claire Brennan,
Ann Bernadette, Lee Ann, and Ann B.

Contents

Introduction

In 1972, Reggie Maudling, a British member of Parliament (MP), was giving an impassioned speech on thirteen unarmed Irish protestors who had been shot the previous week in an earth-shattering event that would later be known as Bloody Sunday. He called the protestors "terrorists" and claimed that the soldiers had fired in self-defense. A petite, twenty-one-year-old woman in a miniskirt promptly walked across the chamber and slapped him hard across the face. Maudling, a senior MP, wavered for a second, raised his fist, and punched her, knocking her out cold—but her slap had more effect. The woman was Bernadette Devlin, the youngest member ever elected to the British parliament and the political leader who would go on to inspire millions across the world. It was the slap heard round the world and a defining moment for Irish people around everywhere. Irish women never take anything lying down again.

The Weeping Woman. Roisin Dubh (the Black Rose). Cathleen ni Houlihan. The Old Woman with the Harp. Mother Ireland. For the past several hundred years, Ireland has been almost exclusively described in feminine terms. And from the first century B.C. through Ireland's independence in 1922 to today, Irish women have fought on the battlefields, right alongside their male counterparts, led revolutions, fought for human rights, and written seminal works. When they began to cross the Atlantic to come to the United States in the nineteenth and twentieth centuries, their influence was just as strong. Women like Mother Jones led American coal miners to victory in unions all over the country, and leaders of the suffragette movement like Clara Dillon Darrow led American women to victory in the voting booth.

Ironically, the very women who helped to create the image of Mother Ireland and fought for her sovereignty—and would later change the face of the American landscape—have largely been written out of her history. Today, there are celebrations all over Ireland, the United States, and England to commemorate the heroes of the great dates in Irish history. The heroines are visibly absent. Most notably, *Mother Ireland*, the most famous and definitive documentary on Irish women ever produced, was banned because it included the voices of women who fought in revolutionary struggles. Books on Irish women are scarce and tend to be incredibly specific (the women of one certain date) and very difficult to find in the United States. And there are no books that celebrate the achievements of Irish and Irish American women in one volume. Even books that cover influential Irish and Irish American figures only include a handful of women. *The Daughters of Maeve: 50 Irish Women Who Changed the World* will serve to correct this omission and will finally give the Irish women the recognition they deserve.

I first conceived of writing this book when I began to give lectures on Irish women in history at a variety of venues in New York City almost ten years ago. I discovered that I could not find any books to help me in mainstream bookstores, and I had to special order any books on the topics I was discussing directly from Ireland through a specialty bookstore in New York. Today, that bookstore is long gone and I have found that the only way to obtain many of these books now is by traveling overseas. While I want this book to be a celebration of women throughout Irish and U.S. history, I also believe it will be an invaluable, much-needed tool for students, lecturers, professors, and writers who have a passion for the subject and have found it impossible to find the information they need.

While this book will obviously appeal to Irish Americans, it is much larger than that. Anyone fascinated by military history, social movements, U.S. history, great literature, politics, art, and women's studies will find this book invaluable. For example, while a majority of Americans have heard of Mother Jones (largely through the magazine), very few know anything about her life, much less that she was Irish born. Even fewer readers will know that Jackie Kennedy's Irish roots rivaled her husband's and that she was asked to downplay them—by her own father-in-law, Joseph P. Kennedy. Our right to vote was fought for and won by several brave Irish American women, but we rarely acknowledge them. And most of us can't even name them. This will not be the case after reading this book. And by exploring the profiles in this book, readers will begin to see how the Irish women who came before them continue to shape the lives of women today. Surely, we can see St. Bridget's dedication to the education of children in the inspired work of Caroline Kennedy; we can hear the fierceness and dedication to social justice that made Dorothy Day such a renowned journalist echo in the columns of Nell McCafferty today; and we can see the outspoken, fearless beauty of Queen Maeve reborn in the image of Sinead O'Connor.

In the *Daughters of Maeve*, we find women who refused to sit down, shut up, lie down, or be tied down. We see women who dedicated their lives to Ireland's freedom (Maud Gonne, Mairead Farrell, and Anne Devlin) as well as women who felt compelled to leave Ireland to find their own (Edna O'Brien, Sinead O'Connor, Mother Jones). And although these fifty women come from a wide variety of time periods, religious backgrounds, and social classes, we will find among them a pervasive sense of social justice and empathy for those who have been disenfranchised, and above all, a refusal to stay silent in the face of adversity and discrimination. We will also find much irony in the stories of these women. For example, Margaret Sanger, a woman of Irish extraction, was the pioneer of birth control in America, yet it would take another century for birth control to become legal in Ireland. Many of the mothers of the feminist movement in late nineteenth century America were of Irish descent, but women in Ireland would not truly become liberated until the late 1990s.

To truly understand these women, it is important to understand the history that gave birth to them. Ironically, women in Celtic societies were far more liberated than they would be during the nineteenth and twentieth centuries in Ireland. The ancient Celts gave women equal property rights, equal status in the household, and equal pay for equal work. They were also equal on the battlefield and in the bedroom. As Jack Holland observes in his book *Misogyny: The World's Oldest Prejudice*, "In Europe, it is much later than the Paleolithic, and only when we come to the Celts, that we find a pre-classical culture offering a basis for some claims, that before the Greeks and Romans stamped their hegemony on history, a form of matriarchy prevailed. The evidence comes in the Celtic myths and sagas, and in the writings of the Greeks and Romans of the time about what seemed to them the shocking freedoms the Celts afforded their women."

With the advent of St. Patrick and Catholicism, women began to feel both their power and their sexuality being impinged, although women like St. Brigid still held positions of esteem. By the sixteenth century, Irish women like Granuaille O'Malley were still every inch as formidable as their predecessors, but they were becoming increasingly rare. By the eighteenth century, when British rule was in full force in Ireland, the image of the warriorlike Irish woman had all but been forgotten. As historian Margaret MacCurtain observes in the documentary *Mother Ireland*, "I think it developed from the eighteenth century, where the image of the very powerful woman had disappeared. Ireland was in a dark period. The Penal Laws (British laws inflicted on Irish citizens) had just come over the country and had subdued the native population. The image was one that represented the idea of being subdued—that this was a country in the shape of a woman being subdued, symbolic of surrender and helplessness."

It was not until the struggle for Irish independence began to gather steam in the late nineteenth century that women again were accepted in the role of soldier, warrior, and leader. With the formation of Cumann na mBann (the women's wing of the Irish Republican Army), women like Constance Markiewicz and Maud Gonne fought right alongside their male counterparts and after independence were elected to office in the newly formed Irish government. But although the struggle for Irish independence had been based on three principles—women's equality, national freedom, and support for the labor movement, the national struggle began to take precedence. Much as the abolitionist movement had subsumed the women's movement in America in the nineteenth century, the struggle for Irish freedom relegated the Irish women's movement to the sidelines. This was even more apparent when Eamonn DeValera, who himself had fought alongside Irish women to gain his country's independence, became president of Ireland in 1937. He immediately added an amendment to the Irish constitution stating that a woman's place was in the home. Ironically, the women who had fought so hard for their country's freedom had just lost their own. So while their Irish-American sisters were beginning to enjoy the right to vote and access to birth control, Irish women were being plunged into the dark ages for another thirty years.

In 1968, discrimination, unemployment, and poor housing among Catholics in Northern Ireland all led to a burgeoning civil rights movement, much like the movement in the American South. By 1971, internment, or imprisonment without trial, had been imposed in the North of Ireland, and young men were being picked up and arrested without charge, sometimes facing imprisonment for years at a time. This new development left women in charge of their homes, and in charge of the struggle. By the early '70s, women were again asking not only for the rights of Catholics, but also for their own right to equal pay and to birth control. As Bernadette Devlin observes, "If you look at young women today, I still think that the best of the feminist movement, the best of the young women today, are those that have come out of the experience of the Republican movement—those who have come to an awareness of their oppression as women, through a growing awareness of all other layers of oppression."

In the thirty years since the civil right movement in Ireland, many battles have been fought and won. Irish women now have access to the Pill, divorce, and many more career opportunities, thanks to women like Nell McCafferty and Mary Robinson. But there is still work to be done—both in Ireland and America. Women in both countries still earn less than their male counterparts, and while Ireland has elected two female presidents in the last fifteen years, the United States has yet to elect one. And although the Good Friday Agreement was enacted in Northern Ireland in 1998 to alleviate some of the prejudice and strife of the Catholic community, injustice and violence still plague that part of the world. It will be up to the next generation of Irish and Irish-American women to take up the mantle. It is my wish that the stories found in *The Daughters of Maeve* will inspire them to do just that.

ACKNOWLEDGMENTS

Without the support of my family, friends, and esteemed academic institutions, this book would not have been possible. I would like to thank my editors, Bob Shuman and Danielle Chiotti, for their endless patience and wisdom; my dear friend and author, the late Jack Holland for his professional and personal support; and my family, especially Martin Sigillito, Sean Sigillito, Louis Colombo, and Beverly Colombo. Grateful acknowledgment also goes to the libraries of Fordham University, St. Louis University, the University of Missouri, and Trinity College, Dublin.

DAUGHTERS
of
MAEVE

1. QUEEN MEDB
Maeve

FIRST CENTURY B.C.
WARRIOR QUEEN

If I married a mean man, our union would be wrong, because I am so full of grace and giving. It would be an insult if I were more generous than my husband, but not if the two of us were equal in this. If my husband were a timid man, our union would be just as wrong, because I thrive, myself, on all kinds of trouble. If I married a jealous man, that would be wrong too. I have never had one man without another waiting in his shadow.

—Queen Medb, putting her husband,
Ailill, in his place

More than 2,000 years ago, women took the battlefield with superior strength and courage. They were the equals of any man, physically strong, morally courageous, and sexually liberated. In the world of the ancient Celts, women enjoyed more sexual and financial freedom in some ways than they do today. The Brehon Laws (ancient laws of Ireland) ensured that women receive equal pay for equal work (a dream that is still yet to be realized today in many countries) and that they retained an equal place in household affairs. In ancient Irish literature, women are the fiercest warriors and teach many of the men how to conquer in battle. In the great Irish epic *The Tain*, it is the women such as Scathach, Aife, and Nes, and most important, Queen Medb (Maeve) who wield the power and call the shots. Beautiful, fearless, and in control of her sexual destiny, Maeve proves to be a worthy adversary to the Irish hero Cuchulainn, and it is she who leads her forces into battle. Known as the "Intoxicating One," Medb awakened desire in even her fiercest enemies. One of

1

the great debates in Irish myth and legend begs the question: Did Queen Maeve really exist? Although no authority seems to have the answer, it is almost immaterial. The legacy that Queen Medb has given Irish women is more important than whether she ever took flesh-and-blood form. Her strength in the face of adversity, her superior intellect, and her sexual potency has given Irish women a role model that has enabled them to overcome the greatest obstacles. The warrior-like spirit of Maeve has given birth to great Irish women everywhere. And it is her legacy that gives inspiration even today. Only such a progressive time could have given birth to such a progressive heroine.

While many believe that Medb was a goddess of Leinster, others believe that she was a flesh-and-blood warrior queen who lived in the first century B.C. She boasted of having thirty lovers a day, many of whom were in her army. Following the Celtic tradition of having warriors sleep together to ensure their loyalty, Medb made sure that her bravest warriors were granted sexual favors, so the men fought hard and courageously on the battlefield for a chance to enjoy Maeve's "willing thighs." She is believed to have lived in County Sligo and to be the wife of Conchobar MacNessa, who she later parted from, and Ailill, the king of Leinster. She then murdered Conchobar's next wife, her own sister, Eithne, while she was pregnant. Eithne's son, Furbaide, was born by posthumous caesarean section. It was a murder that would seal Maeve's own fate. Her husband, Ailill, was just as promiscuous as Medb, but also a fiercely jealous man, as he proves in *The Tain*. He even asserts that it is his wealth and status that have brought value to their marriage, not hers. When she discovers that Ailill owns a more valuable bull, Finnennbach, the White Horned, who has left Medb's herd because he refused to be led by a woman, she becomes furious. Never one to be second best, Medb is determined to acquire the kind of wealth that will give her more leverage in her household. She quickly investigates where she can acquire a bull of similar quality and discovers the brown bull that belongs to the king of Ulster. Maeve's lust for power is mythologized in the "Cattle Raid of Cooley." The warrior queen insists on raiding Ulster to claim the king's prized possession. It is here that she encounters the mighty Cuchulainn, who sacrifices his life to defend Ulster.

Several conclusions have been lent to this story, making the real outcome unclear. One ending states that both armies suffered great losses, but Maeve eventually attained the bull of Ulster, and when it and Ailill's bull were penned together, the two beasts killed each other. And so after all the death and decimation, Queen Maeve and King Ailill finally had equal wealth . . . but not equal power. Ailill eventually chose to leave Connacht rather than live in the shadow of its infamous queen.

Maeve's jealousy eventually got the better of her. In her later years, she often went to bathe in a pool on an island. Her nephew, Furbaide, sought revenge for the death of his mother, Eithne. He took a rope and measured the distance between the pool and the shore and practiced with his sling until he could hit an apple on top of a stake that was Medb's height from that distance. The next time he saw Medb bathing, he put his practice to good use and killed her. She was succeeded to the throne of Connacht by her son, Maine Athramail.

According to legend, Medb is buried in a forty-foot-high stone cairn on the summit of Knocknarea (Hill of the Queen) in County Sligo. Deeply flawed and greatly admired, Maeve is an appropriate heroine for the women who came after her.

2. BRIGID

453–524 A.D.
Patron Saint of Ireland, Religious Icon, Educator

The proud citadel of Allenn
Has perished with its warlike host.
Great is victorious Bridgid,
Faid is her populous name.

—Ancient Gaelic hymn

She is destined for great things.
—St. Patrick on Brigid, at the time of
her final vows

I would have the people of Heaven in my house.
I would like the baskets of peace to be theirs.
I would like the vessels of charity to distribute.
I would like for them to have cellars of mercy
I would like there to be cheerfulness in their drinking
I would like for Jesus too to be there among them.

—Brigid

She has been identified as a feminist, a saint, a healer, and a maiden of plenty. Along with Patrick and Columcille, she remains one of the three most revered saints in Ireland and every February 1, on St. Brigid's Day, millions across the world honor her memory. The pervasiveness of the name Brigid or Bridget in Irish children is further testament to her popularity, and the shrines across Great Britain and Europe only serve to strengthen this "Cult of Bridget" that has developed over the past several hundred years. The name Brigid of Ireland conjures up disparate images for many, but so few are familiar with the real woman behind the myth. In reality, this daughter of a slave girl and a high king was a defiant woman, a vessel of charity, a religious pioneer who paved the way for women in the church, a peacemaker and tireless defender of the poor. She was also thoroughly human—a woman who could be stubborn, willful, and generous to a fault. She was a lover of music and displayed a love of good times. And she was a mass of contradictions—a dairy maid who was dedicated to the exalted ambitions of higher learning and religion; a luminary whose counsel was sought by all, but who worked in the fields until the day she died; and an intellectual who lauded the practical art of agriculture.

But to truly understand Brigid, one must understand the history of Ireland at the time she was born and raised. While it would seem unlikely that a woman could have such influence in fifth- and sixth-century Ireland, it is important to understand the freedoms that women were afforded during that time. According to the Brehon Laws (the ancient laws of Ireland), women had marital rights, property rights, and the right to receive equal compensation for equal work. Daughters had the right to inherit their father's land, and so it is not surprising that Brigid, a woman, would come to take equal place beside her male counterparts. As Alice Curtayne, Brigid's most respected biographer observes in *Saint Brigid of Ireland*, "Women of early Christian Ireland were more emancipated that the women of 1933."

Brigid was born in Faughart, County Louth, in 453 to Dubthach, a married pagan king, and Brocessa, his Christian slave. The age of her birth was a particularly brutal and bloodthirsty time; Celtic warriors took to the battlefield with abandon, and *The Annals of Ulster*, the chronicle of Ireland's history, reveals the death and carnage that took place daily during the fifth century. Having courage on the battlefield and being fearless in the face of death were two of the most prevalent values in pre-Christian and early Christian Ireland, and they were the two values that Brigid would later challenge in her adult life. One story that pays tribute to Brigid's role as peacemaker recalls a war between two brothers, Conale and Cairbre, sons of the high king of Ireland, who were determined to kill each other. Brigid prayed hard so that the brothers would not recognize the other on the battlefield and managed to save both their lives.

According to the ancient Irish law of fosterage, the practice in which a child was sent to another member of the community to be raised, Brigid was raised by a Druid in Connacht, the west of Ireland. Dubthach's jealous wife had also insisted that Brocessa be banished from their house in punishment for her infidelity with her husband. According to myth, Brigid was destined for glory even before she was born. A prophecy by the Druid declared "a fair birth, a fair dignity . . . who shall be called from her great virtues the truly pious Brigid, she will be another Mary, mother of the great Lord." As Curtayne observes, the baby Brigid was said to be born in the presence of "a flame and a fiery pillar" and would soon earn the name "fiery arrow." It was also here that she is believed to have performed her first miracle: angels are said to have appeared at her christening.

Even from an early age, Brigid showed an ability to perform almost Christlike loaves and fish miracles and acts of generosity. One of the most famous Brigid stories tells of her extreme generosity, even at the expense and annoyance of her family. Annoyed by Brigid's early philosophy of taking from the rich (namely Dubthach) to give to the poor, Dubthach decided to sell her into slavery—to the king of Leinster. When she famously gave her father's sword to a leper on the journey, an act of defiance against his warlike tendencies and of selflessness, she said she had done it because the leper was actually appearing to her as God himself, in the guise of an impoverished beggar. When he heard the story, the king ordered Dubthach to free her because he was convinced that Brigid was living and acting according to God's word.

This was not the last time she would stand up to her father. Brigid went to her mother's aid, freeing her from the bonds of slavery by single-handedly taking over her duties. It was here that she displayed the ability to feed the hungry with a wave of her hand—she was observed to create hundreds of pounds of butter in minutes. It was this almost supernatural talent that would eventually win Brigid her own freedom. The Druid was so impressed by her generosity and dedication to her mother that he let her go. As a teenager, Brigid defied Dubthach once more when she refused to agree to an arranged marriage to a poet (this is somewhat ironic as she was later to become the saint of poets). It was this decision that would be the catalyst for her religious life; Brigid vowed to be chaste and to remain unmarried for life, married only to God. It was this milestone in her life that influenced Brigid to dedicate her life to religion. In Brigid's time, Irish nuns lacked their own community and continued to live with their families. Determined to give women in religious life a place as well as a voice, Brigid began to travel Ireland on a mission at the tender age of fourteen, with seven of her fellow sisters in tow, that no one had undertaken before: to support all women who chose a religious life.

After taking her vows before St. Mel, the bishop of Armagh and the nephew of St. Patrick, at Croghan Hill, she took on her most important challenge to date: founding the first-ever convent for nuns at Ardagh. Soon, thousands of young women came to the convent to pursue a religious life. Impressed again by Brigid's miraculous generosity and calling to God's service, the king of Leinster came to play his most important part in Brigid's life yet. He gave her the land that was to become Cill Dara (the church of the oaktree), or the Abbey at Kildare, as it is known today, which remains legendary. Under Brigid's tutelage, it grew in just a short time to epic proportions, consisting of a monastery and convent, a farm, a school for converts, a safe haven for travelers, a school for artisans, and a shelter for the poor. The convent began to produce gloriously illuminated manuscripts like the *Book of Kildare,* which rivals the *Book of Kells* for sheer splendor. Visitors to the church reported on its richness and beauty, and great figures from all over the country came to visit Brigid there and seek her advice. One may imagine a kind of King Arthur's court for religious figures, where St. Brendan the navigator, St. Finnian, and Ailbe, the predecessor of St. Patrick, all came to gather around Brigid and seek her wisdom. Brigid also began to take her ministry on the road, traveling in her chariot and healing the sick and the dying. It is here that she wove her legendary cross of reeds to succor a man who was dying, a cross that remains a tradition to this day.

During her travels, she cured the blind, the mute, and the lepers, and her abbey became the symbol of the Celtic value of generosity. No one was ever turned away from Kildare and gifts were never kept, but immediately given away to the needy. The abbey became the stuff of legend for its practice of allowing men and women to worship together for the first time. As Cogitogus, Brigid's first biographer recorded, "Thus in one great temple, a multitude of people in different order and ranks, separated by partition, but of one mind, worship almighty God." Along with St. Conleth, whom she enlisted to help her with the running of Kildare, Brigid established a school for the arts and metalwork, and the city of Kildare soon became a mecca for art, scholarship, and religious study. By the time of her death, Brigid was the mother abbess of more than 13,000 sisters and de facto governess of the entire town.

Brigid died on February 1, 524, already a worshipped figure—Columcille paid tribute to her and St. Brendan paid homage to her healing powers. According the Celtic custom of burying the dead with great expense and splendor, she was buried in a jewel casket at Kildare. She was later moved and laid to rest alongside St. Patrick and St. Columcille at Downpatrick, where she took her place beside them in history. Dedications and tributes from all over the world flooded Kildare. As Hugh De Blacam observes in *The Saints of Ireland*, "Patrick, Brigid, and Columcille is a phrase that stirs the Irish heart. It symbolizes and concentrates Irish tradition." While it is doubtful that Patrick and Brigid ever crossed paths, they shared a common bond that transcended time and space. As the *Book of Armagh* states, "Between St. Patrick and St. Brigid, the columns on which all Ireland rested, a cordial friendship existed, such that they were one in heart and soul."

In 1962, Brigid became St. Brigid, the patron saint of Ireland and of dairymaids, poets, midwives, nuns, sailors, scholars, cattle, babies, children born out of wedlock (appropriately enough), and chicken farmers. More than 1,500 years later, Kildare remains a center of religious life and study, and the nuns who reside there have never let Brigid's fire die. Her legacy of charity and compassion has been passed down to the sisters who came after her and who now inhabit the abbey, and whose dedication to God was made possible by their indomitable abbess.

3. GRACE O'MALLEY

1530–1603
SEA CAPTAIN

She is a notorious woman in all the coasts of Ireland.
> —Sir Henry Sidney, governor to Queen Elizabeth I

I n the sixteenth century, an intrepid Irish pirate ruled the high seas, striking fear into the hearts of Englishmen everywhere. But this pirate was no man. At a time when men reigned supreme, one woman lived on her own terms, never asking permission. It is said that in her lifetime she commanded a fleet of more than 200 men and was the only Irish woman ever to stand up to Queen Elizabeth I. While the myths surrounding Grace O'Malley are legion, very few know the real story behind the woman known as Granuaile.

Grace O'Malley was born in County Mayo, Ireland, in 1530 into a famous seafaring family. The daughter of the renowned sea captain Owen "Black Oak" O'Malley, Grace always knew she wanted to be a sailor but because she was a girl, she was told that her dream would never be realized. Like so many Irish women, Grace was encouraged only by her father and often sailed with him on his trading missions overseas. Even as a young girl, Grace displayed the bravery that would define her all of her life. Once, after returning from a trip to Spain, their ship was attacked by an English vessel. Grace had been instructed by her father to hide below deck if they were ever attacked, but she refused to listen. Instead, she climbed up onto the sail rigging. Watching the battle from above, she noticed an English pirate with a raised dagger sneaking up on her father. The brave Granuaile leaped off the rigging and sailed through the air, landing squarely the pirate's back. The distraction this caused was enough for the O'Malleys to regain control of the ship and defeat the English pirates.

She spent her young life learning the ways of the sea and grew to be an accomplished sailor—eventually owning her own fleet of ships. Her family had become wealthy mainly through fishing and trade, but in her later life, Grace took up piracy by attacking and capturing Turkish and Spanish pirate ships and even English ships. She grew her estate to include a fleet of ships as well as several islands and castles on the west coast of Ireland.

In her later years, Grace developed her reputation as a fearless leader through her efforts in battle alongside her followers. Legend has it that Grace gave birth to one of her sons while out to sea. The very next day following the birth of the baby, the ship was attacked by Turkish pirates. Though exhausted from giving birth, Grace grabbed a gun, went on deck, and proceeded to rally her men against the Turks, forcing their retreat.

In 1546, at the age of sixteen, Grace married her first husband, Donal O'Flaherty, who was the son of the chieftain of the O'Flaherty clan and next in line for the post as chieftain. The O'Flahertys were a seafaring people, much like the O'Malleys, so Grace was right at home with their clan. Over the course of their marriage, Grace learned more about seafaring from Donal and his clan and added to her knowledge of sailing and trading at sea. Grace was soon in charge of the O'Flaherty fleet of ships and ruled the waters surrounding their lands. Although it was unusual for a woman to lead men, Grace earned the respect of all who followed her through her shrewdness, knowledge of sailing, and bravery at sea. Donal had a reputation for being volatile and his temper eventually cost him his life in battle against a rival clan. They were married for nineteen years and had three children: Owen, Murrough, and Margaret.

According to Irish law, widows were entitled to a portion of their husband's estate. Unfortunately, the O'Flahertys did not follow this tradition, and Grace was forced to rely on the O'Flaherty clan for support. Much too proud to rely on the charity of her husband's family, she set out on her own, taking with her a loyal group of followers and traded on the seas to earn her own way. She used what she learned from her father in her youth and from her husband and was eventually able to break away from the O'Flaherty clan altogether. Grace moved back with the O'Malley clan and brought her followers with her—Grace had become a chieftain in her own right and the heir as chieftain of the O'Malley clan.

In equally as political a move, Grace married her second husband, Richard Burke to strengthen her hold on the west coast of Ireland. Since Donal's death, she had built her empire to include five castles and several islands in Clew Bay, but she needed Rockfleet Castle on the northeast side of the bay to complete her stronghold on the area. Legend has it that Grace traveled to Rockfleet Castle, knocked on the door, and proposed marriage to Richard for a period of one year. She explained that the union would enable both clans to withstand the impending invasion by the English (who were slowly taking over the Irish lands around them). It is believed that after exactly one year, Grace said to Richard, "I release you," apparently offering him the option to end the marriage, but by that time, Richard was already smitten with the lovely Granuaile.

In 1593, after many difficult years of fighting against the English and the capture of Donal-na-Piopa, her brother, and Theobald, her son, by English forces, Grace visited Queen Elizabeth to make peace and ask for the release of her brother and son. Events leading up to the meeting between Grace and Queen Elizabeth had a significant impact on the meeting itself and Grace's behavior afterward.

Over Grace's lifetime, the English had taken over much of Ireland a piece at a time through a process called "Submit and Regrant." The English would convince (or force) clan leaders to submit their lands to the English and in return they were given an English title. While some chieftains surrendered, many rebelled, including Grace. She maintained her independence longer than most of the rest of Ireland, but in her later years, the pressure from English forces began to weigh heavily on her.

At fifty-six years old, Grace was captured by Sir Richard Bingham, a ruthless governer appointed by the queen to rule over the regranted territories. Soon after his appointment, Bingham sent guards to arrest Grace and have her hanged. Grace was apprehended, along with members of her clan, imprisoned, and scheduled for execution. Determined to die with dignity, Grace held her head high as she awaited her execution. At the last minute, Grace's son-in-law offered himself as a hostage in exchange for the promise that Grace would never return to her rebellious ways. Bingham released Grace on this promise but was determined to keep her from power and make her suffer for her insurrection. Over the course of time, Bingham was responsible for taking away her cattle, forcing her into poverty, even plotting the murder of Owen, her eldest son.

During this period of Irish rebellion, the Spanish Armada was waging war against the English along the Irish and Scottish coastlines. It is not known whether Grace assisted the English against the Spanish or if she was merely protecting what little she had left—but around 1588 Grace slaughtered hundreds of Spaniards on the ship of Don Pedro de Mendoza near the castle on Clare Island. Even into her late fifties, Grace was fierce in battle. In the early 1590s, Grace was still virtually penniless thanks to the constant efforts of Bingham to keep tight controls on her. There was a large rebellion brewing and Bingham feared that Grace would run to the aid of the rebels against the English. He wrote in a letter to Queen Elizabeth during this time that Grace was "a notable traitoress and nurse to all rebellions in the province for 40 years."

Grace had written letters to the queen demanding justice, but received no response. In 1593, Donal-na-Piopa and Theobald were arrested and thrown into prison. This was the final straw that prompted Grace to stop writing letters and go to London in person to request their release and ask for the queen's help in regaining the lands and wealth that were rightfully hers.

Grace set sail and managed to avoid the English patrol boats that littered the seas between her homeland and London. The meeting took place in Greenwich Castle, and the only record of this meeting that has survived is an old song that tells of Grace's presence in the court of the queen. Amazingly, Queen Elizabeth agreed to meet with Grace and it is a tribute to Grace's standing and reputation that the queen never had her executed or imprisoned. Grace was fluent in Latin and thus was able to converse freely with the queen. She explained that her actions in the past were not rebellion but acts of self-defense. She told of how her rightful inheritance from both husbands' deaths was wrongfully withheld from her and asked for it to be returned. She also asked for the release of her brother and son. In return for all of this, Grace agreed to use her strength and leadership to defend the queen against her enemies by land and by sea.

The queen accepted the offer and ordered that Bingham release Donal-na-Piopa and Theobald and return Grace's assets. Bingham released the two captives, but he never restored Grace her rightful possessions. Grace set out to sea again, under the guise of fighting for the queen. Bingham knew she would go back to her old ways if she could, so he ordered a captain and a company of soldiers to follow her on all voyages. Grace finally fled to Munster and stayed with an old friend, Thomas, Earl of Ormond. The earl helped Grace petition the queen again, but there is no record of a reply. Grace eventually returned to Rockfleet. It is believed that Grace went back to her pirating ways; there is only one account of an English patrol overcoming one of her galleys on its way to raid the ships of the McSweeneys. Grace died in 1603. While some believe that she died in battle while raiding a ship, others believe that she died in her castle at Rockfleet. In her seventy years of life, she and her family saw the English rule spreading throughout Ireland, but her strength and leadership ensured that her clan and those around her were mostly unaffected by it. It is said that from the year of her death onward no Irish chieftain had been able to preserve the old Gaelic way of life as Granuaile and her family had done.

4. MARY WOLLSTONECRAFT

1759–1797
FEMINIST

She is alive and active, she argues and experiments, we hear her voice and trace her influence even now among the living

—Virginia Woolf

It would be an endless task to trace the variety of meannesses, cares, and sorrows, into which women are plunged by the prevailing opinion, that they were created rather to feel than reason, and that all the power they obtain, must be obtained by their charms and weakness.

—Mary Wollstonecraft

She was one of the world's first feminists who gave birth to one of the most popular novelists of gothic literature. Although her career would span only nine years, her seminal feminist treatise *A Vindication of the Rights of Woman* would give birth to first-, second-, and even third-wave feminism. She lived and loved fearlessly and her exploration of sexual freedom would influence Victorian women who came after her, as they struggled for sexual liberation of their own. And although she would die eleven days after the birth of her daughter, Mary Shelley, her revolutionary philosophies and passion for women's liberation would embolden her daughter and inspire her to create her own legacy. Not surprisingly, Mary Wollstonecraft was the daughter of an Irish woman, and although she died at thirty-eight, her influence has lived for over two centuries.

Mary Wollstonecraft was born on April 27, 1759, to Edward and Elizabeth (born Elizabeth Dixon in Ballyshannon, Ireland) Wollstonecraft.

Her father was a tough, unyielding man and her mother was a meek, subservient woman who favored Mary's older brother, which undoubtedly influenced her own need for emancipation from a very early age. Her grandfather was a wealthy silk merchant who left 10,000 pounds to her father, but Mary's father tried to distance himself from the trade and set up as a gentleman farmer first in Essex, and then near Beverley in Yorkshire. Mary's grandfather bought the family's first farm in Essex, where Mary lived when she was four and five and where her other sister, Everina, was born.

In less than four years, Edward's farm in Essex failed. The failure drove Edward's career across England and Wales, to poorer and more remote farms; he eventually squandered his inheritance and ultimately made his children rootless. He developed a drinking problem and began to verbally, and perhaps even physically, abuse Mary's mother; Mary tried to shield her mother from Edward's aggression by sleeping on the landing near her mother's bedroom door during the night. As a result of the neglect to which her parents subjected her, Mary assumed a mother's role for the children who followed, especially the girls.

In 1768, the Wollstonecrafts moved to a farm outside of Beverley, where Mary attended a local day school for girls; the school was dedicated to teaching the girls the basics of becoming a good housewife and morals, and the curriculum was aimed at making a girl marriageable and ladylike.

The Wollstonecrafts left Beverley for Hoxton, London, when Mary was fifteen. Disinherited both economically and emotionally, Mary became immersed in reading and study and began to participate in discussion groups, public lectures, and clubs. When in Beverley, she attended the lectures of John Arden on experimental science; he also taught her along with his daughter, Jane Arden, how to use globes and how to argue philosophical problems.

In Hoxton, Mary also found mentors in her next-door neighbors, the Reverend Mr. Clare and his wife, who recommended and encouraged her to read proper books. It is through Mrs. Clare that Mary met Fanny Blood, a woman two years her senior who became the emotional center of

Wollstonecraft's life for the following ten years. Fanny was a role model to Mary, who inspired her to think of leaving her unhappy family life and obtaining employment. Mary was prepared to leave, but was begged to stay by her mother; in exchange for staying, she was given a place to live near Fanny, where she lodged with an unusual couple: Thomas Taylor "the Platonist" and his wife. Mary became friends with them and began to read Plato, which helped influence her religious views.

Mary eventually moved in with Fanny and her family after Elizabeth Wollstonecraft's death in 1782, prompting Mary to throw all her energy into supporting the Bloods, as well as her own younger sisters. Early in 1784, Wollstonecraft, her two sisters, and Fanny Blood set up a school on Newington Green, then a village just to the north of London and now part of Islington. The following year, Fanny Blood left the school and sailed to Lisbon to marry. Later, Mary followed her friend to assist her in childbirth, but Fanny died, just as Mary would fifteen years later.

In 1786, Mary closed her school because of financial problems that had mounted during her absence. To raise money and improve her spirits, Mary began to write *Thoughts on the Education of Daughters*; the work was published in 1787 by Joseph Johnson and earned her a nominal fee, which she gave to the Blood family. She also composed *Mary, A Fiction* and "Cave of Fancy" and worked as a reader and translator with Johnson, beginning her career as a published writer.

In 1790, Mary published *Young Grandison,* a translation of Maria van de Werken de Cambon's adaptation of the novel by Samuel Richardson, followed by a translation of *Elements of Morality* by Christian Gotthilf Salzmann. In November of that year, she published *A Vindication of the Rights of Men* anonymously, then, one month later, she published the second edition bearing her name, establishing her reputation as a partisan of reform. One year later, in 1791, she published a second edition of *Original Stories* and started to write *A Vindication of the Rights of Woman;* she also met her future husband and soul mate, the philosopher William Godwin, through Johnson in November of that year

In January 1792, Mary published her most famous work, *A Vindication of the Rights of Woman*, which was received with great acclaim. The first great feminist treatise and revolutionary in its scope, *A Vindication* proposed that men and women were intellectually equal. Mary was also the first to propose that women had been taught to be superficial and simpering, but that they had not been born that way. In opposition to the popular opinion of the time, she maintained that a woman's reproductive system did not disqualify her from learning Latin and Greek or engaging in any other intellectual pursuits. She wrote the book "to persuade women to endeavour to acquire strength, both of mind and body, and to convince them that the soft phrases, susceptibility of heart, delicacy of sentiment, and refinement of taste, are almost synonymous with epithets of weakness." She called marriage "legal prostitution" and declared that women were enslaved by men who wanted to deny them equal education.

In 1793, Mary met Gilbert Imlay, had an affair with him, and although not married, she registered as his wife at the U.S. embassy in London to claim protection of U.S. citizenship. In 1794, their daughter, Fanny Imlay, was born, and in 1795, Mary learned of Imlay's infidelity and attempted suicide twice; she saw Imlay for the last time in 1796 and met William Godwin again in April. She also published *Letters Written during a Short Residence in Sweden, Norway, and Denmark*, started to write *The Wrongs of Woman*, and began her relationship with Godwin by midsummer. True to her tendency to resist the mores of her time, she became pregnant again out of wedlock.

Finally, in 1797, Mary married William, and their daughter, Mary, was born in August. Mary Wollstonecraft died in September of complications resulting from childbirth. In 1798, Godwin, who considered his beloved wife his intellectual superior, published *Mary's Posthumous Works*, including *The Wrongs of Woman*, or *Maria*, "The Cave of Fancy," her *Letters to Imlay*, and other miscellaneous pieces; he also included his own *Memoirs of the Author of A Vindication of the Rights of Woman*, Mary's first biography. Because her husband was every inch the feminist that she was, he raised Fanny and Mary with the same privileges that he would have afforded a male child.

More than 200 years after its publication, *A Vindication of the Rights of*

Woman has remained the seminal work of the feminist movement and would go on to inspire the fight for women's liberation in the nineteenth and twentieth centuries. Women like Elizabeth Cady Stanton and Susan B. Anthony called her the mother of the women's movement, and the feminist thinkers Virginia Woolf and Gloria Steinem took up the cause for women's equality because of her stirring words.

5. ANNE DEVLIN

1780–1851
REVOLUTIONARY

In Dublin town they sing of a brave Wicklow woman
Of her troubles and her times in cruel Kilmainham Jail
All the way from Butterfield Lane Anne Devlin was her name
A friend to Robert Emmett she served his cause in vain
In 1851 Anne Devlin met her maker
But her story's with us still as a lesson for the wise
Not poverty or fear can kill the heart of freedom
Anne Devlin was a servant to the spirit of our land

—Lyrics from the song "Anne Devlin"
by Pete St. John

I'll not say a word against you.

—Anne Devlin to Robert Emmet
before the 1803 rising

When we speak of Robert Emmet and 1803, let us not forget Anne Devlin.
—Pádraig Pearse, Irish Rebellion leader

She was one of Irish history's unlikeliest heroines. A housekeeper who fueled a revolution, Anne Devlin remained obscured in the shadows for years, but without her contributions, there could have been no Countess Markievicz, no Maud Gonne, and certainly no Bernadette Devlin (no relation). The confidante and heroine of Robert Emmet's 1803 Rebellion in Ireland, she remains one of the nation's most revered figures. Fiercely loyal, intrepid, and nationalist to a fault, she became the standard by which Irish female revolutionaries would be measured. Yet despite her eventual renown, Anne Devlin died in poverty and loneliness, and it would be more than 100 years before her legacy was given its full due. As Pat Murphy, the director of the film *Anne Devlin*, observes about Robert Emmet's 1803 Rebellion, Devlin "help set it up and suffered more than anyone as a result."

Anne Devlin was born at Cronbeg, near Rathdrum, County Wicklow, in 1781. Anti-Catholic and anti-Irish discrimination was in full force in Ireland, and Anne's family was fiercely nationalist. Her cousins, Michael Dwyer and Arthur Devlin, were both active in the 1798 Rebellion for Irish Independence and were imprisoned along with Anne's father, Brian. The second oldest of seven children, Anne was called on to carry messages from the Irish rebel Michael Dwyer. Born in 1771, Dwyer was a rebel leader in 1798 and for years after the rising was still in trouble with the British for his revolutionary activities.

Anne was surrounded by stories of Irish heroism from a young age, but was taught to respect authority. The Devlins were a well-respected family but continually harassed by the British authorities. It was after the 1798 rising that her father was arrested and put into the overcrowded Wicklow Jail. During this time, the Devlins were often raided on account of their cousins, the O'Dwyers and the O'Byrnes. Two of Anne's uncles and two cousins were also in prison. One of the O'Byrnes (Hugh) did escape but was later recaptured and executed.

After over two years in prison, her father petitioned for a retrial as no formal charge had been made against him personally. After the trial, he was unexpectedly acquitted.

It was after this that Anne's father decided that it would be safer for the family to move, so, having given up his lease and parting on good terms from his landlord, the family moved to Rathfarnham in County Dublin. Here, he founded a dairy business and kept horses for hire to the local gentry. The Devlins soon met a new neighbor, a man called "Mr. Ellis," who was actually the revolutionary leader Robert Emmet.

At one point "Mr. Ellis" required the services of a housekeeper in his house in Butterfield Lane and asked his neighbor, Arthur Devlin, to advise him on the choice. It was now that another strange twist occurred in the saga that was to have such a tragic ending for those involved. Anne Devlin became the housekeeper at the house in Butterfield Lane and assumed the name of Emmet.

Chaotic, and poorly organized, the Rebellion of 1803 was doomed for failure. But it was an important precursor to the struggle and eventual victory for Irish independence in 1921. Under the guise of a servant, Anne Devlin helped organize the rebellion in Dublin, while Robert Emmet secured the delivery of arms into the city center. Just as she had in 1798, she helped run messages to and from Emmet's estate to his men in Dublin.

But on July 23, the day of the rising, Emmet soon realized that his men had arrived in the wrong places and that he had even fewer men than expected—less than 100. They stormed Dublin Castle and brutally murdered the chief justice, Lord Kilwarden, on their way. In just hours, the British military had rounded up the rebels and managed to kill a number of them. Emmet escaped to the Wicklow Mountains. As Anne recalls in *The Life, Sufferings and Death of Anne Devlin*, "This was a lonely day for me. There were no visitors. Towards evening there were a few messages, principally with regard to arms and ammunition that were under my care."

On Tuesday, July 26, a gang of soldiers raided Emmet's house and brutally threatened and tortured Anne and her sister. They tried to hang Anne from the handles of her own plough, but she refused to speak. As Anne Kinsella reports in *The Women of 1798*, "She was tortured and prodded with bayonets until covered in blood, but she revealed nothing—similarly she resisted a more subtle offer of 500 pounds and was unmoved by unfounded information that her associates had confessed."

The whole Devlin family was arrested—father and mother, three brothers, two sisters, and Anne herself (her youngest brother is said to have been covered in smallpox)—taken to Kilmainham Jail, placed under strict observation, and tortured mercilessly by Major Sirr and Dr. Trevor, the governor of Kilmainham Jail. During the same time, Emmet was arrested in a house in Harold's Cross. Major Sirr now had a warrant issued against Anne for high treason, a crime punishable by death. She was about to meet Emmet for the last time.

During a brief conversation, he begged her to give information about him as he was already a dead man, but she refused, saying that she could not bring herself to be an informer.

Emmet was hanged in Thomas Street on September 20, 1803. Anne witnessed the horror of Emmet's last moments. "Coming down to St. Catherine's Church in Thomas Street, the coach stopped at a signal from the jailor. The windows were on a sudden let down. I looked out. Horror overcame me when I perceived the blood of Mr. Emmet on the scaffold where his head had been cut off. Dogs and pigs were lapping up his blood between the paving stone." She was returned to Kilmainham Jail, where she was confined to a dank, dark cell for three years and "became more the shape of the cow than a human being." Dr. Trevor continued to torture Anne and refused to release her entire family. Seven members of the Devlin family died before she was released because of ill health in 1806.

After her release, Anne found employment as a ladies companion and then later worked in washing and cleaned houses. Ironically, Anne now made her living by becoming a real housekeeper and married a man named Campbell (who died in 1845) and had two children.

In her final days, Anne was poverty stricken and almost blind. Fortunately, she was discovered by Brother Luke Cullen, who recorded her story. Now, Anne Devlin is a bona fide heroine. In 2003, she was honored with a postal stamp in Ireland, and there have been several movies and documentaries dedicated to her life. But on September 18, 1851, she died in extreme poverty and obscurity at the age of seventy. She is buried in Glasnevin Cemetery in Ireland, alongside her sisters, Maud Gonne and Constance Markiewicz.

6. MARY SHELLEY

1797–1851
FEMINIST, AUTHOR

The companions of our childhood always possess a certain power over our minds which hardly any later friend can obtain.
—Mary Shelley

My heart was fashioned to be susceptible of love and sympathy, and when wrenched by misery to vice and hatred, it did not endure the violence of the change without torture such as you cannot even imagine.
—Mary Shelley, *Frankenstein*

Nothing contributes so much to tranquilize the mind as a steady purpose— a point on which the soul may fix its intellectual eye.
—Mary Shelley

Out of that vampire-laden fog of gruesomeness known as the English Gothic Romance, only the forbidding acrid name of Frankenstein remains in general usage. Mary Shelley had courage, she was inspired.
—Muriel Spark

Mary Shelley and her mother, Mary Wollstonecraft, the great feminist thinker, are one of two great mother-daughter pairs featured in *The Daughters of Maeve*. Although Mary Wollstonecraft would die when her daughter was only eleven days old, her legacy, intellect, and strength would give rise to one of the most beloved and popular novelists of all time.

Mary Wollstonecraft Godwin was born on August 29, 1797, in London, England, the daughter of one of the world's first feminists, Mary

Wollstonecraft, and the writer and political analyst William Godwin. Although Mary Shelley is considered a great English novelist, her maternal grandmother, Elizabeth Dickson, was an Irishwoman from Ballyshannon. The author of the brilliant feminist treatise *A Vindication of the Rights of Woman* and the novel *The Wrongs of Woman*, Mary died of puerperal fever eleven days after the grueling birth of her daughter. Mary and William had been married only five months before her death, and William was too distraught by the loss of his wife to attend her funeral. During her life, Mary had been a sexually free, progressive woman who had numerous affairs and had given birth to an illegitimate child—Mary's half sister, Fanny. Devastated by the loss of this vibrant, brilliant companion, William also found himself too overwhelmed to care for baby Mary and her three-year-old sister. He employed a family friend, Louisa Jane, to raise the children while he oversaw their education. Surrounded by the great intellectuals and writers of their time, the Godwin girls received a superior education from their father, who was himself a feminist, and his friends, including luminaries like Samuel Coleridge and Charles Lamb. Both Fanny and Mary proved to be bright, literary children who could read by the age of six. He became dedicated to their education, believing that men and women should receive equal opportunities when it came to learning.

In 1801, two years after the death of his wife William fell in love with and married his neighbor, Mary Jane Clairmont. Neither Mary nor her sister warmed to their new mother and were openly hostile to her. Despite the tensions in his family, William doted on his daughters, especially the intellectual Mary, who so resembled her mother. By ten, Mary had published her first poem and was proving to be the intellectual equal of her mother. Although Mary enjoyed a fairly happy childhood, the Godwin family was constantly in debt. Despite owning the children's press the Juvenile Library, William was plagued by money worries throughout Mary's childhood. But his troubles appeared to be over when he met the young poet Percy Bysshe Shelley, a political free spirit. At the age of twenty-one, Shelley was already a renegade—he had recently been expelled from Oxford and was a tremendous fan of William's work. While he was eager to help William financially, he was also falling deeply in love with Mary. As he became increasingly unhappy in his marriage, he began to pursue her more ardently. By 1814, when Mary was just sixteen, Mary and Shelley were completely in love. William was furious and demanded that Shelley return to his wife, Harriet. Mary and Shelley eloped on July 28, 1814 (even though he still remained married to Harriet). William refused to see or write Mary for years after the marriage.

Beautiful and artistic, Mary and Shelley enjoyed a happy marriage. They both shared a love of language and literature, and Shelley began to laud his wife's interest in and skill for poetry. During this time, Shelley wrote "Alastor, or The Spirit of Solitude," in which he counsels against the loss of "sweet human love" in exchange for the activism that he himself was to promote and indulge in for much of his life.

In May 1816, the couple traveled to Lake Geneva to spend the summer near Shelley's friend Lord Byron. Shelley began work on "Hymn to Intellectual Beauty" and "Mont Blanc," while Mary began to write the novel that would define her life and career: *Frankenstein*. Lord Byron insisted that the other writers who were guests at the house join him in a ghost story writing contest. Uninspired, Mary later had a dream of "the hideous phantasm of a man stretched out, and then, on the working of some powerful engine, shows signs of life, and stir with a uneasy, half vital motion."

Also known as *The Modern Prometheus,* this novel that would captivate readers for the next two centuries, drew heavily from literary references, including the Promethean myth from Ovid, John Milton's *Paradise Lost, The Rime of the Ancient Mariner,* and Mary's mother's own work, *A Vindication of the Rights of Woman,* which discusses the lack of equal education for men and women.

After they returned to England, Mary suffered a double tragedy. Fanny, who had long suffered from crippling depression, committed suicide on May16, 1816. She had been invited to teach at their aunt's school in Ireland. Instead, she traveled to Wales, where she took an overdose of laudanum at a local inn. Heartbroken at the loss of her only sister, Mary sought solace in the completion of her novel, but death would haunt her once again. In December of the same year, Harriet, Shelley's first wife, took her own life by drowning herself in Hyde Park. Six days later, shortly after Harriet's death, Shelley and Mary were officially married. The next year, Mary gave birth to their first child, William.

In 1818, Mary and Shelley moved to Italy, where they lived until he died four years later. It was also the year that *Frankenstein* was published to wide acclaim. Even though she would become one of the most popular novelists of her day, Mary began suffering personally. Shortly after they moved to Venice, the couple's second child, Clara, died suddenly. The next year, William died of malaria, and Mary had a complete nervous breakdown. By this time, Shelley had uprooted the family once again. They eventually moved to Lerici, where Shelley continued to pursue other women and became more erratic. Although Mary suffered a miscarriage in 1822 that nearly killed her, Mary and Shelley had one more child, Percy Florence Shelley, who became the joy of Mary's life. Later that same year, Mary endured her final heartbreak with Shelley, the man whom she later called the love of her life. In July 1822, Shelley drowned at the age of thirty when he got caught in a fierce storm off the coast to Livorno, Italy. As Mary later lamented, "Well, here is my story. The last story I shall have to tell, all that might have been bright in my life is now despoiled. I shall live to improve myself, to take care of my child, and render myself worthy to join him."

Bereft, Mary vowed never to remarry and returned to London with her son in 1823. She remained devoted to her husband's memory and was tireless in promoting his work, including editing and annotating unpublished material. Despite their troubled later life together, she revered her late husband's memory and helped build his reputation as one of the major poets of the English Romantic period. She also continued to hone her own craft as a writer, and in the 1830s, she wrote several novels including *Lodore*, *Faulkner*, *Valpera,* and *The Last Man*. While none of these novels ever matched the lyricism of her masterpiece, Mary Shelley's legacy was sealed when she published what has become one of the most enduring and pervasive myths in literature. Part feminist criticism, part cautionary tale on the evils of science and industry, and part creation story, *Frankenstein* became a classic that would later inspire a whole new genre of novel: science fiction. The inspiration for more than fifty films, *Frankenstein* became the definitive gothic novel. Mary Shelley died of brain cancer on February 1, 1851, at the age of fifty-three in London and was buried at St. Peter's Churchyard in Bournemouth, in the English county of Dorset. At the time of her death, she was already a legend.

7. ELIZABETH CADY STANTON

1818–1902
SUFFRAGETTE

Abraham Lincoln immortalized himself by the emancipation of four million Southern slaves. Speaking for my suffrage coadjutors, we now desire that you, Mr. President, who are already celebrated for so many honorable deeds and worthy utterances, immortalize yourself by bringing about the complete emancipation of thirty-six million women.
> —Elizabeth Cady Stanton, in a letter to President
> Theodore Roosevelt, just hours before her death

If men cannot be trusted to legislate for their own sex, how can they legislate for the opposite sex, of whose wants and needs they know nothing.
> —Elizabeth Cady Stanton

Although she would remain less famous and less mainstream than her dear friend and fellow suffragette Susan B. Anthony, Elizabeth Cady Stanton proved herself to be the fire behind the early movement for women's rights. With her superior oratory skills and sublime gift for writing, she helped galvanize the struggle for women's liberation in a time when women had no legal right to property, land, or even their own children. And more than any other figure who attended the First Women's Rights Convention in Seneca Falls, New York, she fought tirelessly for a woman's right to vote. While some of her fellow suffragettes would compromise on this issue, Elizabeth Cady Stanton stood firm, even at the risk of censure and ostracism.

Elizabeth Cady was born in Johnstown, New York, on November 22, 1918, to Daniel Cady and Margaret Livingston Cady. The Cadys were one of the most prominent and elite families in the Hudson Valley. Daniel Cady was one of the best-known lawyers of his time, and Margaret Livingston hailed from an elite Scots-Irish family and was the daughter of Colonel James Livingston, an officer in the American Revolution. Domineering and outgoing, Margaret was an early proponent of women's property rights and the polar opposite of Daniel, who was a shy, retiring intellectual who introduced his children to artistic and scholarly pursuits. Despite his quiet disposition, Daniel was also a member of Congress from 1815 to 1817.

Elizabeth was the seventh child in a family of ten children. From an early age, she was an outgoing, outdoorsy child who displayed a keen intellect that would entrance her supporters years later. Because she grew up at a time when children were seen and not heard, she felt stifled by her parents, who were strict disciplinarians. By the time she was eleven, five of her siblings had died, including her older brother Eleazer. Her brother's death proved to be a turning point in her life, as Elizabeth found herself assuming a lead role in the family. As Judith Wellman observes in *The Road to Seneca Falls: Elizabeth Cady Stanton and the First Women's Rights Convention*, "Of all the people Elizabeth loved, Daniel Cady would be the least sympathetic to her work for women's rights, yet ironically, in his grief, Daniel Cady sowed the seeds for his daughter's life's work." After Eleazer's death, Daniel expressed his frustration that Elizabeth had not been born a boy. It was then that she decided to fill her brother's place and be equal to any boy. Desperate to become educated, she studied the law books in her father's office and looked up laws pertaining to women. When she discovered just how few rights her sex had, she became more determined than ever to avail herself of every opportunity afforded her.

When she graduated from the co-ed Johnstown Academy at the age of eighteen, she was one of a handful of girls in her class. Although she was determined to attend Union College in Schenectady, New York, she soon found herself up against the first of many obstacles. Union did not allow women, and Elizabeth settled for Troy Female Seminary, the best women's college in the country. When she entered Troy in 1831, she took on the most grueling course load she could find and immersed herself in French, math, the sciences, and critical thinking. The young Elizabeth also spent long hours debating her father's law students, a skill that would stand her the rest of her life. It was during her time at college that she met her cousin, Garritt Smith, a renowned reformer and abolitionist who introduced her to the plight of African American slaves. She spent many hours at the Smith home, and it was where she met the man who would become her husband.

Elizabeth Cady met Henry Brewster Stanton in 1839 during his work with antislavery conventions. Fiery, passionate, and articulate, Henry Stanton was a journalist and skilled orator, and Elizabeth immediately fell in love with both the man and his message. Henry was equally smitten, and the couple soon became engaged. Daniel Cady was opposed to the union from the start: Stanton was a modest reformer with a modest salary, and Daniel feared that he would not be able to care for Elizabeth. Despite her father's concerns, Elizabeth and Henry were married on May 1, 1840. True to her early feminist leanings, Elizabeth insisted that the word *obey* be left out of the ceremony. By this time, Henry was already at the forefront of the abolitionist movement. He had been exposed to violence and mobs at antislavery meetings and had formed a friendship with Angela and Sarah Grimké, two abolitionist women who would also influence his wife to become active in the fight for women's rights. As Angela later recalled, "The investigation of the rights of the slave has led me to a better understanding of my own." Ironically, Henry would be one of the antislavery proponents to believe that the struggle for women's rights would distract its supporters from the abolitionist debate.

Elizabeth and Henry spent their honeymoon at the World's Anti-Slavery Convention in London. Much to Elizabeth's horror, the women delegates, even Lucretia Mott, were not allowed to sit on the main floor. And although her husband was a secretary at the convention, Elizabeth felt "humiliated and chagrined" at the blatant discrimination. These women who had fought so tirelessly for the rights of slaves were now being denied their own. As she recalled, "The movement for women's suffrage both in England and America may be dated from the World's Anti-Slavery Convention." Despite his abolitionist views, Henry did not share the same egalitarian view toward women and marriage and tended to treat his wife as a possession in their early years. Elizabeth and Henry were both strongly passionate people and their early marriage endured its share of difficulties. Elizabeth often found herself rebelling against her husband, asserting "I do in truth think and act for myself knowing that I alone am responsible for the sayings and doings of Elizabeth Cady Stanton." But Elizabeth loved being a mother, and her first child was born in 1841. Three years later, Henry was born, followed by Garritt Smith Stanton in 1845. By this time, the Stanton family had moved to Boston, where Henry opened his law practice and Elizabeth became an expert mother and homemaker. But by 1847, the cold weather had begun to affect Henry's health, so they decided to move to Seneca Falls, where Elizabeth's sister Tryphena and brother-in-law Edward Bayard lived. It was here that Elizabeth gave her first lecture and began teaching Sunday school to African American women. Daniel Cady also gave his daughter her own house, which gave her status as a landowning woman. It was during this same year that Lucretia Mott and Elizabeth began to realize their eight-year dream of forming a women's rights convention. Since their humiliation at the antislavery convention, the two women knew that such an event was long overdue.

Joining forces with the antislavery parties and the women of the Quaker movement, mainly Elizabeth M'Clintock, Lucretia and Elizabeth began publicizing the 1848 Women's Rights Convention in Seneca Falls. It would be held at the Weslyan Church on July 19–20 and feature Lucretia Mott and Frederick Douglass as its main speakers. Much to the surprise of the women, hundreds of people were gathered outside the church on the morning of the convention. Elizabeth immediately drafted the infamous Declaration of Rights and Sentiments. Based on the Declaration of Independence, the document declared that "woman is man's equal" and called for equality in all areas of life, including the right to speak in public, control of personal property, the right to testify in court and preach, access to equal education, legal custody of children, and the right to vote. On the 20, Elizabeth spoke to an impassioned, enthralled convention audience as she proclaimed, "Man had endeavored in every way that he could to destroy her [woman's] confidence in her own powers, to lessen her self-respect, and to make her willing to lead a dependent and abject life." At the end of her speech, the attendees had passed all eleven resolutions and sixty-eight women and thirty-two men had signed the declaration. Elizabeth stood firm on the right to vote, and Douglass gave a rousing speech supporting her. The Seneca Falls convention was an unmitigated success and received publicity from newspapers all over the country—some positive, some disparaging. But it was clear that a movement had been sparked. In August of that same year, a similar convention was held in Rochester, in support of political and industrial rights for women.

Fueled by the support, Elizabeth began speaking at Quaker meeting houses across the country. In 1851, she began a friendship with another Quaker woman who would become her lifelong sister and ally in the struggle for women's equality. During an antislavery meeting in Seneca Falls, she was introduced to Susan B. Anthony, the reformer and school teacher who shared her passion. Soon, the women began conspiring, and Elizabeth began writing speeches, articles, and letters for *Lily*, a temperance publication, and the *New York Tribune*. Later that same year, she gave birth to another son, Theodore Wild Stanton, and one year later, she had the daughter she always wanted, Margaret Livingston Stanton. In 1852, she became the president of the New York Women's Temperance Association. In 1854, she became the first woman to address the New York State Legislature.

For fifty-four years, Elizabeth and Susan would make women's rights their life's work, in the face of every adversity. While the struggle for slave's rights took precedence after the end of the Civil War, from 1865 to 1869 the two women found their resolve shaken but not broken. In 1865, they campaigned in opposition to the Fourteenth Amendment, which penalized any state that denied the right to vote to any of its male inhabitants. For the first time, the issue of gender was introduced into the Constitution in regard to voting rights. In response, Elizabeth fired back, "Do you believe that the African Race is composed entirely of males?" They came up against fierce opposition from their fellow suffragettes, who did not want to be seen as upstaging what was known as the "Negro's Hour" and men like Elizabeth's own cousin, Garritt Smith, who believed that the issue of abolition came first. The struggle for women's voting rights had been subjugated and it would be another fifty-five years before women gained the right to vote. Determined to be heard, Elizabeth became the first woman candidate for Congress on October 10, 1866. Ironically, a woman could run for office, she just couldn't *vote* for anyone running for office. Although she garnered only 24 out of 22,026 votes in New York's Eighth Congressional District, she had made her point. Women were not going anywhere. Two years later, Elizabeth addressed the Constitutional Convention of New York State, where she demanded that women's suffrage be granted during the redrafting of the state constitution. She and Susan began a petition campaign and secured more than 20,000 signatures. In 1868, they founded the paper *Revolution*, which was dedicated to women's rights.

The next year, in 1869, they founded the National Woman's Suffrage Association (NWSA), an organization dedicated to gaining women the right to vote. Elizabeth began lecturing on controversial issues, much to the chagrin of fellow suffragette and NWSA member Lucy Stone. In response to Lucy's concerns, she fired back, "When I think of all the wrongs that have been heaped upon womankind, I am ashamed that I am not forever in a condition of chronic wrath, stark mad, skin and bone, my eyes a fountain of tears, my lips overflowing with curses, and my hand against every man and brother." Meanwhile, in 1887, while women in Wyoming and Utah were granted the right to vote, New York state defeated a women's suffrage amendment by a vote of thirty-four to sixteen. The next year marked the fortieth anniversary of Seneca Falls. In celebration, Elizabeth and Susan formed the International Council of Women and welcomed women from England, Finland, Ireland, France, Norway, Italy, and India to join them in the struggle. In 1890, Elizabeth opposed a merger with the American Woman Suffrage Association, which created the National American Woman Suffrage Association (NAWSA). Despite her opposition, she became its first president, with Lucy Stone as chairwoman. The next year, Susan and Elizabeth wrote A *History of Women's Suffrage*, a six-volume anthology that chronicled the women's movement. More controversially, in response to her belief that organized religion played a major role in the subjugation of women, Elizabeth published *The Women's Bible*, a collection of biblical quotes with comments that were deemed "too radical" by the NAWSA. By 1892, the icon of the suffragette movement had begun to go blind and resigned as president of the organization, but she never stopped working for the cause that she loved so dearly. She dedicated herself not just to the cause of women's suffrage but to female equality in all areas. In 1898, she published her autobiography *Eighty Years and More*. Four years later, on October 26, 1902, eighteen years before the passage of the Nineteenth Amendment, Elizabeth Cady Stanton died in her home, but her legacy lives on to this day. Her daughter, Harriet Stanton Blatch, took up her mother's cause and oversaw the celebration of the sixtieth anniversary of Seneca Falls. In 1920, the women of Seneca Falls celebrated the right to vote by erecting a marble monument to Elizabeth Cady Stanton, Lucretia Mott, and Susan B. Anthony. The precedent that these brave women set gave birth to the formation of groups like the National Organization of Women, the Equal Rights Amendment, and the Women's Political Caucus. In 1977, the United Nations Decade of Women organized a marathon from Seneca Falls to Houston in commemoration of the First Women's Rights Convention. While women now enjoy many of the same rights as men, they still do not receive equal pay for equal work, and many of the reproductive freedoms they have gained are now in danger of being eroded. There is still much work to be done and as Elizabeth Cady Stanton stated at the anniversary of Seneca Falls, "I urge the young women especially to prepare themselves to take up the work so soon to fall from our hands."

8. MARY WARD

1827–1869
SCIENTIST

One of the most multi-skilled scientists in the microscopic and telescopic fields, Mary Ward's death was almost as extraordinary as her life. On August 31, 1869, Mary Ward and some others were traveling along a quiet Irish road in a steam-driven car when it jolted suddenly, tossing Mary under one of its heavy iron wheels. She died almost instantly in what many believe was the first fatal automobile accident. But if Mary's death was remarkable, so was her life. While other women spent their time in genteel pursuits such as music or sewing, Mary spent hers with her eyes glued to either a microscope or telescope. She was a Victorian woman with a passion for science who had the good fortune to belong to one of the most inventive families in Ireland. But her remarkable family was her misfortune too: if her ingenious cousins had not invented the steam car in the first place, there would have been no accident, and Mary might have made history of a different kind.

Mary Ward was born in Ballylin, near Ferbane, County Offaly, in April 1827. She belonged to an aristocratic family and had two sisters and one brother, and was a first cousin of the famous astronomer Lord William Rosse and a frequent visitor to his home at Birr Castle. As was the norm at that time, Mary Ward and her sisters did not go to school but were taught by a governess at home. Ward showed an interest in plants and animals from an early age, collecting butterflies at the age of three. Later, she particularly liked looking at specimens through a magnifying glass, then drawing them. She was also an avid microscope user and created beautiful drawings of the plants and animals that she saw. She taught herself to make her own microscope slides from ivory, as glass was not plentiful at that time. Her parents encouraged her in these activities, and when she was eighteen, on the advice from the renowned English astronomer, Sir James South, they bought her a microscope, made by Ross of London. At the time it was probably the finest in Ireland, and she continued to use it and demonstrate it to others until her death.

When she was growing up, her cousin William Parsons was building what became the world's largest telescope for over fifty years, the fifty-eight-foot Leviathan Telescope at Birr Castle. Mary Ward was involved in recording its different stages of construction and both her drawings and the photographs of Mary Rosse (Sir William's wife) were crucial for the recent restoration of the Leviathan at Birr castle.

In 1835, the Reverend Henry King and his wife were entertaining at their home in the rural Irish backwater of Ballylin. Suddenly, their youngest daughter, Mary, burst into the room. She had, she announced to the assembled guests, been looking for Halley's comet with her telescope—and she had found it. She was only eight years old.

Mary also drew insects, and astronomer South observed her doing so one day. When Scottish physicist David Brewster wanted microscope specimens, he asked her to make them. He admired her drawings too, and used them to illustrate his papers and books.

The fact that universities and learned societies were exclusively male didn't hold her back. Mary kept abreast of things by begging or borrowing copies of books and papers from her growing circle of eminent friends. It was even easier when Sir William, now the third Earl of Rosse, became president of the Royal Society in 1848. Visits to his London home were as good as sitting in at the Society. At dinner, Mary was surrounded by scientists. Sometimes, though, it was Mary who was the expert. On one occasion, a guest's question had the host stumped. "My cousin Mary King knows rather more than I do on that subject," Sir William confessed. "I recommend that you address your question to her."

In 1854, she married the honorable Henry William Crosbie Ward, of Castle Ward, near Strangford, County Down. Over the next thirteen years, she gave birth to eight children, two of which died very young.

This marriage proved to be a one-sided arrangement. Mary was left to raise the large family and maintain the finances while Harry continued his varied interests and social activities. For the next few years, the family moved from one rented house to another, before finally settling for a number of years near Dun Laoghaire; they had little money and no home. But though Harry burdened her with family responsibilities, he didn't actively stand in her way.

Her next scheme was to write a book, a how-to guide for would-be microscopists. She knew no publisher would touch it because she was a woman. Women at this time could not even become members of any learned societies or obtain any degrees or diplomas. So in 1857, she had 250 copies of *Sketches with the Microscope* printed privately along with hundreds of handbills advertising it. The book sold out in weeks, incentive enough for one London publisher Groomsbridge to ignore her sex and sign her up. Retitled *The World of Wonders as Revealed by the Microscope*, the book became a best-seller, being reprinted eight times in the next twenty years. In 1859, *Telescope Teachings*, a companion volume featuring her drawing of the Birr Leviathan on its cover, was published. Her books, simply written, appealed to all. She also published articles in journals like *Recreative Science* and *The Intellectual Observer*. In England, she was added to the Royal Astronomical Society's mailing list, one of only three women to have this privilege, the others being Queen Victoria and Mary Sommerville of Oxford College. Two of her books were selected to be displayed at the international exhibition at the Crystal Palace in 1862.

Encouraged, Mary wrote a popular guide to astronomy, explaining based on her own experience how to get the most from a small telescope—what to look for and where. Her advice on observing a comet was to "discover" one "humbly in the newspaper," then follow its progress. Despite husband and growing family, she did exactly that when Donati's comet unexpectedly appeared in 1858, turning out in the dead of night or early hours of the morning to examine and draw the spectacle. In September and early October of that year, she kept her two-inch telescope fixed on the comet, recording its changing form as time passed. As she recalled, "The nucleus was very bright, and glittered in the telescope more like a star than a planet." Two days later "the appearance of the comet on that cloudless evening suggested the shape of a bird of paradise feather, and was beyond imagination graceful and beautiful."

An exceptionally fine artist and painter, she illustrated all her own books and papers, and also those of others. Sir David Brewster, F.R.S, came to visit her father's house, and soon she was preparing microscopic specimens for him. These specimens she drew and painted, and the colored illustrations are on display in the *Transactions of the Royal Society of Edinburgh* in 1864. She also made the original drawings of Newton's and Lord Rosse's telescopes, which can be seen in Brewster's *Life of Newton*. In 1864, Sir Richard Owen asked Mary to send him a copy of her painting of the natterjack toad for the collections of the British Museum. An article by Mary, "Natterjack Toads in Ireland," had been published in a scientific journal, and this paper was reprinted in full in *The Irish Times* in May 1864 with a very complimentary editorial comment.

Castle Birr remained a favorite place, and was always a hive of activity. Sir William—and now his sons—spent much of their time in the workshops, making mechanical devices of their own designs. Around 1865, the two youngest Parsons boys, Clere and Charles, hardly in their teens but already proficient mechanics, decided to build a steam car.

There were a few rich enthusiasts who wanted steam cars, and they either found a willing engineer or built one themselves. The Parsons boys built a four-wheeled carriage, with boiler and engine mounted on a flat base at the rear and a bench seat for the driver and passengers at the front. With its young stokers keeping the steam up, the car could travel at a racy seven miles an hour.

After Sir William died in 1867, the boys still took the carriage out occasionally. During the holidays, in August 1869, Mary and her husband joined Clere and Charlie and their tutor for a ride. The car was gliding along when it reached a bend in the road. Mary was thrown from the seat and under one of the rear wheels. Rushing to the scene, a local doctor found her cut and bruised, and bleeding from her ears. She died moments later. At the inquest, one witness testified that "the wheel hit the lady and pushed her to one side." The fatal injury, said the doctor, was a broken neck. The death certificate records the cause of death as "Accidental fall from steam engine. Sudden." The family was so distraught, they broke up the car and buried it.

Following her death, her family moved to Castle Ward. Today, her microscope, accessories, slides, and books can be found on display there in a room dedicated to her. The early death of this remarkable young woman was tragic. She had proved herself as one of the best-known nineteenth-century writers on the use of the microscope. Castle Birr, the home of William Parsons (Lord Rosse) in County Offaly, is also open to the public.

9. MOTHER JONES

1837–1930

SOCIAL REFORMER, UNION ORGANIZER

She is a wonder.

—Carl Sandburg

Pray for the dead, fight like hell for the living.

—Mother Jones

Now Mother . . . the trouble lies here: if I put the pardoning power in your hands there would be no one left in the jails.

—President William Howard Taft
to Mother Jones

I'm not so sure of that, Mr. President. A lot of those who are in would be out, but some of those who are out would be in.

—Mother Jones in reply to President Taft

I f one were to pick up a copy of *Mother Jones* magazine, one would see the rather innocuous sweet visage of a white-haired old woman and below it the words "Mother Jones is an independent non-profit whose roots lie in a commitment to social justice implemented through first rate investigative reporting." Mother Jones's name has become synonymous with social justice, and for most modern readers, the very name Mother Jones conjures up images of the radical magazine first made famous in the 1960s. Others may imagine a petite old woman with rosy cheeks clothed in a black dress and black hat who fought tirelessly for coal miners in the United States. But very few know the remarkable woman behind the icon. This woman who will be forever known as "the Miner's

Angel" was born Mary Harris in a small village in Ireland. She began her adult life as a mother to four children and transformed herself into the mother of a nation. Ironically, in her day she was the most influential and famous woman of her time, but her legacy remained somewhat clouded after her death in 1930. But during the resurgence of political activism and commitment to social justice in the late 1960s in the United States, Mother Jones once again became a household name and inspired a whole new generation to fight for rights of the oppressed.

Born in Inchigeelagh, County Cork, in the 1830s (she claimed May 1, 1830, as her birthday, but church records confirm that she was baptized on August 1, 1837, so she was more than likely born in that same year), Mary Harris was exposed early to the plight of the oppressed. The daughter of Richard and Ellen Harris, she was one of five children born into a devoutly Catholic family. Ireland was still dominated by the Protestant population, and Catholic families were the victims of abject poverty, unemployment, disease, and emigration. The Potato Famine would occur just ten years after Mary's birth, during which over a million people would die of starvation and millions more would flee to the United States, Canada, England, and Australia in search of opportunity. To escape anti-Catholic discrimination and crippling poverty that was now pervading Cork, Richard Harris immigrated to Toronto, Canada, in 1845 to work in the burgeoning railroad industry. In the early 1850s, the rest of his family joined him.

The Harrises settled in St. Mary's Parish and soon discovered that although they had escaped the squalor and poverty of Cork City, they had not escaped anti-Catholic sentiments. According to Elliot Gorn's biography *Mother Jones,* "The Canadian Press abetted discrimination, even violence against Irish Catholics. The *Toronto Globe* declared 'the monstrous delusion of Catholics' to be the enemy of the human race." This sense of injustice and social awareness cannot have been lost on young Mary Harris and would later fuel her own social passion. Despite the anti-Catholic climate, Mary and her siblings did manage to receive a first-class education in Canada. In 1857, she attended Toronto's normal school and became certified to teach. Just three years later, the twenty-three-year-old acquired her first teaching position at a convent in Monroe, Michigan.

She soon became bored with the stringent set of rules at the school and decided to use her dressmaking skills to earn a living. At this point in her life, we begin to see Mary's wanderlust in effect. She traveled to Chicago and then onto Memphis, Tennessee, an exciting, burgeoning city that was teeming with Irish immigrants. It was here that Mary began to put her social passion into effect. In Memphis, the new Irish immigrants and newly freed black slaves worked side by side. Mary's own experiences with anti-Catholic and anti-Irish discrimination made her especially empathetic to the anti–African American racism that she began seeing in Memphis.

It was also in Memphis that Mary Harris became Mary Jones. She met and soon married George Jones, an iron molder for the Union Iron Works and Machine Shop and a member of the International Iron Molders Union, one of the most powerful unions in the country. Because George was a skilled laborer, he and Mary enjoyed a comfortable existence. The couple had four children between 1862 and 1867: Catherine, Elizabeth, Terence, and Mary. Coincidentally, they soon settled in St. Mary's Parish, an Irish stronghold. But in 1867, the life they had built for themselves began to deteriorate. Yellow fever began to invade the port city of Memphis and spread like wildfire, bringing with it a vicious illness that caused its victims to endure extreme blood loss, fever, liver failure, and eventually death. As Mary Jones observed in her autobiography, "The dead surrounded us. They were burned at night quickly and without ceremony. All about my house I could hear weeping and the cries of delirium. One by one, my four little children sickened and died. . . . My husband caught the fever and died. I sat alone during my night of grief." It was a cruel twist of fate. Mary's family had fled Ireland to escape famine and disease and now at the age of thirty, she had lost her entire family to a much crueler fate.

Consumed with grief and with no means of income, Mary returned to Chicago to take up her career as a dressmaker. After suffering unspeakable tragedy, she was determined to put her energy into relieving the suffering of others, particularly the poor and disenfranchised she saw on the Chicago streets everyday, much as she had seen on the streets of Memphis and Cork years before. As Gorn observes, "It was the tragedies of her early days that energized the life of Mother Jones." In 1871, Mary suffered another setback when the Chicago fire destroyed her home and everything in it. She was just thirty-four years old. Undaunted by her own personal tragedy, she began to step up her own interest in labor unions and the struggle of the working man. She had been attending Knights of Labor meetings during her time in Chicago, and in 1873 the American worker was in deep need of help. Workers in Chicago and Pittsburgh began protesting for higher pay and better working conditions, but they were too unorganized to make any kind of impression. But in the next decade, the U.S. economy would plunge into another depression and the pivotal events of the Haymarket riots and the government's recent practice of union busting only served to fuel support for labor unions. By the early 1880s, the Knights of Labor claimed more than a million members. It was Mary's work with the knights that spurred her passion, but it was an event called Coxey's Army in 1894 that helped put her name on the map. Jacob Coxey organized a movement that demanded that the government create jobs for the unemployed. The organization traveled to Washington, D.C., in protest and Mary became the star speaker and fund-raiser for the group, and even though the army failed to get its demands met, the world had been introduced to Mary Jones.

Fueled by her newfound success as a speaker and organizer, Mary joined the United Mine Workers of America (UMWA) and began to fight for the plight of the more than 500,000 coal miners who were working in one of the most treacherous jobs in the United States. Coal workers in the late 1890s and early 1900s endured grueling hours and were in constant danger of contracting black lung or being crushed to death in the mines. They were also forced to relocate to mining towns where they were isolated. The miners had begun to strike in protest of the injustices in the 1860s and by 1890 the UMWA was a force to be reckoned with. It was here that Mary Jones became Mother Jones and began to take her "boys" under her wing, educating them and advocating for them. She was already sixty-five years old and just getting started. Her past tragedies had made her fearless and her gift for eloquence commanded attention. And as many of the members were Irish, they gave her a sense of family that she had been seeking for years. When Mother Jones joined the UMWA, the organization boasted 300,000 members and was the largest labor union in the United States. She soon began galvanizing women and children and involved them in the strikes, and because of her efforts, the coal miners of Pennsylvania received a well-deserved pay raise.

Between 1900 and 1902, Mother Jones became known as an "international organizer" and traveled the country to involve workers' wives, held meetings, and organized rallies. She spoke at the UMWA national convention and also began to lock horns with its president, John Mitchell, and accused him of cowtowing to President Theodore Roosevelt and giving short shrift to miners in West Virginia, where the rate of death was the highest in the United States and coal miners were suffering from crushing poverty. Mother Jones soon stepped in to rally the troops and organized the Strike of 1902 in West Virginia, despite a court-ordered injunction. She was arrested for the first time, at the age of sixty-seven, and her sentence was suspended. After her victory, she moved on to help the workers in Colorado who had walked out of their jobs and had been evicted from their homes. Less than a week after her arrival, the union and its employers had reached a settlement.

Despite her successes, Mother Jones resigned from the UMWA in 1905, tired of battling Mitchell, but under her tutelage, the UMWA was still the most powerful union in the United States. Its 500,000 members were now working under much safer conditions and for a good living wage. Mother Jones may have resigned from the miner's union, but she had no intention of retiring from the worker. She returned to West Virginia, where she took on the plight of the mill workers—particularly that of the child laborers. It was here that her maternal instinct took over again. When she saw children working ten-hour days in appalling conditions, she began organizing strikes in Pennsylvania and New Jersey demanding a reduction in working hours and an increase in wages. In 1906, she conceived one of her most renowned marches, the March of the Mill Children, in which 100 boys and girls would march with factory workers from New York City to Philadelphia. The march took three weeks and despite the unbearable heat of the journey, the march grew in number. The protest garnered attention from President Roosevelt and put child labor on the U.S. political agenda.

Between 1905 and 1912 (despite entering her seventies), Mother Jones never wavered in her tenacity or passion. She was a speaker for the Socialist Party, supported labor leaders and textile workers, raised money for Mexican revolutionary leaders, and organized women workers. The next year, she returned to Virginia to aide the struggling miners, where she rejoined the UMWA and took part in the most volatile strike in U.S. history at Point Creek. The governor declared martial law in response and arrested Mother Jones on charges of rioting and insurrection. Even though she was placed under house arrest for three months, the workers won their conditions: a nine-hour day and a bi-weekly paycheck. The next year, she returned to Colorado and was imprisoned again for her part in organizing the miners, testified in Washington, D.C., on behalf of the workers, and took on John D. Rockefeller, a fierce opponent of organized labor. By this time, she was also organizing dressmakers and street car workers.

But just a few years later in 1919 anticommunist hysteria was reaching an all-time high in the United States. Mother Jones's association with labor unions and socialists was beginning to backfire on her. She fell victim to accusation, but she remained true to the cause, making speeches and raising hell in West Virginia. She was also falling victim to crippling rheumatism, which was preventing her from traveling the country as she once had. She published her autobiography in 1922, and it sold less than 2,000 copies. The indomitable legacy and body of Mother Jones were beginning to fade.

Mother Jones died on November 30, 1930, of a condition that was referred to as senility. She was buried in the Union Miners Cemetery in Mount Olive, Illinois. She was ninety-five years old, and even though she was one of the most famous (and infamous) women of the early nineteenth century, she had fallen into the shadows by the time of her death. It would be another thirty years before Mother Jones once again blazed her name in history. In 1960 *Mother Jones* magazine was founded in San Francisco, and it remains a symbol of revolutionary and progressive thought in the United States. Her autobiography has been reprinted and the UMWA carries her legacy to this day. Just before her death, Mother Jones had requested one wish, "I hope it will be my consolation when I pass away to feel I sleep under the clay with those brave boys." It is this statement that so defines Mother Jones's legacy. In the end, she was a woman whose tireless compassion gave voice to the voiceless: workers, children, former slaves, and immigrants, and a woman whose own tragedy only made her more determined to ease the tragedies of others. And though her fiery oration and steel will made her seem larger than life, she considered herself humbled in the wake of the working man. As she so eloquently stated in a speech at the 1901 UMWA convention: "The foundation which you lay with aching backs and your bleeding hands and your sore hearts will not perish with the years. It will grow and live." The same words can be applied to her own legacy.

10. JENNY HODGERS

1844–1915
SOLDIER

Historians have documented more than 400 women who are known to have fought in disguise for either the North or South during the Civil War, and many were never detected. Among the 36,312 names on the Vicksburg, Illinois, monument is the name Albert Cashier, whose real name was (Irene) Jenny Hodgers (sometimes spelled Hogers) from Ireland. Private Albert Cashier was, in fact, a woman—an Irish immigrant from Belfast named Jenny Hodgers. While this may seem implausible, many farmwomen of the time did the same work as men, dressed in men's clothing, and became used to a hard life. In the ranks of both sides were many boys in their early teens, so it was not unusual for a soldier not having to shave. Furthermore, Civil War medical exams were often limited to a few health questions. These factors made it relatively easy for women to enter the service.

Once enlisted, they bunked alone, used the latrine only at night, and avoided going to the hospital altogether. Some learned to smoke cigars, chew tobacco, curse, and play cards to appear convincing. Hodgers's story is particularly intriguing, not only because of her heroism but also because she had already been playing dual roles in her life, as an Irish immigrant who had relocated to the United States.

Irene "Jenny" Hodgers claimed to have been born in Belfast around 1843 or 1844. Accounts verified by researchers indicate that her family lived in Clogherhead, County Louth. Jenny told many stories about her past to hide her true identity. In fact, few facts about Jenny's early life can be verified because she told so many conflicting stories about her background. She may have been an illegitimate child who lived with or worked for her uncle, who was a shepherd. How she came to the United States is also unclear. She told some people that her mother later married a man named Cashier, and the family emigrated from Ireland to upstate New York. Some reports indicate that she stowed away on a ship. Other sources claim her stepfather dressed her up as a boy, called her Albert, and got his "son" a job. The one fact that does seem to be true is that she grew up in poverty and never learned to read or write.

When Jenny's mother died, she went west to Illinois, where she supported herself as a shepherd, farmer, and laborer. She apparently always used the name Albert Cashier. In July 1862, when President Abraham Lincoln sent out a call for an additional 300,000 men to serve in the Union army, she wondered if she could enlist. She learned from some young men that the medical examination for new recruits was often limited to a few health questions and a quick exam in full clothing. She decided to see if she could fool the examiner. Dressed in men's clothing, she went to the recruiting office in Belvedere, Illinois, and volunteered for military service. Fortunately, reading and writing were not required of volunteers, so she marked an X on the enlistment papers. Jenny Hodgers was transformed into Albert D. J. Cashier, Private First Class, Sixth Company, Ninety-fifth Illinois Infantry Volunteers.

After Jenny and her fellow recruits completed several weeks of training, the company was mustered into service on September 4, 1862. Hodgers's regiment left on November 4 for Kentucky to serve under the command of Major Ulysses S. Grant. Because she had a light complexion, blue eyes, and auburn hair, she looked like the many other Irish Americans who served in the Union army. However, at five feet, three inches tall and weighing 110 pounds, she was the smallest person in her regiment. Although she was small, she refused any special treatment. If someone helped her, she always returned the favor by doing washing or sewing in return. While the other soldiers hated those tasks, she not only did not mind this "women's work" but she also seemed to have a talent for it.

In battle, Private Cashier was the equal of any man in the unit at handling a musket. Jenny's fellow soldiers did joke about her lack of facial hair, but during the Civil War many other soldiers were too young to have facial hair. She was often referred to as a "a short, well-built man." In *They Fought Like Demons: Women Soldiers in the American Civil War*, DeAnne Blanton and Lauren M. Cook speculate that her gender was never discovered because soldiers spent the majority of their time outdoors and could easily pretend to be modest men and seek privacy. In addition, she seemed to be a shy boy who did not want to participate in the usual male banter and games. Regardless, she still had to be vigilant to keep her secret. When she had to go to the hospital due to severe diarrhea, she had to fool the doctor. Some accounts propose that she may have even conducted some sort of affair with another woman. "Throughout the war Cashier corresponded with the Morey family of Babcock's Grove, Illinois," Blanton and Cook write. "Three of Morey's letters to [Cashier] inquire about a 'sweetheart,' wondering if Albert had brought her a new dress. The Morey family, like the soldiers with whom Cashier served, did not know Cashier was a woman. Since Cashier's letters to the Morey family have not been found, further information about the relationship . . . is unavailable." Long after the war when her identity was revealed, her fellow soldiers were shocked. As one said, "I never suspected at any time all through the service that Cashier was a woman." Another one said, "She seemed to be able to do as much work as anyone in the company."

During the next three years, Jenny Hodgers and the Ninety-fifth encountered some of the fiercest fighting of the war, including the siege of Vicksburg, the Red River Campaign, and the Battle of Guntown in Mississippi. On May 18, 1863, she was with Grant during the siege of Vicksburg. The Union army had shelled the city relentlessly for weeks. During the battle, she was captured while conducting a reconnaissance mission, but escaped from capture by grabbing a Confederate guard's rifle and knocking him to the ground. Although the guards chased her, she was able to run back to her unit. If she had been interrogated, her captors would have tried to force her to provide details about Union troop movements and General Grant's tactics. Soldiers in her unit also remembered that she exposed herself to sniper fire when she climbed a tall tree to attach the Union flag after it was shot down.

By the end of the war, Jenny had fought in more than forty battles, earning a reputation for bravery and perseverance under fire. Remarkably, she escaped the war without serious injury, which helped her keep her true identity a secret. The gender of other women soldiers was usually discovered when they were injured. According to Blanton and Cook, "She served a full enlistment, and long after the war, her fellow veterans remembered the diminutive Private with the Irish brogue as a good and brave soldier, and expressed a great deal of admiration for her heroic fighting." Her final battle was the capture of Mobile, Alabama.

When the Ninety-fifth Illinois Infantry Volunteers were finally discharged in August 1865, four months after General Robert E. Lee surrendered and the Civil War came to a close, Jenny and her fellow soldiers returned to Illinois, where they were honored with a huge public rally. Each man then went his own way and Jenny remained in her male guise, living as Albert, a quiet bachelor. Albert settled down. She worked for a while as a farm hand before taking a job as a dry goods clerk in Saunemin, Illinois, in 1869. She lived there for the next forty years and held a variety of jobs, including janitor and lamplighter. Every year on Decoration Day she put on her Union army uniform and marched in the local parade. And every year on election day, she did what no woman would be permitted to do in her lifetime: she voted. She voted in several presidential elections before Illinois gave women the right to vote and before the Nineteenth Amendment became a part of the U.S. Constitution in 1920. Although no voter registry was kept in those early days, Saunemin residents remember that Albert marked an X on the ballot in the voter's booth. In 1899, Albert filed for a military pension.

In 1911, Jenny's secret was finally discovered by the town doctor. While Albert was working for Illinois state senator Ira Lish, Lish accidentally ran over Cashier with his car. In the course of treatment, the town doctor discovered Albert was in fact a woman, but the doctor and the senator agreed to keep the matter a secret. Because her leg never healed properly, the senator secured a place for her in a rest home for veterans. Her secret was never revealed.

However, the Pension Bureau launched an investigation to determine if Jenny Hodgers had defrauded the government to receive the veteran's pension she had been receiving since 1890. After careful review of the evidence and interviews with dozens of Hodgers's fellow soldiers in the Ninety-fifth, the bureau decided that Hodgers and Cashier were one in the same and maintained the pension. They verified that she was indeed the small yet brave soldier who performed many dangerous missions. Although she was granted status as a veteran, tragically she was judged to be insane for masquerading as a man. She was sent to a mental asylum, where she was forced to wear dresses. According to Blanton and Cooke, "She was a frail 74-year-old who did not know how to walk in such apparel, having worn pants her entire adult life and probably for a good part of her childhood as well. Cashier tripped, fell, and broke her hip. She never recovered from this injury, and spent the rest of her life mostly confined to her bed." Her comrades tried to gain her release from the asylum, but they were unsuccessful. On October 10, 1915, Albert D. J. Cashier died at the Watertown State Hospital for the Insane.

Newspapers across the country reported her death and noted that she was buried in a Union army uniform with full military honors with a marker reading: "Albert D. J. Cashier, Co. G, 95 Ill. Inf." Jenny is also honored on the Illinois memorial at Vicksburg with the inscription, "Cashier, Albert D. J., Pvt." As Tom Deignan notes in *Irish America* magazine, "Roughly sixty years after her death, another headstone was erected next to Private Cashier's grave marker. It reads: 'Jenny Hodgers.'"

11. KATE MULLANEY

1845–1906

FOUNDER OF THE FIRST WOMEN'S LABOR UNION

They fought for equal pay for equal work, and we still do so today. They fought for better working conditions, and we still do so today. They fought for respect at work and at home, and we still do today.
—Hillary Rodham Clinton, on the women
of the Collar Laundry Union

By the time she was nineteen years old, the Irish immigrant Kate Mullaney became the founder of the first all-female union in the United States. Exhausted from fourteen-hour workdays as a laundress in upstate New York, Kate was supporting her mother and two younger sisters on a salary of just $2 a week.

She was born in Ireland in 1845, one of four children, and immigrated to Troy, New York, with her parents and her older sister Mary to seek more opportunity. She enjoyed a relatively carefree childhood in America until her father died and her mother, Bridget, became gravely ill. At the age of just nineteen, Kate had become the head of the household.

She began working in one of the fourteen commercial laundries in Troy, and although she considered herself fortunate to have a job, she and her other female co-workers were subjected to grueling conditions. More than three thousand women worked in these factories, spending as much as twelve to fourteen hours every day bleaching, washing, and boiling the detachable collars that had become fashionable among affluent men in the mid to late nineteenth century. Even by standards of the time, the women were working in deplorable conditions. Because of the dangerous chloride and sulfur used to clean the collars as well as exposure to boiling hot water and unwieldy irons, the workers often suffered severe burns. And if any shirts were ruined, a woman would have to pay for them out of her own meager salary of three to four dollars a week.

Like so many of her fellow Irish women, Kate knew that she would have to be the one to summon the courage to fight for her rights as a woman and as a worker. She took inspiration from the male members of the nearby Iron Molders Union, who impressed upon her that much could be accomplished through organized protest. Because she had become the head of her household, she had experience in organizing and had already gained a sense of maturity far beyond her years. In February 1864, with encouragement from the Iron Molders, Kate and her coworkers Esther Keegan and Sarah McQuillan organized three hundred women into the Collar Laundry Union—the first female union in the country. Just a few weeks later, on February 23, the women decided to strike over low wages and dangerous conditions. It was an ambitious strike. By noon, all of the women from the fourteen laundries walked out of work. Within a week the owners gave in to their demands for a twenty-percent wage increase.

Two years later, in 1866, the Laundry Collar Union donated a thousand dollars to the Iron Molders Great Lock Out, and they also received a substantial wage increase of their own. In just two years, their salary had risen from three dollars a week to fourteen dollars. Kate was now becoming a major force in the labor movement. With her fellow union heads, she was able to garner higher wages for her members and establish a substantial fund from which to care for their workers when they became ill or injured.

Kate went on to play a sterling role in organized labor. In 1868, she went to New York City to attend the convention of the National Labor Union, along with Mary Kellogg Putnam and Susan B. Anthony. There she was nominated for the position of Assistant Secretary of the Union, the first time a woman had been appointed to national office in the labor movement. As William Sylvis, leader of the Iron Molders later remarked, "We now have a recognized officer from the female side of the house— one of the smartest and most energetic women in America; and from the great work which she has already done, I think it not unlikely that we may in the future have delegates representing 300,000 working women." In this same year, Kate and her fellow members supported the thousands of members in the Bricklayers Union in New York City, who had organized their own strike. One year later, in 1869, Kate and her family moved to a comfortable three-story brick house in Troy. By now, the Laundry Collar Union had more than 450 members and was stronger than ever. They began to demand raises of one to two cents per dozen collars, and they also began to incur the wrath of the laundry owners. When the workers decided to strike again, their rally drew more than seven thousand supporters.

But now the collar manufacturers were holding the laundry owners hostage by refusing to send their products to any laundry that used union labor. Kate responded by forming a cooperative laundry, which the laundry owners succeeded in destroying. They also began to defame the members of the Laundry Collar Union in the local press. Refusing to be shaken, Kate formed the Union Line Collar and Cuff Manufactory, and began to sell shares in the company. By 1869, the Manufactory appeared to be making money. However, collar manufacturers had recently invented a new paper collar, which rendered the old collars obsolete. By 1870, it appeared that the laundry owners and manufacturers had won—there was a new product on the market and the Iron Molders could no longer afford to contribute to the Laundry Collar Union. Kate was forced to disband the union that same year, but her legacy remains. With her courage and tenacity, she helped improve the lives of working women everywhere, and gave women the determination to forge their own way in labor movements across the country.

Kate Mullaney died on August 17, 1906, and was buried in Troy's St. Peter's Cemetery. For many years, she remained in an unmarked grave until local supporters and union groups raised enough money for a grave marker in the shape of a Celtic Cross. In 1998, First Lady Hillary Clinton spoke at the landmark designation ceremony of the Kate Mullaney House in Troy, New York.

12. KATHARINE O'SHEA

1845–1921
IRELAND'S UNCROWNED QUEEN

On October 6th, 1891, nearly twenty-three years ago, Charles Stewart Parnell died in the arms of his wife; nearly twenty-three years ago, the whole civilized world awoke to laud—or to condemn—the dead chief. It ranked him with the greatest heroes, or with the vilest sinners, of the world because he had found and kept the haven of her arms with absolute disregard of that world's praise or blame, 'til death.

—Katharine O'Shea

I was Parnell's messenger, and in all other work I did for him, it was understood on all sides that I worked for Parnell alone.

—Katharine O'Shea

It is quite impossible for me to tell you just how much you have changed my life, what a small interest I take in what is going on about me, and how I detest everything which has happened during the last few days to keep me away from you.

—Charles Stewart Parnell in a letter to his wife, Katharine O'Shea

The name Charles Stewart Parnell, perhaps more than any other name in Irish history, conjures up images of a fallen hero who met his end far too soon. Called "Ireland's Uncrowned King," the Irish revolutionary leader has been mythologized by Irish literary giants like William Butler Yeats and James Joyce as the man who could have gained Irish independence from the hands of the British. In Joyce's *Portrait of the Artist As a Young Man*, the dinner scene in which Stephen Dedalus's father and his friend Mr. Casey lament Parnell's fall and cries, "Oh, Parnell! More poor dead king!" is one of the most famous in Irish literature. By 1882, Parnell had founded the Irish Parliamentary Party and garnered support for Irish self-determination (or Home Rule) from the British prime minister William Gladstone. But while Parnell was being hailed as Ireland's savior, his career was about to erupt in scandal. In 1880, he fell in love with Katharine O'Shea, the wife of another man. When Parnell fell, many throughout Ireland blamed "Kitty O'Shea," as they cruelly called her, pegging her as an evil temptress who led their hero astray. History judges Katharine more kindly. While it is true that the affair wrecked Parnell's career, it is also true that without Katharine, it would have been impossible for Parnell to progress as far as he did with Gladstone. She was his confidante, advisor, and best friend. And although Charles Stewart Parnell loved Ireland, he loved Katharine O'Shea more. As Joyce Marlow observes, "In 1890, the previously unknown name of Kitty O'Shea rang round the world, and among other things, she was called a proved British prostitute and the 'were-wolf' woman of Irish politics; when she died it was said that she had done more to affect Anglo-Irish relations that any female of the Nineteenth century."

Katharine Wood was born in London on January 30, 1845 into a well-educated, creative, and exceptional family. The daughter of Sir John Page Wood, an Oxford-educated vicar, and Emma Caroline Michell, an artist, novelist, and daughter of an admiral, Katie, as her family called her, was the last of thirteen children. A politically active Whig and skilled orator, John became the secretary to Queen Caroline and chaplain to the Duke of Sussex. After Katie was born, the family moved from London to Rivenhall Place, an ideal setting in which to raise children. Inspired by her gifted family, Katie began writing short adventure stories at an early age, which her father affectionately called "blood-stained bandits." These delightful stories soon inspired Lady Wood and Katie's sister Anna to write novels of their own, including *Sorrows of the Sea* and the book of poems *Ephemera*. Katie also wrote several songs that were eventually published by Boosey's music publisher in London. Although she never had any formal education, Katie was surrounded by artistic and intellectual expression that fostered her own creativity. The author Anthony Trollope often visited the house, and Kate later struck up a friendship with the writer George Meredith. Surprisingly, the woman whose name would become synonymous with sexual impropriety and desire was no great beauty as a child and teenager, but she was charming and vivacious and had, according to Marlow, "a strong strain of coquettishness and an acceptance of the traditional female role as sexual playmate." It was this allure that would capture the heart of Captain William ("Willie") O'Shea, her future husband, and seal her fate forever.

In 1862, when she was eighteen, Katharine's brother Frank introduced her to Willie O'Shea (a member of the Eighteenth Hussars Regiment) at a review near his house in Aldershot, England. O'Shea was dashing, Irish (from County Limerick), and completely smitten with Katie. A horse enthusiast, Willie began visiting the Woods at their home and took full advantage of their stable of horses. Although the pair was deeply in love, the couple seemed ill fated from the beginning. Katie's parents thought she was too young too marry. Willie was Catholic, Katie was Protestant, and Willie's mother, Countess O'Shea, found Kate completely unsuitable. However, in 1866 Kate's father died suddenly, leaving her mother virtually penniless. Fortunately, Lady Wood's sister set up a fund for the family that would allay any of the family's financial anxiety. Soon after, William returned from his post in Spain more determined than ever to marry Kate. Willie and Katharine were married in Brighton on January 25, 1867. Years later, Kate moved to the same town to live with her great love, Charles Stewart Parnell.

Soon after the wedding, Willie took up a partnership in his uncle's bank, O'Shea and Company, in Spain. The couple lived there for a year before returning to England, where they bought a horse farm. While the couple led a glamorous life and gave grand dinner parties, the marriage was already beginning to show signs of strain. Willie racked up heavy expenses, was often unreliable, and traveled often on business. Bored, lonely and frustrated, Kate was already feeling that her marriage was a mistake. As she recalls in her book *Charles Stewart Parnell*, "What a curious life mine was, I thought, narrow, narrow, narrow, and so deadly dull." By the time her son, Gerard William Henry, was born in 1870, the couple was already partially separated. While Willie stayed in London, Kate went to

live at a house owned by her aunt in Eltham. Although Willie and Kate
had two more children during their marriage, Norah in 1873 and Car-
men in 1874, their union was almost entirely for show. By this time,
Willie was growing increasingly interested in Irish politics. As an Irishman living in England, he believed that he could be instrumental in fix-
ing Ireland's problems. After a visit home, he decided to run for
Parliament in County Clare. It was then that he met Charles Stewart Parnell, the leader of the Irish Parliamentary Party and the man who would
become his wife's lover.

By 1879, Parnell was already hailed as "Ireland's Uncrowned King."
Of Anglo-Irish ancestry, Parnell was the relative of the poet Thomas Parnell. Like Kate, he was raised in England, but he detested the English
government. While studying at Cambridge, Parnell learned about the
English atrocities in Ireland and soon joined the Fenian movement. He
became passionate about the prisoners and soon formed the Home Rule
League, the nationalist movement that sought to establish an autonomous
government in Ireland. By the late 1870s, he became president of the Land
League, which advocated the abolition of landlordism in Ireland and
would lead to independence. Parnell began raising funds in the United
States and Canada, thus securing his position as the leader of the nationalist movement. O'Shea backed Parnell to the hilt and soon returned as a
member of Parliament for County Clare. Ironically, it was Willie's idea to
invite Parnell to dinner at Eltham. Despite several invitations from Kate
and Willie, Parnell never showed. Finally, he accepted and Kate immediately became enraptured by the passionate and regal Irish leader. The two
began meeting for dinner in London and discussing the Irish situation.
What followed was a series of ardent letters between Parnell and Kate.
While it is difficult to pinpoint when the affair began, it probably started
in 1880, as Kate was already pregnant with Parnell's child by 1881. Kate's
own letters show that Parnell began calling her "My own Love" in his letters rather than "Mrs. O'Shea." In one October 17, 1881, letter, Parnell reveals his growing love, "You cannot imagine how much you have
occupied my thoughts and how very greatly the seeing you again com-
forts me."

While Parnell was spending a great deal of time at Eltham with Kate, the Irish servants in the house, who were in awe of Parnell, kept the affair a secret. However, Parnell was cavalier about the entire affair and it is probable that his nationalist colleagues knew as early as 1881, as they were already opening his mail for "security" reasons. Pregnant with Parnell's child, Kate was trying to allay her husband's already growing suspicions. She persuaded Parnell to let Willie be his intermediary with Prime Minister Gladstone, and she had sex with her husband in the interim to cover the pregnancy. By this time, Parnell was traveling between Ireland and England to promote his "Relief of Distress," which would allay the impending eviction of Irish tenants. He gave an incendiary speech in Leeds, which the English saw as promoting lawlessness against the government. He was put on trial as part of "a conspiracy to impoverish landlords." O'Shea, being a landlord himself, was appalled by Parnell's convictions, but Kate was in total sympathy with the tenants, many of whom were left homeless on the roadside and whose homes were destroyed while they were still in them. As she recalls, "Remembering these and so many other tales of some of the 50,000 evictions that he afterwards calculated had taken place in Ireland, I have never wondered at the implacable hatred of England that can never really die out of the Irish heart."

The house in Eltham soon became Parnell's headquarters, and he hid his papers under the watchful eye of his mistress. Kate hid him there during his impending arrest, cooked for him, and nursed him during his bout of illnesses. Before his arrest, he gave her a hollow gold bracelet containing his secret papers that she kept on her arm for three years. While it seems implausible that O'Shea was blind to the affair, it is more likely that he wanted to be. Having no real money of his own, it seems that Willie was willing to turn a blind eye to his wife's indiscretions as long as they weren't thrown in his face. However, Parnell's letters were becoming less and less discreet. He eventually began referring to Kate as "my dearest wife" and "my Queen." And he declared, "For good or ill, I am your husband, your love, your children, your all. And I will give my life to Ireland, but to you I give my love, whether it be your heaven and your Hell." Soon afterward, O'Shea returned to Eltham only to find Parnell's suitcase. In a fury, he challenged Parnell to a duel, which never came to fruition.

On April 7, 1881, Gladstone's land bill became law, but Parnell had his reservations, stating that the act should be tested on selected cases in Ireland. Kate began working on Parnell's behalf, mainly in monitoring the government's intention to arrest him. She wired him a code that warned him of the warrant for his arrest. Irritated that he had given Parnell much of what he wanted in the Land Act and that he still insisted on causing political fireworks, Gladstone had Parnell formally arrested, accusing that he was "pre-eminent in the attempt to destroy the authority of the law." Parnell was taken to Kilmainham Jail in Dublin. While O'Shea attempted reconciliation with Kate, she was already pregnant with Parnell's child. As Parnell was already a celebrated figure, he was able to sneak daily letters to Kate through a messenger, many of which alluded to her pregnancy by ending those letters with the phrase, "Best love to our child." Although some of the letters may seem cloying by today's standards, the sentiment is sincere. Parnell expressed concern about Kate's health and vowed to resign from politics rather than worry her. Kate was enduring a difficult pregnancy but as she recalls, "The joy of carrying Parnell's child carried me through my troubles." On February 16, 1882, Kate gave birth to their daughter, Sophie Claude (named after Parnell's sister). Amazingly, O'Shea did not suspect the paternity of the child, but misfortune soon followed the birth of the baby. Sophie soon became gravely ill. Parnell was granted leave to attend his nephew's funeral, and he immediately rushed to Eltham, where Kate placed the baby in his arms. While their child was dying, Parnell and O'Shea met to discuss the future of Ireland. The situation in Ireland was worsening by the minute, and Gladstone needed Parnell's help. It was here in Eltham that O'Shea and Parnell conceived the Kilmainham Treaty, which called for Ireland's autonomy through constitutional change rather than through armed resistance. Soon after, Parnell was released from prison and O'Shea delivered the news. It was here that Kate seemed to have the most influence over Parnell's point of view. The letter to Gladstone regarding the Kilmainham Treaty was actually drafted by Kate and Parnell, and she was starting to lead her lover to a more moderate, antiviolent agenda. Even Gladstone would later agree that Kate had a great influence on Parnell.

As she affirmed later, "I was very anxious that he should reign by constitutional means."

On May 6, 1882, the infamous Phoenix Park murders shocked Ireland. Two high-ranking English officials, Lord Frederick Cavendish and Thomas Henry Burke, were brutally murdered by nationalists, and Parnell considered resigning from politics altogether. In another instance of foreshadowing, a picture depicting O'Shea and Parnell in Parliament that hung in the O'Sheas' Eltham house came crashing to the ground. Anxious that Parnell should stay in politics, Kate wrote to Gladstone and persuaded him to meet with Parnell. Gladstone, eager to keep the Irish vote, agreed to a private communication. Kate became the intermediary between the two and advised Parnell, "Why not see Gladstone yourself privately, and get what you can from him in return for the Irish vote." Besides being Gladstone's envoy, Kate advised the prime minister on a number of issues, including a death sentence that was being unfairly passed on a young Irishman. She persuaded him to reverse the decision. In 1884, Parnell had written a proposed constitution for Ireland that gave "the power to make enactments regarding all the domestic concerns of Ireland, but without the power to interfere in any imperial manner." The new Tory government was determined to secure the Irish vote and Parnell was now the de facto head of the House of Commons. It seemed that Irish self-determination would become a fait accompli.

Parnell was given the Freedom of the City of Dublin, the city's highest honor, and his celebrity was growing, but trouble in his political life was already beginning. Kate opened all his correspondence and was forced to keep some of the more upsetting death threats from him. She kept him from falling for traps and warned him that Forster had a vendetta against him. In addition, Parnell was already ill with gastric trouble and exhaustion. Kate traveled with him, nursed him through illness, and waited for him secretly in every train station in Ireland and England. By March 1887, reports of their relationship were beginning to leak out. On March 7, 1887, the Parnell letters appeared in the *London Times*. While the letters were a forgery, they were an omen of the growing conspiracy against Parnell. That year, he was given the Freedom of the City of Edinburgh, but

Parnell was growing weary of keeping his love affair a secret. In 1890, he told Kate, "I have given and will give, Ireland what is in me to give. That I have vowed to her, but my private life shall never belong to any country, but to one woman." Parnell was officially served in a copy of the petition in the divorce case of O'Shea versus O'Shea. While his personal life was finally taking a positive turn, his political future was about to be destroyed.

The Irish Parliamentary Party was afraid of shocking Gladstone with the scandal, but Parnell was prepared to fight. Although Gladstone knew of the affair for more than ten years, he had to be seen as morally upright. All of Parnell's followers turned on him, including Gladstone, who issued a statement declaring that Parnell's continued service in government would be "disastrous" for Ireland. Home Rule was officially dead. Struggling to maintain support, Parnell's already fragile health began to worsen. Anti-Parnellites began using the name "Kitty O'Shea" as the ultimate insult in Parliament. Undeterred, Parnell married Katharine O'Shea on June 25, 1891, in Brighton, the town where she had married Captain O'Shea. Three months later, broken by betrayal and suffering from rheumatism, the embattled leader died in her arms. His last words were, "Kiss me, sweet wife, and I will try to sleep a little."

Heartbroken, Katharine was dissuaded from attending her own husband's funeral in Glasnevin Cemetery. By now, she had very little income and was also trying to gain custody of Katie and Clare, the two children she had with Parnell in 1883 and 1884 (interestingly enough, she does not mention these children in her memoirs). Crippled with grief, she moved frequently and suffered one of many breakdowns. In 1913, she published her memoirs, mainly because she needed the money. On February 5, 1921, she died of heart disease. While her death made front-page news all over the world, only four mourners attended her funeral.

13. LADY GREGORY

1852–1932
DRAMATIST

Think like a wise man, but to express oneself like the common people.

—Lady Gregory

The greatest living Irishwoman.

—George Bernard Shaw

Alas! A woman may not love!
For why should she bestow in vain
The riches of that treasure trove
To win but a recipient of pain
For never will the gainer pay
In full the love she gives away.

—Lady Gregory

Along with her contemporary William Butler Yeats, Lady Gregory has captivated the Irish literary imagination for more than eighty years. One of the founders of the Celtic literary revival, she will forever be known as the woman who helped found the Irish Literary Theatre and the Abbey Theatre and who translated lost Irish poetry and literature. What is less well known about Lady Gregory is the role she played in fostering the great literary figures of her time. She was the woman who paid James Joyce's fare to Europe, helping him escape the stifling clutches of Catholic Ireland and therefore conceiving one of the most illustrious writing careers in history. Her dedication to Irish nationalism helped to inspire such women as Maud Gonne and Countess Markievicz.

Isabella Augusta Perse was born on May 21, 1852, the youngest daughter of an Anglo-Irish landlord-class family in Roxborough, County Galway. Her mother, Frances Barry, was related to Standish Hayes O'Grady, the first Viscount Guillamore, and her family home, Roxborough, was a 6,000-acre estate that was later burned down during the Irish Civil War. She was educated at home, and her future career was strongly influenced by the family nurse, Mary Sheridan, a Catholic and a native Irish speaker who introduced the young Isabella Augusta to the history and legends of the local area. This early introduction probably had a greater impact on her than it otherwise would because the house had no library and her mother, who was a strict evangelical Protestant, forbid her to read any novels until she was eighteen.

She married Sir William Henry Gregory, a widower with an estate at Coole Park, near Gort, County Galway, in 1880, at a Protestant church in Dublin. As the wife of a knight, she became entitled to the style "Lady Gregory." Sir William Gregory, who was thirty-five years older than his bride, had just retired from his position of governor of Ceylon, having previously served several terms as a member of Parliament for Westminster. He was a well-educated man with many literary and artistic interests, and the house at Coole Park housed a large library and an extensive art collection, both of which his bride was eager to explore. He also had a house in London, and the couple spent a considerable amount of time there holding a weekly salon that was frequented by many of the leading literary and artistic figures of the day, including Robert Browning, Lord Tennyson, John Everett Millais, and Henry James. Their only child, Robert Gregory, was born in 1881. He was killed while serving as a pilot during World War I, an event that inspired Yeats's poems "An Irish Airman Foresees His Death" and "In Memory of Major Robert Gregory."

The Gregorys traveled to Ceylon, India, Spain, Italy, and Egypt. While in Egypt, Lady Gregory had an affair with the English poet Wilfrid Scawen Blunt during which she wrote a series of love poems, *A Woman's Sonnets*. Blunt later published these poems under his own name. Her earliest work to appear under her own name was *Arabi and His Household* (1882), a pamphlet in support of Ahmed Arabi Bey, the leader of an Egyptian nationalist revolt against the oppressive regime of the

Khedives. She later said of this booklet, "Whatever political indignation or energy was born with me may have run its course in that Egyptian year and worn itself out." Despite this, in 1893 she published *A Phantom's Pilgrimage, or Home Ruin*, an antinationalist pamphlet against William Gladstone's proposed second Home Rule Act. She also did charitable work in the parish of St. Stephen's, Southwark, London, and wrote the pamphlet *Over the River* (1887) about her experiences there.

She also worked on more literary prose during the period of her marriage. In 1883–1884, she worked on a series of memoirs of her childhood home under the title *An Emigrant's Notebook*, but these were never published. She also wrote a number of short stories in the years 1890 and 1891, although these also never appeared in print. A number of unpublished poems from this period have also survived.

When Sir William Gregory died in March 1892, Lady Gregory went into mourning and returned to Coole Park, where she edited her husband's autobiography and had it published in 1894. She later wrote, "If I had not married I should not have learned the quick enrichment of sentences that one gets in conversation; had I not been widowed I should not have found the detachment of mind, the leisure for observation necessary to give insight into character, to express and interpret it. Loneliness made me rich—'full,' as Bacon says."

A trip to Inisheer in the Aran Islands in 1893 inspired an interest in the Irish language and in the folklore of the area in which she lived. She organized Irish lessons at the school in Coole and began collecting tales from the area around her home, especially from the residents of Gort workhouse. This activity led to the publication of a number of volumes of folk material, including *A Book of Saints and Wonders* (1906), *The Kiltartan History Book* (1909), and *The Kiltartan Wonder Book* (1910). She also produced a number of collections of Kiltartanese versions of Irish myths, including *Cuchulain of Muirthemne* (1902) and *Gods and Fighting Men* (1904). In his introduction to the former, Yeats wrote, "I think this book is the best that has come out of Ireland in my time." James Joyce was to parody this claim in the Scyla and Charybdis chapter of his novel *Ulysses*.

Toward the end of 1894, and encouraged by the positive reception of her editing of her husband's autobiography, Lady Gregory turned her attention to another editorial project. She decided to prepare selections from Sir William Gregory's grandfather's correspondence for publication as *Mr. Gregory's Letter-Box 1813–30* (1898). This entailed researching Irish history of the period, and one outcome of this work was a shift in her own position from the "soft" Unionism of her earlier writing on Home Rule to a definite support of Irish nationalism and what she was later to describe as "a dislike and distrust of England."

Edward Martyn was a neighbor of Lady Gregory, and it was during a visit to his house in Tulira that she first met Yeats. Discussions between the three of them over the following year or so led to the founding of the Irish Literary Theatre in 1899. Lady Gregory oversaw the fund-raising, and the first program consisted of Martyn's *The Heather Field* and Yeats's *The Countess Cathleen*. During this period, she effectively coauthored Yeats's early plays, including *The Countess Cathleen*, specifically working on the passages of dialogue involving peasant characters.

Lady Gregory remained an active director of the theater until ill health led to her retirement in 1928. During this time she wrote more than forty plays, mainly for production at the Abbey. Many of these were written in an attempted translation of the Hiberno-English dialect spoken around Coole Park that became widely known as Kiltartanese, from the nearby village of Kiltartan. Her plays, which are rarely performed now, were not particularly popular at the time. Indeed, the Irish writer Oliver St. John Gogarty once wrote, "The perpetual presentation of her plays nearly ruined the Abbey." Besides her plays, she wrote a two-volume study of the folklore of her native area called *Visions and Beliefs in the West of Ireland* (1920). She also played the lead role in three performances of *Cathleen ní Houlihan* in 1919.

During her time on the board of the Abbey, Coole Park remained her home and she spent her time in Dublin, staying in a number of hotels. In these, she ate frugally, often on food she brought with her from home. She frequently used her hotel rooms to interview would-be Abbey dramatists and to entertain the company after opening nights of new plays. She spent many of her days working on her translations in the National Library of Ireland.

She also gained a reputation as being a somewhat conservative figure.

For instance, when Denis Johnston submitted his first play *Shadowdance* to the Abbey, it was rejected by Lady Gregory and returned to the author with "The Old Lady says No" written on the title page. Johnston decided to rename the play, and *The Old Lady Says "No!"* was eventually staged by the Gate Theatre in 1928.

When she retired from the Abbey board, Lady Gregory returned to Galway to live, although she continued to visit Dublin regularly. The house and demesne at Coole Park had been sold to the Irish Forestry Commission in 1927, with Lady Gregory retaining life tenancy. Her Galway home had long been a focal point for the writers associated with the Irish literary revival and this continued after her retirement. On a tree in what were the grounds of the now demolished house, one can still see the carved initials of John Synge, Æ (George Russell), Yeats, and his artist brother Jack, George Moore, Sean O'Casey, George Bernard Shaw, Katharine Tynan, and Violet Martin. Yeats wrote five poems about or set in the house and grounds: "The Wild Swans at Coole," "I walked among the Seven Woods of Coole," "In the Seven Woods," "Coole Park, 1929," and "Coole Park and Ballylee, 1931."

The woman Shaw once described as "the greatest living Irishwoman" died at home at the age of eighty from breast cancer and is buried in the New Cemetery in Bohermore, County Galway. The entire contents of Coole Park were auctioned three months after her death and the house was demolished in 1941. Lady Gregory's plays fell out of favor after her death and are now rarely performed. She kept diaries and journals for most of her adult life, and many of these have been published since her death. In 1992, a visitor's center dedicated to her memory opened in Coole Park.

14. MAUD GONNE MACBRIDE

1865–1953

REVOLUTIONARY, AUTHOR, ACTRESS

The English may batter us to pieces, but they will never succeed in break-ing our spirit.

—Maud Gonne

To me Ireland was the all-protecting mother, who had to be released from the bondage of the foreigner, to be free and able to protect her children.

—Maud Gonne

What could have made her peaceful with a mind
That nobleness made simple as a fire,
With beauty like a tightened bow, a kind
That is not natural in any age like this,
Riding high and solitary and most stern?
Why, what could she have done, being what she is?
Was there another Troy for her to burn?

—William Butler Yeats, "No Second Troy"

Maud Edith Gonne was born on December 20, 1865, in Aldershot, England, to Tommy Gonne, a wealthy British army colonel of Irish descent, and Edith Cook, a beautiful English socialite. After her mother died of tuberculosis in 1871, Maud was educated in France by a governess, then moved to Dublin in 1882. Her father set the family up in Donnybrook, an affluent suburb, where Maud enjoyed a happy life with her sisters, May and Kathleen. Always a beautiful child, Maud was her father's favorite and he taught her to be strong, independent, and willful, qualities that would become invaluable later in life. He also gave her in-

credible freedom. When she came out to society at the age of just eighteen, she was already one of Ireland's most celebrated socialites, and essentially the head of the Gonne household.

Despite her privileged existence, Maud was already becoming aware
of the Irish peasant class in the countryside and their cruel treatment at
the hands of the British. As an upper-class Dubliner, she often came into
the company of landlords who treated their tenants with utter contempt.
At one dinner party, she recalled meeting a man who had observed a ten-
ant's wife who was dying of hunger. When Maud expressed outrage at his
callousness, the landlord reportedly shouted, "Let her die. These people
must be taught a lesson." Maud became so furious that she immediately
left the house.

Maud's beloved father died in 1886, at the age of fifty-one, leaving
Maud devastated. She and her sisters were sent to live in Ascot with her
uncle Charlie, and Tommy had left Maud with a substantial inheritance.
By this time, Maud had developed an interest in acting—a scandalous
profession at the time. She had, however, inherited her mother's lung
problems and it was during a rehearsal that one of her lungs collapsed.
Lung problems would plague her all of her life. When her doctor prescribed a holiday in a warmer climate, Maud traveled to the spa town of
Royat, France, where she met and fell in love with French journalist Lu-
cien Millevoye, who would become the love of her live. He also fueled her
love for revolutionary politics. She began to engage in political work for
Millevoye and was soon carrying papers for the Russian Tsar, in an effort
to gain Russian support for the French revolutionary movement. While
she enjoyed the intrigue, she wanted to work for Ireland more. She returned home and began to fully immerse herself in Irish politics.

While in Dublin, Maud met John O'Leary, the renowned republican
and leader of the 1848 uprising. Though naïve, Maud was beautiful,
young, and fearless, and O'Leary and the other leaders in the movement
began to realize how useful she could be to the cause. She soon rented a
flat in Dublin and took up the cause of the Land League. However, when
she attended a League meeting at the Gresham Hotel, she was told by one
of the male attendees that she could not join, because she was a woman.
She replied, "Surely, Ireland needs all her children." Tim Harrington,

who was a Member of Parliament and a head of the National Land League felt differently from other men. He immediately entrusted her with working with evicted tenants in Donegal, where poverty and hunger were rampant among Irish citizens.

During this time, Maud met the man who elevated her from revolutionary to muse: William Butler Yeats. Yeats was infatuated with Maud, as his poetry and plays reflect, but Maud refused his many proposals of marriage, seeing him only as a friend. However, Yeats did share her passion for Irish politics and soon became involved along with her in the national struggle. In turn, she became involved in the Celtic literary revival and helped Yeats found the National Literary Society of London in 1891. Yeats called Maud his "glimmering girl" and wrote the play *The Countess Cathleen* for her.

By 1889, Maud had become a legend in Ireland and a pariah to the British authorities. In imminent danger of being arrested, she returned to Paris to live with Millevoye. She started a nationalist newsletter called *L'Irelande Libre* and continued to travel to the United States and Scotland to raise funds for prisoners. In 1890, she gave birth to a son, George, out of wedlock, and gave her first political speech to a crowd of fifteen hundred, in which she opposed the British government. Tragically, her son died just a few months later. Though wracked with grief, she continued to give lectures in France and campaigned tirelessly for republican prisoners. In 1894, she gave birth to a daughter, Iseult. Interestingly enough, in her autobiography, *A Servant of the Queen*, Maud refers to her daughter as her "niece," probably to seem more acceptable to the Catholic community, who had come to revere her. Maud and Millevoye eventually ended their relationship, which many observers attribute to her aversion to physical passion.

After her breakup with Millevoye in the late 1890s, Maud returned to Ireland, where she was already being referred to as "Ireland's Joan of Arc," and co-founded the Transvaal Committee, which supported the Afrikaners in the Boer War. In 1900, she co-founded Inghinidhe na hÉireann (Daughters of Erin) along with Constance Gore-Booth (later Countess Markiewicz) and wrote for its newspaper, *Bean na hÉireann* (Women of Erin).

In 1900, while visiting Paris, Maud met Major John MacBride, who had been second in command of the Irish Brigade in the Boer War. She converted to Catholicism before marrying MacBride in 1903 in what would become one of the great political alliances in Ireland. The two made a formidable pair—he was a hero and she was a living legend. Maud gave birth to their son Seán in 1905, who would later form Amnesty International to assist Irish political prisoners and their families. But it was a marriage between political comrades, not a great love, and the couple soon separated. MacBride stayed in Dublin, while Maud returned to Paris with the children, where she would remain until 1917. Maud continued her political work, and volunteered with the Red Cross in France during World War I. When she returned to Ireland after the Easter Rising, she found that her beloved country was forever changed and her husband had been executed, along with the other leaders of the Rising.

Although she was already in her fifties, her passion never wavered. Along with Hanna Sheehy Skeffington, Kathleen Clarke, Countess Markievicz, she was arrested and imprisoned for her involvement in the anti-conscription movement. In 1922, during the Irish civil war, Maud supported the anti-treaty side and helped to form the Women's Prisoners Defense League which gave aid to Republican prisoners. The next year, the Irish government imprisoned her on conspiracy charges. In protest, she immediately went on hunger strike and was released a month later.

In 1938, she published *A Servant of the Queen*, and although it has many factual inaccuracies, it remains an impressive document of a woman who was ahead of her time politically and personally. Maud died on April 27, 1953, at the age of eighty-six, but her legacy lives on. To this day, she is the most revered woman in republican history, and it is impossible to take a class on Yeats without hearing her name. Her son Seán, a leader of the IRA in the 1920s, would become a hero in his own right through his work with Amnesty International, and he was awarded the Nobel Peace Prize in 1974. Maud Gonne MacBride is buried in the Republican plot in Glasnevin Cemetery, near her comrade Countess Markievicz. As Margaret Ward observes in her biography, *Maud Gonne*, "her personality remains as beguiling and compelling as it was 100 years ago, when she first began working for the Irish cause."

15. ANNE MANSFIELD SULLIVAN

1866–1936

TEACHER, MIRACLE WORKER

A fire of hatred blazed up in me which burned for many years.

—Anne Sullivan

My teacher is so near to me that I scarcely think of myself as apart from her. All of the best in me belongs to her.

—Helen Keller

The lives of Anne Sullivan and Helen Keller were so intertwined that it is impossible to write about one without mentioning the other. Many biographers have questioned how much of Helen Keller was actually Anne Sullivan. In fact, critics of both women have proposed that Anne Sullivan did not just make Helen Keller what she became (as in serving as a teacher-mentor). They allege that Anne's influence on Helen was so profound that she created Helen Keller in her own image. While Helen always acknowledged the debt she owed to Anne for bringing her back to the world and teaching her how to interact with the world, the two women were distinct individuals with very different personalities and beliefs.

From her birth in 1866 until she was fourteen years old, Anne Sullivan (baptized as Johanna Mansfield Sullivan) experienced the worst life the child of immigrant Irish parents could possibly imagine. Forced out by the Potato Famine, her parents, Thomas Sullivan and Alice Cloesy, immigrated from Limerick, Ireland, to the United States. They settled near some uncles in Feeding Hills, a village outside Springfield, Massachusetts. While many Irish immigrants were poor, Anne's parents were among the most impoverished, partly because her father was an alcoholic who had no skills and seldom worked. He was also an abusive man who eventually abandoned the family.

Misfortunes and illness plagued the family. Two years after Anne was born in April 1866, she contracted trachoma, which gradually destroyed her vision. By age five, Anne had lost the majority of her vision. Anne's mother had tuberculosis and was always frail. One of Anne's brothers, Jimmie, also contracted tuberculosis, which resulted in a tubercular hip. When Anne was eight, her mother died. After her mother's death, her father could not care for the children, so all the children except for Anne were taken in by family members. Anne was left to take care of her father in a run-down cabin on her uncle's farm. Anne's father told the children stories from Irish folklore, but he was angry about the treatment of the Irish and shared stories with Anne about Irish history and the injustice of Irish landlords and the British. Two years later, her father abandoned the entire family and Anne lived with an uncle. Eventually, the family decided they could not deal with all the children. They sent Anne's sister Mary to live with an aunt and Anne and Jimmie to the poorhouse in Tewksbury, Massachusetts. Anne was just ten years old. Jimmie died in the poorhouse three months later and Anne never saw Mary again.

Life in the Tewksbury Almshouse was very difficult for Anne. The residents of the poorhouse included not only poor adults and children but also prostitutes with syphilis and the mentally ill. Years later, Anne wrote, "I doubt if life or for that matter eternity is long enough to erase the terrors and ugly blots scored upon my mind during those dismal years from 10 to 14." Besides living in horrible conditions, she had almost no usable sight and received no formal education. The almshouse did have a small library but no teachers. Some reports allege that the prostitutes taught her to read while others indicate that some of the workers read to her or convinced other girls to read to her. Apparently, those who read to her selected many books written by Irish authors, including pulp novels that featured stories similar to those told by the inmates of Tewksbury. Anne also heard about world events when inmates read the *7th Pilot*, a newspaper published by a Boston Irish immigrant. Despite her vision impairment and lack of formal education, Anne became literate by her early teens. She acquired knowledge about literature, history, and current events, albeit from a distinctly Irish perspective. In Tewksbury, she learned of the Protestant persecutions, Charles Stewart Parnell's political exploits, and the Potato Famine, and she witnessed the day-to-day life of the almshouse women, who were pregnant, sick, or widowed individuals living with poverty, rape, violence, unemployment, and disease. Her experiences in Tewksbury left her with the belief that life is "primarily cruel and bitter."

As Anne became more literate, she realized she needed formal education. When Frank Sandborn, the state board of charities chairman, came to Tewksbury to investigate the living conditions, Anne threw herself in front of him crying, "Mr. Sandborn, I want to go to school." Soon after this visit, Anne was sent to the Perkins Institute for the Blind in 1880. While she attended Perkins, the staff arranged for multiple surgeries on her eyes. These surgeries were designed to relieve the pain and shooting light in her eyes but often left her vision blurry. Some accounts say that two of the operations restored some of her vision so that she could see some print, but she remained visually impaired for the rest of her life.

At Perkins, she learned to study with her fingers, and later to use her vision. She met Laura Bridgman, another famous student at Perkins who was blind and deaf, and learned the manual, or finger, alphabet, so that she could communicate with Laura. This experience prepared her for her future work with Helen Keller. Although Anne was a good student academically, she was rebellious, outspoken, and angry. She talked back to the teachers and questioned their teaching. She was ridiculed because of her speech, her dress, and her inability to read. Because she could not read, she was placed in beginning classes with the youngest children and called Big Annie. Nevertheless, she excelled and in 1886 she graduated as valedictorian of her class.

After graduation, she had trouble finding work. Although the Howes, the founders of the Perkins Institute, took an interest in her while she was there, they apparently did not help her find employment. When Helen Keller's father wrote to the institution asking for help for Helen, the head of Perkins, Michael Anagnos, referred Anne to the Kellers. Although she had no experience or formal training, Anne was chosen to be Helen's teacher. After learning some details of her new work, Anne went to Helen's home in Tuscumbia, Alabama. Anne was twenty-one when she arrived at the Keller home on March 3, 1887. When she met Helen, she realized her work with this "wild child" would be a challenge, but she said later that it was "the most important day I remember in all my life."

Immediately after she arrived, she began to sign words into Helen's hand, trying to help her associate objects with names. Helen's behavior problems made it difficult to work with her. Because Helen's parents did not know how to teach or manage her, Helen had become a spoiled, angry child who ruled the house with her tantrums. Anne realized that Helen needed discipline, but it would be difficult to change her behavior if they lived in the same house with her parents. She convinced Helen's parents that it would be best if she and Helen lived alone in the cottage on the Keller property. Although Helen's tantrums continued until she learned to communicate, she did begin to make progress.

Anne used the natural or immersion method. Rather than teach a series of lessons, Anne immersed Helen in a total environment of language, thereby allowing her to experience her environment. She approached teaching Helen as parents approach teaching an infant. As she said, "I shall talk into her hand as we talk into the baby's ears." From the beginning, she finger-spelled words into Helen's hand. Many accounts report that on the first day Anne gave Helen a doll as she spelled *doll*. For a while, Helen did not understand the connection between the signs and the names of objects. In the incident depicted in the movie *The Miracle Worker*, Anne tried to teach Helen the difference between a cup and the water in the cup. She took her to a pump, pumped water over one hand, and spelled *water* into the other hand. Helen finally understood the association of words and objects. She then pointed to Miss Sullivan, who spelled *teacher*. Helen called Anne "teacher" for the rest of her life. This breakthrough allowed Helen to learn thirty words that same day and over a hundred words within three weeks.

Although Anne had no formal training as a teacher, she took all she had learned at Perkins about teaching a deaf-blind child and used a variety of methods. She devoted some time each day to teaching Helen new words but she spelled words all day. She also realized that this deaf-blind child could learn much using her three remaining senses of touch, smell, and taste. Because Helen loved the outdoors and naturally explored her environment using her senses, Anne taught many lessons outdoors. She treated Helen as a typical child rather than as a child with multiple dis-abilities. She signed full sentences and believed Helen would learn the meaning of individual words from the context of the full sentences. She talked to Helen as she would to a "seeing and hearing child" and insisted that others do the same. In Helen Keller's biography *Teacher: Anne Sulli-van Macy*, she described Anne's approach as natural, because Teacher taught her to read in the same way that normal children were taught to read. Sullivan did not give her every word but left her "to puzzle out the meaning for herself." She noted that Teacher "dropped the verbs in one at a time" or supplied a word or two at a time. In her visualization of Sul-livan's teaching, she used the metaphor of melting snow. As she learned nouns, adjectives, and then verbs, some of the snow began to melt. Not long after beginning to read, she began to write. She wrote letters to all kinds of people, even surprising Anne.

Anne's success with Helen was regarded by others as amazing. She sent progress reports in letters to Anagnos. He published these in the school's annual reports. As Anne wrote, "Something within me tells me that I shall succeed beyond my dreams. . . . I know that [Helen] has re-markable powers, and I believe that I shall be able to develop and mould them." These reports led to more publicity about Helen's achievements. Alexander Graham Bell, the inventor of the telephone and a teacher of the deaf, who had referred Helen's parents to the Perkins Institute, gave a New York newspaper a picture of Helen and one of her letters to him. As a result, several newspapers published stories with pictures showing Helen's accomplishments such as reading William Shakespeare. Anne, Helen, and Helen's mother also traveled to Washington, D.C., and Boston, where they met many famous people, including President Grover Cleve-land, Samuel Clemens (Mark Twain), Oliver Wendell Holmes, John Green-leaf Whittier, Edward Everett Hale, and many prominent Bostonians.

They spent time with Bell and were Anagnos's guests at the Perkins Institute. Soon after, Anagnos persuaded Helen's father to let Helen study at Perkins. While most people were interested in Helen, Clemens gave Anne the credit for Helen's success when he called her a "miracle worker."

When Helen learned to spell words, Sullivan put them into raised print and on pieces of cardboard, and then Helen matched names to objects and created sentences. She eventually read from beginning readers and then Anne introduced Helen to literature. One of her first novels was *The Scarlet Letter*. Later, Anne suggested another book that became one of Helen's favorite childhood books, *Little Lord Fauntleroy*. Anne spelled the book to her by finger; then Anagnos had it produced in raised print because Helen loved it so much. Helen loved this because as she said, she "preferred reading [by] myself to being read to, because I liked to read again and again things that pleased me."

From 1888 to 1894 Helen attended the Perkins Institute. While she was there, Anne introduced her to the literature in the Perkins library, including Charles Dickens's *A Child's History of England*, Charles Lamb and Mary Lamb's *Tales from Shakespeare*, Johanna Wyss's *The Swiss Family Robinson*, Daniel Defoe's *Robinson Crusoe*, Louisa May Alcott's *Little Women*, and Johanna Spyri's *Heidi*. By age ten, Helen was proficient in reading Braille and in manual sign language and she now wanted to learn how to speak. Anne took Helen to the Horace Mann School for the Deaf in Boston. Sarah Fuller, the principal, gave Helen eleven lessons. Then Anne took over and Helen learned how to speak. But she was never really happy with her speech, which was intelligible to Anne and Fuller but very difficult for others to understand. The method that Anne used, called Tad-Oma, was pioneered in the United States by Sophia Alcorn, a teacher at the Kentucky School for the Deaf in Danville, Kentucky. The children were taught to speak by touching their teacher's cheek and feeling vocal vibrations.

In June 1892, Anne was elected a member of the American Association to Promote the Teaching of Speech to the Deaf. In 1894, Bell asked her to give a speech at an association meeting but she was so shy that Bell had to deliver the speech for her. Bell was a major influence in Anne's life. As an educator of the deaf, he strongly supported Anne's great talent as a teacher. He also provided emotional support and helped her in dealing with others. He understood the struggles she had to overcome as a child and was patient with her difficult temperament. He came to her defense when she was accused of being too controlling or having too much influence over Helen. Anne relied on him as a friend and mentor.

Anne and Helen met John D. Wright at the American Association to Promote the Teaching of Speech to the Deaf meeting. He convinced them to move to a new school in New York City that he and a colleague had founded. In 1894, Helen was enrolled in the Wright-Humason Oral School for the Deaf in New York as the only deaf-blind student. Despite the fact that Anne did not always agree with the teaching methods used there, which were very different from hers, she and Helen stayed there for four years.

Although the publicity about Helen's accomplishments was generally positive, critics attacked Helen and Anne several times. Laypeople and experts questioned Helen's abilities, alleging she was too extraordinary to be authentic. One particular incident brought more criticism. Anne had sent Anagnos a story by Helen titled "The Frost King." When critics noticed that Helen's story was remarkably similar to one written by Margaret Canby, Helen was accused of plagiarism. Helen did not remember reading the book and Anne did not remember reading it to her. Bell, Clemens, and others defended Helen and Anne, saying that everyone unconsciously plagiarizes. However, the critics argued that Anne must have been shaping Helen's thoughts and opinions. An investigation found that Helen had read Canby's book when she was about eleven years old at a friend's house. She did not remember it but the story had become part of her own thoughts. Although Anne and Anagnos had been very close, this incident led to a rift between Anne and Helen and Anagnos that eventually ended their friendship. At other times, Anne had disagreements with educators and with Helen's benefactors. Some accused her of controlling Helen and of even being cruel to her. These accusations plagued Anne and Helen for many years.

In 1896, Anne and Helen enrolled in the Cambridge School for Young Ladies in Cambridge, Massachusetts, to prepare Helen for entrance examinations to Radcliffe College. Later, Helen's sister Mildred came to visit and was allowed to attend the school with Helen. Anne and the school's director, Arthur Gilman, struggled over who would control Helen's education. Gilman alleged that Anne had too much control over Helen and was overworking Helen. When he wrote to Helen's mother, Kate, she sent a telegram authorizing him to take charge of Helen. Helen and Mildred refused to go to Gilman's home without Anne. Anne sent telegrams to several people, including Kate Keller, Bell, and the philanthropist Eleanor Hutton. She returned to the school and refused to leave until she had seen Helen and Mildred. After many people became involved in the argument about what should happen, Helen did not return to the school. Anne and Helen moved to Joseph E. Chamberlin and his family's home in Wrentham, Massachusetts, and Helen completed her preparation for the Radcliffe exams with a tutor.

In 1900, Helen passed the Radcliffe entrance examinations and was admitted as the only deaf-blind student at a higher education institution. Anne manually signed all the class lectures to Helen and also signed all the texts and books that were not available in Braille. The workload took a toll on both Helen and Anne. As Helen wrote in her biography *Teacher,* the reading affected Anne's eyes so much that she had to consult an ophthalmologist. When he discovered that Anne read to Helen at least five hours a day, he told Anne that she "must rest her eyes completely." He also prescribed the smoked glasses that Anne is often seen wearing in pictures. Helen completed all of her studies successfully and also began to write about her life. She learned to use a typewriter and also wrote her story in Braille. When Anne met John Albert Macy, a professor at Harvard, she introduced him to Helen. Macy became Helen's manager and editor and helped Helen edit her first book *The Story of My Life* and *The Practice of Optimism,* both of which were published in 1903. Helen graduated in 1904 cum laude with a bachelor's degree in English. Although Anne completed four years of college with Helen, no one offered her a college diploma.

In 1904, after Helen graduated, Anne and Helen bought a farm and seven acres of land in Wrentham. When Helen and Anne were at Radcliffe, John had become Anne's suitor and repeatedly asked Anne to marry him. She refused his proposals for many reasons, including her temperament, the differences in their religious backgrounds, and her concerns about Helen. Finally, John won her over and they married in 1905. Macy was an integral part of Helen's life and career. He negotiated the terms of the domestic and foreign publications of Helen's works. He learned manual sign language and helped Helen edit several books. John was a socialist and he corresponded with socialist writers such as Upton Sinclair. He discussed socialism with Helen and Anne and gave Helen books by Karl Marx, Friedrich Engels, and H. G. Wells. He convinced Helen to join the Socialist Party, but Anne was not swayed and never believed in change through political action. The three lived together until 1912, when Anne and John separated. The reasons for the separation are not known but authors speculate that the causes may have been Anne's fiery nature, their shaky financial situation, and John's feelings of neglect by Anne in favor of Helen. Their marriage ended in 1914.

After Anne and John separated, she and Helen began a fifteen-month lecture tour in the Northeast to supplement their income from Helen's writing. In the fall of that year, a young Scotswoman, Polly Thomson, joined the two women as a secretary for Helen.

Anne was often exhausted by the travel. Finally, in the fall of 1916 Anne had to stop work when she was diagnosed with pleurisy and incorrectly diagnosed with tuberculosis. She and Polly went to Lake Placid, New York, without Helen so Anne could recover. While they were there, Anne saw an ad for travel to Puerto Rico and bought two tickets for herself and Polly. Anne stayed in Puerto Rico for five months of rest and later said it was one of the happiest times of her life. In April 1917, Helen wrote Anne and Polly in Puerto Rico that the United States had declared war on Germany. They immediately returned to the United States. Anne and Helen decided to sell the house in Wrentham and bought a home in Forest Hills, New York. Anne and Polly traveled with Helen as she delivered antiwar speeches and visited blinded servicemen.

During the early 1920s, Anne and Helen traveled extensively to publicize the new American Foundation for the Blind, which was founded 1921. They advocated for the rights, improved living conditions, and increased opportunities for the blind. Anne and Helen were always in demand to give lectures and to raise money for the foundation, but they needed to also earn an income. They produced the movie *Deliverance*, but it was unsuccessful financially. So they accepted work on the vaudeville circuit. They re-created the famous scene at the pump when Helen learned the word *water* and engaged in a scripted question-and-answer dialogue. Then Anne interpreted for Helen when she answered questions from the audience. Although Helen enjoyed the tours and the income that supported them, Anne did not enjoy the experience.

Between 1927 and 1930 Anne's sight continued to deteriorate. She taught Polly manual sign language so that she could take over the reading and daily workload. In 1928, Anne struggled to help Helen finish her biography *Midstream*. Helen tried to get Anne to let her describe Anne's traumatic childhood but she refused. In 1929, Anne's right eye was removed, and Anne, Helen, and Polly traveled to Scotland, England, and Ireland to allow Anne to recuperate. While they were in Ireland, Anne wrote, "There is nothing in the world, it seems to me, like the sadness that prevails in parts of Ireland. It is the accumulated sadness of centuries of hunger, evictions, and emigrations. It is impossible for anyone in whose veins flows Irish blood to stand on the quay of any port in the country without heartache and tears."

By 1930, Anne had less than one-tenth normal vision. Polly began traveling with Helen on lecture tours because Anne was physically unable to do so. In October of that year, Temple University in Philadelphia, Pennsylvania, wanted to honor both Anne and Helen with honorary degrees. Anne initially refused the honor while Helen graciously accepted the award. Eventually, Anne received recognition from Temple University, the Educational Institute of Scotland, the Roosevelt Memorial foundation, and the Order of St. Sava from the King of Yugoslavia for her tireless teaching and commitment to Helen Keller.

By 1936, Anne's health was continually declining. She had surgery on her remaining eye but soon after she again had pain. She was diagnosed with gastric pains and senility. Despite trips to Canada and eastern Long Island, she did not recover. Finally, Anne collapsed and died in October 1936 from a coronary thrombosis. Anne was cremated and her ashes were placed in an urn in the National Cathedral in Washington, D.C. She was the first woman to be given this honor on her own merits. Later, Helen Keller's and Polly Thomson's ashes were placed next to Anne's along with a plaque that reads: "Helen Keller and her beloved companion Anne Sullivan Macy are interred in the columbarium behind this chapel."

While Anne was living, her teaching methods were often praised and rarely criticized, perhaps because at that time there were no research-based methods. However, Anne's methods did have some detractors. In 1933, the clinical psychologist Dr. Thomas D. Cutsforth wrote a book that questioned whether or not Anne's goal was to make Helen as much like a sighted person as possible or to develop her own potential. Never-theless, Anne's legacy as a teacher continues to this day. In 2003, Anne Sullivan Macy was inducted into the National Women's Hall of Fame in Seneca Falls, New York, for her work "in breaking down the educational barriers for people who are deaf, blind and visually impaired" and for "teaching practices [that] are still very much in use today."

Anne Sullivan saw her role as secondary to Helen's and thought her legacy was Helen. "My own life," Anne once said, "is so interwoven with my Helen's life that I can't separate myself from her." However, she re-mains as well known as Helen. Anne Sullivan is the focus of *The Miracle Worker*, not Helen Keller. *The Miracle Worker* was first performed as a television play. In 1959, it was rewritten as a Broadway play that ran suc-cessfully for two years. In 1962, it was made into a film that earned Oscars for Ann Bancroft, who played Anne, and Patty Duke, who played Helen.

Throughout her life and after her death, people have wondered what would have happened if Anne had chosen a different path for her life. Anne overcame a horrible childhood to become a literate adult with many talents. John Wright praised her musical talent and Helen recorded that her teacher had a love and aptitude for sculpture. Clemens often praised her ability as a writer. She was also an excellent equestrian. Biog-raphers speculate that Anne's talents would have allowed her to pursue other careers. However, she became a teacher—a great teacher. At Anne's sixty-seventh birthday party, Helen summarized Anne's legacy in her toast to her teacher: "Here's to my teacher, whose birthday was the Easter morning of my life."

16. MARGARET TOBIN BROWN

1867–1932
HEROINE OF THE TITANIC

After being brined, salted, and pickled in mid ocean I am now high and dry. . . . I have had flowers, letters, telegrams from people until I am befuddled. They are petitioning Congress to give me a medal. . . . If I must call a specialist to examine my head it is due to the title of Heroine of the Titanic.
—Margaret Brown

While the legend of the "Unsinkable Molly Brown" conjures up images of an elite, privileged woman who would go on to inspire movies, myths, and even musicals, the real Margaret Brown bore very little resemblance to the woman who has been lionized in film and literature. This high-society miner's wife was actually the daughter of poor Irish immigrants who worked her way up from humble beginnings to become a national heroine. A lifelong philanthropist and a champion of women's rights, Margaret Brown, or "Maggie" as she was known to her family, became one of the first advocates of women's suffrage and one of the first women to run for Congress, second only to Elizabeth Cady Stanton. While the *Titanic* made her a legend, she was already a woman who had changed the world long before the disaster happened.

Margaret Tobin was born on July 18, 1867, in Hannibal, Missouri, one of six children of Irish immigrants John Tobin and Johanna Collins. Her parents were both widowed and each had one child when they married. Raised near the Mississippi River, Margaret learned to steer riverboats at a young age, a skill that would save her life, and the lives of many others, later. She attended the grammar school run by her aunt until the age of thirteen, when she went to work at Garth's Tobacco Factory. Later, she became a waitress at the Park Hotel, where one of her customers Samuel Clemens, told her about the fortune that could be made in Colorado. Just eighteen, she moved to Leadville, Colorado, with her sister Mary Ann, and her husband, Jack Landrigan. She eventually found a job in Daniels and Fisher Department Store. In 1886, she met James Joseph Brown (JJ), an enterprising, self-educated man who was also the son of Irish immigrants. Tired of being dirt poor, Maggie had set out to find a rich husband, but she fell in love with JJ's resolve and strength of character. She recalled, "I wanted a rich man, but I loved Jim Brown. I thought about how I wanted comfort for my father and how I had determined to stay single until a man presented himself who could give to the tired old man the things I longed for him. Jim was as poor as we were, and had no better chance in life. I struggled hard with myself in those days. I loved Jim, but he was poor. Finally, I decided that I'd be better off with a poor man whom I loved than with a wealthy one whose money had attracted me. So I married Jim Brown." The couple was married on September 1, 1886, and went to live in a small Irish community. One year later, Margaret gave birth to a son, Lawrence, in 1887. Her daughter, Catherine Ellen, was born two years later.

It was also in Leadville that she first became involved in women's rights, helping to establish the Colorado chapter of the National American Woman's Suffrage Association, and worked in soup kitchens to assist miners' families. Despite a crippling depression that affected the town, JJ was about to become one of the most affluent miners in the country. He had discovered a new method of mining gold, and by the early 1890s Brown was awarded a seat on the board of the Little Jonny Mine and 12,500 shares of stock.

In 1894, the family moved to an opulent house on Pennsylvania Street in Denver, Colorado, and Margaret became a founding member of the Denver Woman's Club, which promoted improvement of women's lives through literacy, education, and the right to vote. She also worked to raise funds for local charities, including St. Joseph's Hospital. With her new social prominence and fund-raising skills, she befriended Judge Ben Lindsay and together they formed the first juvenile court in the country.

In 1901, she became one of the first students to enroll at the Carnegie Institute in New York, where she studied drama, French, German, and literature. In 1909, Margaret ran for the U.S. Senate, eleven years before women were granted the right to vote. By this time, Margaret spoke five languages and was already a household name. Margaret and JJ were the most celebrated couple in the area and the publicity caused an eventual strain on their marriage. They separated later that same year.

In April 1912, Margaret was on a European tour with her daughter Catherine Ellen, who was studying at the Sorbonne. She learned that her first grandson, Lawrence, was ill and decided to leave for New York immediately on the first ship that was available. When she boarded the *Titanic* in France, she could never have known the impact her decision would have on the rest of her life. After the ship hit the iceberg and began to sink, Margaret helped hundreds of passengers onto lifeboats before being forced into Lifeboat No. 6. She and the other women worked together to row and keep spirits up, in contrast to the inept leadership of the quartermaster Robert Hichens. Despite the chaos all around her, Margaret remained calm and directed the lifeboat to safety. According to Kristen Iverson's *Margaret Brown: Unraveling the Myth*, Margaret threatened to throw Hichens overboard when she tired of his fatalistic and hysterical ranting.

When the ship *Carpathia* arrived to save the survivors, Margaret assisted with the rescue efforts. Because she was fluent in five languages, she helped non-English-speaking survivors reunite with friends and family members, radioed information ahead to those awaiting news in New York, and raised funds with other wealthy passengers to help those less fortunate among the surviving passengers and crew. By the time the *Carpathia* reached New York, she had collected $10,000 and had established a Survivor's Committee. For her calm action in the disaster, the media called her "the heroine of the hour." When asked how she kept her cool in the face of adversity, she said "typical Brown luck . . . we're unsinkable." The moniker stayed with her, and she became known as the Unsinkable Molly Brown for the rest of her life. Ironically, Margaret became the most famous *Titanic* survivor, but because she was a woman, she was banned from giving testimony during the *Titanic* hearings. Undaunted, she told her own version of her story in newspapers in New York, Paris, and her hometown of Denver. She also helped establish the *Titanic* memorial in Washington, D.C., and became chair of the Survivor's Committee. Margaret's fame helped her publicize other issues that she had felt passionately about her entire life: the rights of workers and women, education and literacy for children, and historic preservation. In 1914, she formed an alliance with the feminist Alva Vanderbilt Belmont and organized an international women's conference in Newport, Rhode Island, which was attended by human rights advocates from all over the world. That same year, despite her prominence as the wife of a mining tycoon, Margaret showed her pro-labor sympathies when she promoted the cause of the Ludlow massacre in Trinidad, Colorado. One of the most violent events in Colorado labor history, the Ludlow massacre saw the deaths of twenty striking coal miners and their family members during a standoff between the strikers and militia. During World War I, she worked in France with the American Committee for Devastated France to rebuild areas behind the front lines, and helped wounded French and American soldiers. In 1932, she was awarded the French Legion of Honor for her "overall good citizenship," including her relief work in France.

After JJ's death, with whom she had always remained close, despite their separation, Margaret rediscovered her love of the stage and performed for audiences in Paris and New York. She also began helping young actresses in New York hone their craft. After suffering a stroke on October 26, 1932, the indomitable Margaret Brown died in New York City. She died thirty years to the day after her fellow congressional candidate and women's rights advocate, Elizabeth Cady Stanton.

In the end, Margaret Brown's efforts for *Titanic* survivors and her other activism and philanthropy in the United States and Europe have made her legacy what it is today. While she has become immortalized as a brash clothes-horse in the Broadway play and film *The Unsinkable Molly Brown* and later by Kathy Bates in the 1997 film *Titanic*, the real Margaret Brown was an accomplished, fearless, and benevolent woman who paved the way for women's and children's rights and helped save the lives of many of her fellow women passengers.

17. CONSTANCE GORE-BOOTH

Countess Markievicz

1868–1927
MILITARY LEADER

Dress suitably in short skirts and strong boots, leave your jewels in the bank, and buy a revolver.

> —Countess Markievicz, when asked what "fashion" advice she would give the women of her day

She was a child of privilege who later became one of the most important Irish revolutionaries in history. Like her contemporary, Maud Gonne MacBride, she was beautiful, Protestant, independently wealthy, and fearless. As one of the captivating women who also caught the eye of William Butler Yeats (he famously called her "a gizelle" when commenting on her beauty), she could have chosen an advantaged, serene life; instead, she chose the arduous path of a nationalist and suffragette. A socialite who was presented at court in London, she later became the second in command to James Connolly, the leader of the 1916 Easter Rebellion, and would be sentenced to death for her role in the uprising. Hailed as "the new Irish beauty", at her coming out, she preferred to be a soldier and would come to reshape Ireland in the twentieth century.

Constance Gore-Booth was born into the landed Gore-Booth family of Lissadell, County Sligo (Yeats described them as "a very pleasant kindly, inflammable family"), on February 4, 1868, in London. The daughter of Sir Henry Gore-Booth, an explorer and philanthropist, the countess, as she would later be known, was an ancestor of Vice President Al Gore. Although they were of the upper classes, Constance's family instilled a sense of benevolence and tolerance in their girls at an early age. Her sister Eva would grow up to become a famous labor leader and champion of women's liberation in her own right. Artistic and sensitive, she was a skilled equestrian who flourished in the west of Ireland. Because Yeats was a friend of her family and frequented the family estate, Constance soon began to benefit from his creative influence. She would later go on to study at the Slade art school in London.

In 1897, she was presented at court in London and spent several seasons there. The following year, she traveled to Paris to study art at the Julian School, where she would meet and fall in love with the penniless Count Casimir Markievicz, who would give Constance her famous namesake. Markievicz was a widower with one son who owned a house in Ukraine. Casimir and Constance married on September 29, 1901. Overnight, Constance Gore-Booth became Countess Markievicz.

Their daughter Maeve was born at Lissadell in 1901 and was given to Lady Gore-Booth (Constance's mother) to raise. In 1903, the couple moved to Dublin and Constance began to make a name for herself as a landscape artist. While she and Casimir enjoyed their social life in Dublin, their marriage was not a happy one. They soon separated when Constance became passionate about nationalist politics. In 1907, she joined the Inghinidhe na hÉireann (Daughters of Erin), where she met Maud Gonne MacBride, and wrote for the monthly journal, *Bean na hÉireann* (Women of Erin). Still influenced by her arts background, she designed the journal's masthead. She also joined Sinn Féin and became a member of its executive three years later. The next year she founded the Fianna, a youth organization for boys that trained them in military exercises. As Pádraig Pearse observed, "the Volunteers of 1916 would not have arisen" without the Fianna. In 1908, she also tried her hand at politics when she went to England and stood for election—against Winston Churchill.

In 1911, now as an executive member of both the Daughters of Erin and Sinn Féin, she went to jail for the first time for her part in a demonstration against the visit of George V. Constance had also involved herself in the labor unrest of the time, running a soup kitchen during the lockout of union workers in 1913 and supporting the labor leaders James Larkin and James Connolly.

In 1913, war was just beginning in Europe and the self-determination that the Irish had been promised was suddenly on the back burner. In 1914, Irish soldiers were fighting for England in World War I, yet were being denied their own independence back at home. Much as Belfast would erupt in violence some fifty years later, Dublin was on the verge of all out war. The military groups Cumann na mBan and the Irish Citizen Army (both of which the countess was now an integral part) were organizing a rebellion on Easter Sunday for April 14, 1916. And the countess was right there at the front lines, beside the men. Her prowess on the battlefield made her the natural choice to be second in command to Michael Mallin when the rebel forces took over St. Stephen's Green. She attacked snipers, protected civilians, and blew the lock off the door of the College of Surgeons when the Citizen Army attempted to overtake it. Mallin and Markievicz were triumphant in the Green and managed to stave off the British for almost a week. However, their fellow rebels were not so lucky. Connolly was seriously injured in the General Post Office, and the rebel army's official surrender was already being negotiated. Sixteen of her fellow comrades, including Eamon de Valera, Pearse, and Connolly were moved to Dublin Castle and then to Kilmainham Jail, where they were housed eight to a cell. As Anne Marreco observes in *The Rebel Countess: The Life and Times of Countess Markiewicz*, "Soon Constance was isolated from her comrades. They feared for her life—but she would have welcomed death."

The countess was put into solitary confinement, along with seventy other women prisoners, and eleven of her fellow rebels had already been shot, including Mallin. The countess was also sentenced to death, but her sister Eva soon stepped in to work tirelessly to have her sentence commuted. Nevertheless, the countess waited alone in her cell, listening to the gunfire as her friends were executed one by one. She never knew who would be next. She told the officer who brought her the news, "I do wish your lot had the decency to shoot me." Weary and heartbroken, she pleaded to her sister, "Why won't they let me die with my friends?" Nevertheless, because she was a woman, she was sent to Aylesbury Jail and held until

1917. Even though she was given a life sentence, she was released under the general amnesty.

In solidarity with her nationalist contemporaries, the countess converted to Catholicism in 1918, just as Maud Gonne had done. That same year, she became the first woman ever elected to the House of Commons, but she refused to take her seat in keeping with the Sinn Féin policy of abstentionism. When the first Dáil Éireann, the parliament of the Republic of Ireland, was seated two months later, she was appointed the first minister of labor but was in jail during most of this time. She would go to jail twice during the course of the Irish War of Independence and was only released to attend the Anglo-Irish treaty debates. She strongly opposed the treaty and had an angry exchange with Collins the day the antitreaty forces walked out of the hall. She called the protreaty advocates "traitors."

During the Irish Civil War, which erupted in 1921, the countess again took part in the fighting and later toured the United States to raise funds for the Republican cause. After the civil war, she regained her seat in the Dáil, but again she was jailed for her strong nationalist politics. Along with ninety-two other women prisoners, she went on hunger strike and was released after a month. She joined de Valera's Fianna Fáil Party in 1926 at the beginning of its foundation, and was elected to the Dáil in 1927. Prison, battle, and revolution had finally taken their toll on the countess. She died one month later, on July 15, in Sir Patrick Dun's Hospital. She had been operated on for appendicitis and developed peritonitis. The entire country mourned her loss. When Countess Markievicz was taken to the Republican plot at Glasnevin Cemetery in Dublin for burial, it was said that as many as 300,000 people turned out on the streets to bid her good-bye. At the graveside, de Valera, her comrade and now Ireland's president, gave the eulogy: "Madame Markievicz is gone from us. Madame the friend of the toiler, the lover of the poor. Sacrifice, misunderstanding and scorn lay on the road she adopted, but she trod unflinchingly."

18. MARY MACSWINEY

1872-1942
ACTIVIST

A rebel is one who opposes lawfully constituted authority and that I have never done.

—Mary MacSwiney

It is easier for you than it is for us, but you will not find in Ireland a woman who has suffered, who today will talk as the soldiers here today have talked, and I ask the Minister of Defense, if that is the type of soldier he has, in heaven's name, send the women as your officers next time.
—Mary MacSwiney in the Dáil, speaking
in opposition to the Treaty of 1921

She was a founder of Cumman na mBan and one of the first women ever elected to the Dáil Éireann. Although she was born in England and attended Cambridge University, she would become a formidable opponent of British rule in Ireland. Like the great Irish women of her day, she survived imprisonment, hunger strikes, intimidation, and excommunication to become one of the foremost revolutionaries in Irish history. As Margaret Ward observes in her book *Unmanageable Revolutionaries*, she was one of the most uncompromising members of Cumann na mBan.

Mary MacSwiney was born in London on March 27, 1872, the eldest child of Irish parents. Her brother Terence would later die on hunger strike during the war for Irish Independence, her sister Annie was also a republican prisoner, and Mary herself would become the first woman ever to go on hunger strike. She was educated in the Ursuline Convent in Cork before training as a teacher at Cambridge University. At twenty, Mary had obtained a loan from a student's aid society and was admitted to a teacher-training program normally reserved for men at Cambridge. She taught in London for some time, then returned to Cork on the death of her mother to look after the younger members of the family and find employment as a teacher. In 1914, she joined Cumann na mBan and founded the first the Cork branch.

At the time, she refused to join Sinn Féin because, as she said, "I will never accept the Kings, Lords and Commons of Ireland." Influenced by her brother Terence, she also joined the Gaelic League and Inghinidhe na hÉireann (Daughters of Erin.) She later became a member of the Cumann na mBan Executive, and like many female republicans, she was on the front lines during the Easter Rising and was eventually arrested.

When she returned home, she discovered that she had been dismissed from her teaching position. She then founded St. Ita's School for Girls in Cork City with her sister Annie. Mary was now becoming a force in the republican movement. She also finally joined Sinn Féin, as she felt it was now taking a more republican stance. In the winter of 1920, she went to America to give evidence of the atrocities committed by the Black and Tans (British soldiers) to the American Commission of Inquiry on Conditions in Ireland. As she testified of the appalling conditions in her hometown in Cork: "The shops were not allowed to be opened, and the Black and Tans stood there and refused point-blank to allow the women and children to get the food that was waiting for them. . . . And the fourth day they allowed certain women to buy bread and milk . . . and nothing else."

During her trip, she met Éamon de Valera, who was so impressed with her testimony that he asked her to begin speaking on republican issues, and she lectured for nearly a year throughout the United States. It was also in 1920 that Mary suffered a wrenching loss—the death of her brother while he was on hunger strike. Devastated, but determined to go on, she immersed herself in politics.

In 1921, Mary was elected to the First Dáil Éireann as a Sinn Féin TD for Cork. There were now five women in the Dáil—Countess Markiewicz, Kathleen Clarke, Ada English, Kate O'Callaghan, and Mary. Although she had taken her seat in Dáil, she was facing a moral dilemma. She was vehemently opposed to a treaty between Britain and Ireland that would essentially dissolve the Irish Republic and divide Ireland in two: the twenty-six counties of the independent Free State and the six counties of Northern Ireland, which would remain under British rule. Mary made an impassioned speech to her colleagues in the Dáil, saying, "I will fight against compromise to the death. Are you, His Majesty's Ministers, going to send soldiers to arrest me?" However moving her words, five delegates from the Dáil traveled to London to meet with Prime Minister Lloyd George, and the Treaty of 1921 was ratified. It is an agreement that still holds today.

Mary continued to campaign against the treaty, despite opposition and imprisonment. On November 4, 1922, she was imprisoned in Mountjoy Jail and immediately went on hunger strike. Her comrades in Cumann na mBan held nightly vigils in support. When her sister Annie came to visit her in jail and was refused admittance, she too went on her own hunger strike. By the twentieth day of the strike, Mary became critically ill and was given last rites. Supporters from Ireland petitioned the government and she was released four days later. As she recalled, "The only kind of strike was when the striker realized fully the probability of death and was ready for it."

Mary continued to be persecuted for her beliefs, and the continuous cycle of imprisonment and hunger strikes were beginning to take a toll on her health. Despite her ill health, she continued to be returned as a TD for Cork in the Third Dáil Éireann. In 1927, she became vice president of Cumann na mBan and a member of the Sinn Féin Executive, despite vehemently continuing to criticize the organization. She began to see Sinn Féin as a classist, elitist organization, and in 1934, she finally split with the group in opposition to their practice of allowing their members to accept IRA war pensions. As Margaret Ward asserts, "The stern guardian of the Republican conscience was now a lonely figure crying in the wilderness of intransigent principles."

Later that year, she was excommunicated by the Catholic Bishop of Cork, Daniel Colohan. In doing so, he accused her of having embezzled money collected for the republican prisoner's dependent fund. She fought him and refuted his false charges, but the damage had been done. Although she had resigned from Sinn Féin, she remained active in republican politics and continued to defy British rule. Following the end of the Civil War she became legal guardian to her brother Terence's daughter, Máire.

Although she lived the rest of her life in relative obscurity, she remained true to her principles to the end. Mary was one of the last surviving loyal members of the Second Dáil who transferred their authority to the Army Council of the IRA in December 1938. Mary MacSwiney died at her home in Cork on March 8, 1942, at the age of seventy, still believing in a socialist, thirty-two-county Ireland.

19. MARGARET SANGER

1879–1966
BIRTH CONTROL PIONEER

A free race cannot be born of slave mothers.

—Margaret Sanger

Woman must not accept; she must challenge. She must not be awed by that which has been built up around her; she must reverence that woman in her which struggles for expression.

—Margaret Sanger

No woman can call herself free who does not own and control her body. No woman can call herself free until she can choose consciously whether she will or will not be a mother.

—Margaret Sanger

Throughout the *Daughters of Maeve*, we will see Irish women who devoted their entire lives to the legalization of birth control. While birth control would not be fully legal in Ireland until 1992, it was ironically a young Irish American nurse who would coin the term *birth control* and put it on the national agenda for good. Before Margaret Sanger bravely took on the fight for women's reproductive rights, women in the late nineteenth and early twentieth centuries were slaves to their own bodies. Women who wanted to limit the size of their families were often forced into desperate measures—brutal self-inflicted abortions during which they used knitting needles, coat hangers, or a variety of homemade herbal remedies that endangered their lives, or illegal $5 back-alley abortions that most likely would cause them to bleed to death. If she chose to carry her pregnancy to term, a woman who had already endured grueling pregnancies might further risk her health and possibly her life. Only the very rich had access to any information about the only two forms of family planning available at the time: withdrawal and condoms. The very poor were subjected to endless unplanned pregnancies, resulting in sick, malnourished, and mentally compromised children. It was estimated that more than 8,000 women died in New York in the nineteenth century alone because of illegal abortions. In the early twentieth century, one woman would change all that, putting reproductive rights on the map and engendering a revolution that would change the lives of women everywhere. As *Time* magazine asserts in its choice of Margaret Sanger as one of the Top 100 Leaders of the Century, "She taught us, first, to look at the world as if women mattered."

Margaret Higgins was born in Corning, New York, on September 16, 1879, to Michael Hennessy Higgins, an Irish graveyard statue sculptor, and Anne Higgins. From the beginning of her marriage, Anne was besieged by pregnancy. By the time she died, she had endured eighteen pregnancies, of which eleven children lived. As the sixth child in the Higgins family, Margaret witnessed what the onslaught of children had done to her mother's body. In one of her earliest memories, she recalls helping her father make a death mask for her four-year-old brother. She also observed that the richer families in Corning had few children, in contrast to the teeming families with which she grew up. While her father had moved to New York from Ireland at the age of thirteen, he was a skilled tradesman and former med student who imparted his own sense of tenacity and social justice to his daughter. Michael Higgins was also an intellectual who organized local lectures in Corning. On one occasion, he invited the crusader Colonel Robert Ingersoll to speak. Instead of welcoming the colonel, the local townspeople called him a blasphemer and turned on Higgins and his children. When they went to school, Margaret and her siblings were called "Devil Children" and "Heathens" by their neighbors. Eventually, Michael lost his livelihood in the town and had to go outside Corning to find work.

Buoyed by her father's example, Margaret was a brave and resilient child who never shied from physical challenges. At the age of twelve, she tried to cross the tracks of the Erie Railroad that spanned the Chenung

River. The tracks had very wide gaps and Margaret became terrified and fell between the rungs. It was an incident that ensured her belief that she could achieve whatever she wanted.

Even as a teenager, Margaret showed a keen interest in learning and set her hopes on attending Cornell University and becoming a doctor. Her older sisters arranged for her to attend a co-ed Presbyterian school called Calverack in the Catskills. Early on, she displayed a great talent for elocution and dramatic skills and gave her first talk on women's rights. Ironically, it was her father, not her mother, who fostered her interest in women's equality, extolling the achievements of great women throughout history like Susan B. Anthony and Cleopatra. While Margaret was blossoming at school, she suffered her first tragedy. Her long-suffering mother became ill and died on March 31, 1886, leaving Margaret to take over a lion's share of the household chores. Without his wife, Michael became cruel and dictatorial. Margaret knew she had to leave home, and while she still had dreams of becoming a doctor, she knew that her family had no money to send her to medical school. She took up nursing training at White Plains and even though she was still uncertified, she showed a rare courage and compassion with obstetric patients. She soon began delivering babies and even at an early age she became the touchstone for women who wanted to prevent pregnancy.

During her last assignment at the Manhattan Ear and Eye Hospital, Margaret met the handsome and socially important architect William Sanger at a hospital dance. Although she fell for him immediately, she was apprehensive about marriage. Eager to obtain her degree first, Margaret kept dodging Bill's proposals until he finally gave her an ultimatum. Within the first six months of their marriage, Margaret became pregnant with their first child. Like her mother before her, she had an incredibly difficult birth that nearly killed her. Her baby, Stuart, was healthy, but Margaret developed tubercular symptoms that rendered her bedridden. She fell in to a deep depression and lingered in a comatose state through much of her recovery. Anxious to speed her convalescence, Bill moved them into a beautiful house in Hastings on Hudson in February 1908. Idyllic and peaceful, it was the perfect place to raise children, but it also removed Margaret from the intellectual excitement of New

York City. In the next few years, she gave birth to her second son, Grant, and her daughter, Peggy. Her infection soon came back and Margaret became increasingly disenchanted with suburban life. As she recalls, "I was not able to express my discontent . . . but after my experience as a nurse with fundamentals, this quiet withdrawal into the tame domesticity of the pretty riverside settlement seemed to be bordering on stagnation." Like so many women of her generation who could not voice their frustration of staying in the home, she was not satisfied to lead a life of quiet desperation. In addition, her husband was cavalier with money, and Margaret was eager to return to work and contribute to the household.

The couple moved to 135th Street in Harlem and soon found the intellectual and political atmosphere Margaret had been craving. Their apartment became a haven for socialist friends and thinkers like the journalist John Reed and Lincoln Steffans. It was then that Margaret met Mabel Dodge, who began hosting evenings for New York City's intellectuals. The women were immediately drawn to each other, and Mabel convinced Margaret to join Local 5, where she recruited other women for the Socialist Party and wrote for their paper, *The Call*. She soon began giving speeches on labor and women's health, which began to draw more and more women. Because of the high demand for her speeches, Margaret started writing the health column "What Every Mother Should Know" for *The Call* that tackled sex and pregnancy. The column became so popular that she conceived a regular second column, "What Every Girl Should Know," which advised teen girls on sexuality. One Sunday, Margaret discovered that her article had been censored by Anthony Comstock, the Puritanical post master general. He had pulled the article in the interest of "preserving purity" and replaced the text with the word "Nothing!" Ironically, as her main adversary, Comstock would make Margaret Sanger a household name. As Emily Taft Douglas observes in *Margaret Sanger: Pioneer of the Future*, "It was in the cause of labor and again as nurse that Margaret first attracted national attention."

Margaret earned more acclaim during a textile workers strike in Lawrence, Massachussetts. When the leaders were arrested, the Italian workers in New York decided to adopt their children temporarily. They agreed that as a nurse, Margaret should bring the children to New York.

When she gave them physical exams, she found rampant malnourishment and diphtheria. Six weeks later, the children were well fed and healthy and Margaret became a star. When the congressman Victor Berger started an investigation into workers' conditions, Margaret agreed to testify. She made a compelling, eloquent case for the children, one that helped sway Congress's opinion of the strikers, and her photo appeared in newspapers across the country.

When she continued her work as a nurse, she began tending to the very poor of New York's Lower East Side, where women were exhausted by pregnancy. It was here that she began advising women on the withdrawal method and the use of condoms, but the women wanted birth control that they could rely on, not feeling that they could rely on their husband's discipline. She also found women who would rather commit suicide than face another unwanted pregnancy. Furthermore, she saw the savage aftermath of women who almost died from back-alley abortions. But in 1917, she nursed a woman who would drive her crusade for legalized birth control. Sadie Sachs was a poor mother who had just survived a botched home abortion. Margaret helped nurse her through her recovery, but was at a loss when Sadie asked her how to prevent another pregnancy. Months later, she received a call from Sadie's husband; his wife had attempted another abortion. She died instantly, and her image haunted Margaret so that she vowed to keep women from being slaves to their own bodies.

Finding a solution proved more difficult. Margaret discovered that most doctors had no real idea of how to prevent pregnancy. The situation was further complicated because the distribution of birth control advice was banned by New York State law. In addition, the camps in which she thought she would find the most support failed to back her—the feminists refused because they didn't yet have the vote and the socialists wanted to gain support for their own cause first. By now, Margaret's personal life was also in turmoil; her daughter Peggy was ill with muscular atrophy, and her marriage was beginning to dissolve, as Bill believed that Margaret was neglecting their children in favor of her cause. On the suggestion of the labor leader Bill Haywood, Margaret began studying the practices of the French, where the birth rate was low and contraception was in common use. A move to France would also allow Bill to pursue his passion for painting and seemed an ideal solution for their waning marriage. In 1913, the Sanger family moved to Paris and Margaret began studying the practices of French wives, who were already sophisticated in the art of preventing pregnancy through a variety of homemade devices such as douches and tampons. From her research, Margaret planned a journal geared toward low-income women under the name *The Woman Rebel*.

Margaret moved back to New York to work on her magazine, but she was already facing resistance by Comstock, who had already introduced a bill in Congress in 1873 to ban obscenity that included "the prevention of contraception." Comstock showed no waning in his crusade against "obscene" material. His mission also included banning art and literature that he deemed offensive. Anyone who violated this law could expect lengthy jail terms.

But this threat did not deter Margaret. She immediately coined a new term for her passion—*birth control*—and formed the National Birth Control League. In March 1914, the first issue of *The Woman Rebel* appeared on newsstands in the United States, with an inspiring quote from Margaret: "Look the world in the face with a go-to-Hell look in the eyes; to have an idea, to speak and act in defiance of convention." *The Woman Rebel* addressed issues like child labor, women in the workplace, hygiene, and contraception and advised that a woman should be the "Mistress of her own body." Thousands of wives began writing from all over the United States in enthusiastic response to the journal. Comstock responded by refusing to mail the paper, and he banned the next few issues. Margaret and her friends began delivering copies of the paper personally.

By this time, Margaret wanted to devote her time solely to her cause. She wrote to Bill asking him for a divorce, and was immediately arrested on nine counts of obscene violations. She was now facing a prison sentence of forty-five years, but the federal agents who came to arrest her were so impressed by her arguments on birth control that they took her side. The judge postponed the case and her father, who initially disapproved of Margaret's work, called her a "brave, clean warrior." Anxious to carry on with her work for women everywhere, she sent her son Stuart to boarding school, and her two youngest children to live with her sister, Nan. She began writing *Family Limitation*, the seminal pamphlet that would become a treatise for birth control for the next century. Since its initial publication of 100,000 copies, it has grown to 10 million copies and has been translated into thirteen languages. Despite her successes, Margaret's court case was looming. Faced with the choice of pleading guilty and receiving a lighter sentence or serving long imprisonment, Margaret wrote to the court and told it she would be traveling abroad for a while. With the help of friends, she took a train to Montreal and then traveled by boat to England. She took a terrible risk and became a bona fide celebrity overnight. She changed her name for traveling purposes and arranged for friends to release *Family Limitation*.

The trip to London proved a boon to her cause. It was there that she met Dr. C.V. Drysdale, a proponent of family planning in Britain who became one of her greatest advocates, as well as Havelock Ellis, the author of *The Psychology of Sex,* which had inspired Margaret so many years before. Ellis was a sexual pioneer, and like Margaret, had his own work banned, and immediately began guiding her course of study. She began studying the sexual practices of ancient civilizations from China, Persia, and Egypt and discovered that they used contraceptives. She was also inspired by the teachings of Jeremy Bentham and Francis Place, who had discovered the use of the contraceptive sponge and of suppositories. Furthermore, she discovered that the condom was legal because it prevented the spread of disease. Ellis taught Margaret that birth control would change not just women's lives, but those of humanity. Margaret became Ellis's spiritual companion, much to his wife's chagrin, who was deeply jealous of the beautiful, famous Sanger. Margaret also discovered that birth control clinics already existed in Holland, a country in which there was very little venereal disease or illegitimacy.

By the time Margaret returned to New York in 1915, her mission was clear. Upon her arrival, the *National Pictorial Review* credited Margaret with the use of the term *birth control* and her nemesis, Comstock, had died. But she discovered that the National Birth Control League had shunned her, claiming that it disagreed with her radical tactics. That same year her daughter Peggy caught pneumonia and died soon after. Margaret was bereft, but the tragedy garnered her sympathy from supporters all over the country. Heartbroken, she was still facing trial but she received a letter of support addressed to Woodrow Wilson, the governor of New Jersey, from English authors such as H. G. Wells, Arnold Bennett, and Dr. Marie Stopes. Now, Margaret was officially mainstream and began enjoying the support of upper-class suffragettes. The National Birth Control League decided to back its fallen leader again. On February 18, 1916, the *National Pictorial Review* reported that 97 percent of Americans supported birth control, and the indictment against Margaret was dropped. Birth control was now on the national agenda, and statewide birth control leagues began appearing in Cleveland, Detroit, Milwaukee, and Pittsburgh. Margaret began touring the country and her presence started a riot in heavily Catholic St. Louis, but she later received a thousand letters of support from the city. In Washington, she attended a protest rally where she was arrested for the first time. Still passionate about her main cause, the establishment of birth control clinics, she returned to New York and took up residence in a cold-water flat.

With the help of fellow nurses and her sister Ethel, she established the first birth control clinic in the United States in Brownsville, Brooklyn, in October 1916. She circulated flyers that advised, "Do not kill, do not take life, but prevent." The first day, the clinic served more than 140 women of all faiths—Jewish, Catholic, and Protestant. Their success was short lived: a policewoman raided the office with a warrant for Margaret's arrest and confiscated all the patient records. Margaret was imprisoned in Raymond Street Jail and released on $500 bail. She had the fortune of securing the help of the prominent lawyer J. J. Goldstein and the judge postponed her trial. Her sister Ethel was also arrested and sentenced to thirty days in a workhouse. Influenced by the English and Irish female prisoners, Ethel decided to go on hunger strike, and even refused water. The strike gained incredible publicity for the cause, but jeopardized Ethel's help. The strike ended after five days when Ethel was force-fed through a feeding tube—a brutal practice that would be used on prisoners on hunger strike in England and Northern Ireland more than half a century later. As her sister was becoming gravely ill, Margaret agreed to abide by all future laws to save her sister's life. As she later said of Ethel,

"No single act of self-confidence in the history of the birth control movement had done more to awaken the conscience of the public or to arouse the courage of women."

During her trial on January 28, 1917, she stated, "I cannot promise to obey a law I do not respect." She was incarcerated in Queens County Jail in Long Island and sentenced to a workhouse for thirty days. The press was in total sympathy, and thanks to a colleague, Roger Blossom, her *Birth Control Review* was printed. While it seemed Margaret's star was on the rise, the onslaught of World War I put birth control on the back burner. However, a few victories gave Margaret hope. She found that the U.S. Army was using the column "What Every Girl Should Know" for its sage advice on venereal disease. That same year, the New York State Supreme Court ruled that "birth control could be used to protect ailing mothers." In 1920, Margaret wrote *Women and the New Race,* which espoused the right of women to determine their own fertility and stipulated that overpopulation led to the world's problems. It sold more than 250,000 copies, and H. G. Wells declared, "When the history of our civilization is written, it will be a biological history and Margaret Sanger will be its heroine."

The next year she held the First National Birth Control Conference, where she taught doctors about methods of birth control—including a commercial chemical contraceptive jelly she discovered in Germany. At New York City's Town Hall, she held the lecture "Birth Control: Is It Moral?" The police, under the advisement of Cardinal Hayes, tried to stop the lecture. They arrested Margaret and 200 supporters, and Margaret's battle with the Catholic Church began. In 1921, she was invited to speak in Japan along with Albert Einstein, Bertrand Russell, and Wells. She discovered the appalling lives of Japanese women, their repressed sexuality, and their servitude to Japanese men. In a flurry of interviews, she exposed the plight of these women and began helping them set up outlets for birth control information. That same year, she married the millionaire Noah Slee, who would become one of her biggest financial and emotional supporters. In 1925, with her husband's funds and those of another supporter, Clinton Chance, she set up another clinic on West Fifteenth Street, which was fully staffed with doctors, nurses, and social workers and served more than a thousand patients a year. That year, she started a second clinic in Chicago, and more in New Jersey, California, and Cleveland. With the help of Drs. Hannah Stone and James Cooper, who had developed a contraceptive jelly that was 98 percent effective, Margaret and Noah formed the Holland Rantos Company, which was recreating the German diaphragm for use in the United States. Much to Margaret's delight, the U.S. medical community publicly addressed the issue of birth control.

Over the next few years, she founded the Clinical Research Bureau and the American Birth Control League. Now in her late forties, Margaret had found affluence and professional satisfaction. Arthur Schlesinger called her "the most outstanding social warrior of the century." She continued lecturing to women's groups all over the world, including India. Despite continued resistance from the Catholic Church, the courts continued to rule on Margaret's side and allowed her to continue to run her clinics. In 1930, the National Council of Jewish Women advocated birth control, as did the Anglican clergy. The next year, the National Council on Christian Churches did the same. In 1935, she attended the India Women's Conference, where she met with Mohandas Gandhi and Motilal Nehru. The delegation voted in favor of birth control and within months forty-five medical societies started birth control programs in India. By the beginning of the 1940s, Margaret had enjoyed much personal achievement, and even though her husband Noah died in 1943, she continued to be a featured speaker at conferences around the world. In 1949, Smith College awarded her with an honorary degree and the American Birth Control League that she had founded became the Planned Parenthood Federation of America.

Fortunately, Margaret saw many of her dreams realized before she died. In 1960, the first birth control pill that she had helped Drs. John Rock and Gregory Pincus develop was marketed, and in 1965, the U.S. Supreme Court overturned the ban on contraception in the state of Connecticut. Although she was suffering from angina, Margaret never stopped working until the day she died. She continued working for reproductive rights for the women of Japan, China, and India. She died on February 13, 1966, seven years before abortion was made safe and legal.

20. HELEN KELLER

1880–1968
AUTHOR, DISABILITY ADVOCATE

The education of this child will be the distinguishing event of my life.
—Anne Sullivan on Helen Keller

I have seen more of the divine than has been manifest in anyone I have ever met before.

—Alexander Graham Bell

Helen Keller was internationally famous throughout her life. From the time that her teacher, Anne Sullivan, began working with the blind and deaf "wild child," Helen became one of the most renowned persons with a disability. Helen's triumph over her disabilities made her a role model and gained her the respect of people throughout the world, including many famous individuals. Samuel Clemens commented that she was the most remarkable person he had ever met and probably the most remarkable woman since Joan of Arc. However, Helen's detractors not only attributed most of Helen's success to Anne but also claimed that Helen was really a clone of Anne. Throughout her life, Helen gave credit to Anne for being the only one who could reach and teach everything she needed to be part of the world. The controversy about how much of Helen Keller was really Helen Keller does not diminish her remarkable story, nor does it diminish appreciation of her innate intelligence and talents. Helen graduated cum laude with a bachelor's degree in English from Radcliffe, wrote fourteen books, and became an international speaker. From the time that Helen learned how to communicate, there was no stopping this highly intelligent, persistent, and optimistic woman.

Helen was born on June 27, 1880, on the Keller homestead in Tuscumbia, Alabama. Her father was a captain in the Confederate army and later a farmer, but he never earned a reliable living. Her mother, Kate Adams, was a homemaker who cared for and advocated for Helen from birth to adulthood. Helen was a precocious child who spoke at six months and walked before she was a year old. When she was eighteen months old, she contracted an illness called an "acute congestion of stomach and brain" or "brain fever." This illness caused her to lose her sight and hearing at the time when she was just learning language. For the next five years, her parents tried to teach her and she did invent some signs for objects and people. She used her own gestures to communicate her needs and tried to move her mouth to speak, but she did not learn any words. Because she could not communicate effectively, she became increasingly frustrated and difficult to manage. She kicked and screamed until she became exhausted and sometimes hurt her nurse and other children. She also engaged in mischievous and even dangerous behaviors such as locking her mother in the pantry and setting fires.

Eventually, her parents determined that they could not deal with her even with the assistance of a nurse. They decided she needed a teacher, so they contacted Laura Bridgman, who referred them to Alexander Graham Bell. Bell, who was a pioneer in deaf education, examined Helen and referred the family to the Perkins Institute for the Blind in Boston. Anne Sullivan, who was a visually impaired student at Perkins, was selected to be Helen's teacher. Anne arrived at the Keller home in 1886 when Helen was almost seven years old. When Helen met Anne, she was so out of control that she was regarded as a "wild child." Anne referred to her as a "tyrant" whose violent temper made it impossible for her family to control. She attributed Helen's destructive behavior to the fact that she had "untaught, unsatisfied hands." Anne also recognized that Helen knew she was different and knew that other people did not use signs. She saw Helen's behavior as a result of her inability to communicate and immediately began to try to teach her to associate language with objects. Anne also insisted that she and Helen move to a cottage on the Keller property to allow her to deal with Helen's discipline problems. Helen's outbursts and acting out behaviors continued until Anne made a major breakthrough with her.

At the time, few research-based methods existed for teaching students who were blind or deaf, let alone blind and deaf. Although Anne had learned some theory and techniques as a student at the Perkins Institute, she did not have formal training as a teacher. Anne had some definite ideas about the best approach for language acquisition and she did get support from Michael Anagnos, the head of the Perkins Institute. However, many of Anne's methods were based on instinct and trial and error. In the beginning, Anne used finger spelling with Helen to identify common, everyday objects. For example, she gave Helen a doll and finger-spelled *doll* in Helen's hand. Helen imitated Anne but she did not understand the idea that objects had names for several weeks. Eventually, she became so frustrated that she smashed the doll. In the famous "miracle" event depicted in films about Helen and Anne, Anne took her to the well outside the house and pumped water over Helen's hand while she finger-spelled *water* in Helen's other hand. Helen finally understood that this cool liquid was called "water." This understanding allowed her to learn many new words that same day. This was the breakthrough that allowed her to learn the names of other objects and eventually words for ideas, concepts, people, and everything else in the world.

Anne continued to teach Helen at home using a variety of techniques. She knew the sense of touch would need to be Helen's main method of comprehending the world. She continued to use finger spelling but also made word cards with raised letters and placed them next to objects. In one significant lesson, when Anne spelled *think* on Helen's forehead, Helen began to understand the concept of abstract ideas. Since Anne believed children learned from experiences in their natural environment and Helen loved to be outdoors, they often spent much of the day exploring the outdoors. Anne noticed that Helen smelled vines, flowers, and other plants as well as touching them. So she used all of Helen's senses and her curiosity about the environment to teach many lessons. In addition, because Anne believed in teaching the whole child, she designed her instruction to focus not only on cognitive and language skills but also on moral values. Helen later realized that as she was acquiring language, she began to feel remorse, guilt, love, and other emotions and to understand the concepts of emotions and morals. Later, Anne used literature as a "moral template." She noted that Helen became "transported" into the story and reacted to the moral implications in literature. Helen read literature, poetry, and history and later studied French and Latin. She also attempted to learn to speak when Anne arranged for speech instruction by Sarah Fuller at the Horace Mann School for the Deaf in Boston. Later, she studied speech with Mary Swift Lamson, but she never learned to speak intelligibly. When she was thirteen, she began formal instruction in subjects. The instruction she received was advanced for the typical student and certainly advanced for a student with multiple disabilities.

During this time, Helen's remarkable progress brought her to the attention of prominent professionals in education and several famous people. Anagnos promoted Helen, calling her a "phenomenon" in one of the numerous articles on her that he wrote. Newspaper articles about Helen increased her public visibility, particularly those showing her reading William Shakespeare. Her home instruction continued, but Anne, Kate Keller, and several benefactors also ensured that Helen traveled during her childhood. She made several trips to the Perkins Institute and other locations in the East. In addition, she attended the World's Fair with Bell and the Chatauqua for the American Association to Promote the Teaching of Speech to the Deaf and she visited President Grover Cleveland in the White House.

In 1888, Helen attended the Perkins Institute for the Blind and in 1894 she and Anne moved to the Wright-Humason Oral School in New York for the Deaf to study vocal culture, lipreading, and academic subjects. After two years at Wright-Humason, she entered the Cambridge School for Young Ladies in Cambridge, Massachusetts, which was a prep school for Radcliffe. Helen completed the same work as the other students. Her only accommodations were some of her books were in Braille and Anne interpreted for her in class, which was difficult because she had to finger-spell everything. This was the first time that Helen had been in the company of both hearing and seeing girls. Later, her little sister Mildred came to the school and Cambridge allowed her to stay at the school with Helen. Eventually, the school decided that Helen was working too hard and tried to cut back her classes, which meant that she would not graduate with her class. Although Kate, Helen's mother, and Anne argued with the school, the administration held firm and Helen's mother withdrew both Helen and Mildred. Helen studied with a tutor and Anne to prepare for college.

In 1899, she took the exams for admission to Radcliffe and was admitted in 1900, becoming the first deaf-blind person ever enrolled in a higher education institution. Helen's experience at Radcliffe was very difficult for both Helen and Anne. Not only was the workload tremendous but also Anne's eyesight continued to deteriorate. Nevertheless, Helen completed all of her studies successfully and she began to write about her life. She learned to use a typewriter and also wrote her story in Braille. When Anne met John Albert Macy, a professor at Harvard, she introduced him to Helen. Macy helped Helen edit her first book *The Story of My Life*, and *The Practice of Optimism,* both of which were published in 1903. Helen graduated in 1904 cum laude with a bachelor's degree in English.

Although Helen's academic accomplishments were remarkable even for someone without a disability, at times she was involved in controversy and became the target of critics and skeptics. In 1892, she wrote the short story "The Frost King" as a birthday present for Anagnos. When the story was published in the Perkins Institute Annual Report, critics said she plagiarized "The Frost Fairies" by Margaret Canby. Helen did not remember reading the story and Anne did not remember reading it to her. Later, an investigation indicated that Anne had read her the story when she was eleven years old. Helen was humiliated and shaken by the accusations and was worried that her writing was really not her own thoughts. She thought she might not write again because she could not distinguish between what she had read and her own thoughts. In addition, the incident created a rift between Helen and Anne and Anagnos that ultimately ended their friendship. Anagnos felt that he was betrayed and made to appear foolish by Helen's deception. Later, blind critics argued that too much of her education had been language and literature and not enough had been based on real experiences. Helen responded to that criticism by saying that she had been shaped by words and literature.

Other skeptics questioned whether she was a fraud. In the article "Is Helen Keller a Fraud?" published in the *Journal of the Association to Promote the Teaching of Speech to the Deaf,* the principal of the Institutes for Deaf-Mutes defended Helen. He argued that Helen could not be a fraud because the many experts who had examined her verified that she was authentically gifted. Like many other famous people, Helen found that the publicity about her attracted supporters and detractors.

After Helen graduated from college, she continued living with Anne and writing books. John Macy remained friends with Helen but his friendship with Anne evolved into a romantic relationship. In May 1905, John and Anne were married and Anne became Anne Sullivan Macy. After the marriage, Helen continued to live with John and Anne in Wrentham, Massachusetts. With John's help, Helen wrote her third book, *The World I Live In* (1908), which was a treatise about her thoughts on her world. During this time, Helen and Anne also traveled extensively giving lecture tours. Helen's remarks about her experiences and beliefs were interpreted sentence by sentence by Anne. These lecture tours were very popular and allowed Helen and Anne to make a living until 1918, when the demand for Helen's lectures decreased.

This decrease in demand is often attributed to negative publicity about her political beliefs. After college, John had introduced her to socialism, and Helen read H. G. Wells's *New Worlds for Old* and other books by Karl Marx and Friedrich Engels that changed her thinking. In 1909, Helen became a member of the Socialist Party of Massachusetts and a member of the International Workers of the World in 1911. In 1913, her series of essays on socialism, *Out of the Dark*, was published. This had an immense impact on Helen's public image because everyone now knew about Helen's political views. Despite the criticism, she continued to actively support demonstrations, strikes, and other acts of civil disobedience and supported the Socialist Party candidate Eugene V. Debs in each of his campaigns for the presidency. Critics called her an anarchist and journalists attacked her as well as John and Anne. They blamed John and Anne for Helen's views, claiming that they had exploited Helen, despite the fact that Anne was not a socialist. While journalists had previously focused on Helen's intellect and achievements, they now focused on her disability.

Some critics posited that Helen could not really think for herself and her limitations made her vulnerable to the influence of others. Her books about socialism did not sell well and her support of socialist and union causes cost her the support of many in the public as well as longtime benefactors.

Finances had always been an issue in the Keller family and her father had been forced into debt to pay for Helen's education and travel. Despite assistance from wealthy benefactors throughout her life, Helen and Anne needed to continue to work to earn a living. Helen became less active in socialist causes and from 1919 to 1923 they performed in a vaudeville show. Although these shows were very popular, lucrative, and enjoyable for Helen, Anne found them demeaning. During this time, they were also offered an opportunity to make a film about Helen's life, *Deliverance*. Helen was not happy with the film because she felt it glamorized her life. Also, the film was not the financial success they had expected, so it did not help Helen and Anne's financial situation. In 1921, Helen and Anne experienced more adversity. Helen's mother, Kate, died in 1921 from an unknown illness, leaving Anne as Helen's caretaker. Then Anne contracted several illnesses including bronchitis that damaged her vocal cords and left her unable to speak above a whisper. Because Anne could no longer work with Helen on stage, they recruited a new interpreter, Polly Thomson, who had started working for Helen and Anne in 1914 as a secretary.

In addition to their paid lectures, Helen and Anne and later Polly toured the world raising money for blind people. Helen, Anne, and John had raised funds for the American Foundation for the Blind and in 1915 Helen founded Helen Keller International, a nonprofit organization for preventing blindness. To raise money for these organizations, Helen traveled with Anne or Polly to over forty countries, often meeting with famous people and world leaders, including King George and Queen Mary and several of the U.S. presidents. Besides fund-raising, Helen also campaigned to improve the conditions for blind people. At that time, most blind people were living in asylums and received little to no education. Helen's efforts were successful in increasing awareness and improving those conditions.

Significant events in the late 1920s and early 1930s changed Helen's life. John and Anne's marriage ended and then John died in 1932. Anne's health continued to decline and she died in October 1936. After Anne died, Helen and Polly moved to Arcan Ridge, in Westport, Connecticut, which would be Helen's home for the rest of her life. During a fund-raising trip, Helen and Polly were informed that a fire had destroyed the Arcan Ridge home. This fire destroyed many valuable items including mementoes from Helen's life and the manuscript for Helen's latest book about Anne Sullivan, *Teacher: Anne Sullivan Macy*. Then Polly's health began to deteriorate and she had a stroke while they were in Japan. They followed Polly's doctor's advice to stop touring for a while but after Polly recovered, they began traveling again. Helen wrote two additional books during the 1920s: *My Religion* (1927) and *Midstream: My Later Life* (1929).

Helen continued her political activism in the late 1920s. She had always been a strong advocate of women's rights and became a suffragette. She also fought for improvements in women's and children's health, including reproductive healthcare for all women regardless of income. She became close friends with Margaret Sanger, the founder of Planned Parenthood Federation of America. Later, she channeled her political efforts into supporting the New Deal, disarmament, and world peace.

In 1953, *The Unconquered*, a documentary film about Helen's life, won an Academy Award as the best feature length documentary. Helen also began work again on her book *Teacher*. Seven years after the original had been destroyed in the fire, the book was finally published in 1955. Helen's other books include *The Song of the Stone Wall*, *Peace at Eventide*, *Helen Keller in Scotland*, *Helen Keller's Journal*, *Let Us Have Faith*, and *The Open Door*. Helen's companion, Polly Thomson, had a major stroke in 1957 and died on March 21, 1960. The nurse who cared for Polly in her last years, Winnie Corbally, took care of Helen the rest of her life. In the same year that Polly died, *The Miracle Worker* was first performed as a television play. In 1959, it was rewritten as a Broadway play that ran successfully for two years. In 1962, it was made into a film that earned Oscars for Anne Bancroft, who played Anne, and Patty Duke, who played Helen.

In 1961, Helen suffered her first stroke. This was the first in a series of strokes that ended her travel and public life. She lived the rest of her life at Arcan Ridge and was cared for by Winnie. However, she still made public appearances and received numerous awards. In 1964, Helen was awarded the Presidential Medal of Freedom, the nation's highest civilian award, by President Lyndon Johnson. The next year she was elected to the Women's Hall of Fame at the New York World's Fair. Radcliffe College granted her its Alumnae Achievement Award and also dedicated the Helen Keller Garden in her honor. In recognition of many scholarly achievements, she received honorary doctoral degrees from Temple University, Harvard University, and the Universities of Glasgow, Scotland; Berlin, Germany; Delhi, India; and Witwatersrand in Johannesburg, South Africa. She was also an Honorary Fellow of the Educational Institute of Scotland.

Furthermore, she received many international awards including Brazil's Order of the Southern Cross, Japan's Sacred Treasure, the Philippines' Golden Heart, Lebanon's Gold Medal of Merit, the Americas Award for Inter-American Unity, and the Chevalier of the French Legion of Honor.

On June 1, 1968, Helen Keller died peacefully in her sleep. She was cremated in Bridgeport, Connecticut, and a funeral service was held at the National Cathedral in Washington, D.C. The urn containing her ashes was placed next to those of Anne Sullivan and Polly Thomson. An inscription written in words and Braille on the bronze plaque at the memorial chapel reads: "Helen Keller and her beloved companion Anne Sullivan Macy are interred in the columbarium behind this chapel."

Helen Keller changed our perceptions of the disabled. By achieving far more than most people without disabilities, she challenged the public perception of what people with disabilities could accomplish. She was able to integrate into a seeing and hearing world, showing that the disabled could function independently. She also devoted most of her adult life to advocating for and raising funds for the blind. She was always deeply concerned about the suffering of others. From a young age, she wrote and spoke about human suffering and questioned why people had to suffer. However, she never wanted sympathy for people with disabilities. She believed that she needed to work to fix society and therefore focused on broader social issues. Although she is most remembered as a blind-deaf woman who overcame her disabilities to become successful in life, she was really a social activist who campaigned tirelessly for civil rights, human rights, women's rights, and world peace. As Helen said, "Although the world is full of suffering, it is full also of the overcoming of it."

21. NORA BARNACLE JOYCE

1884–1951
MUSE

I guess the man's a genius, but what a dirty mind he has, hasn't he?
—Nora Joyce on her husband, James

How on earth can you possibly love a thing like me?
—James Joyce in a letter to his wife

She was the sixteen-year-old girl from the west of Ireland who captured the heart of one of the greatest writers of the twentieth century. The chambermaid who became literature's most celebrated muse, Nora Barnacle has served as the model for James Joyce's most memorable female characters: the mournful Greta Conroy in "The Dead," the lusty Molly Bloom in *Ulysses*, and the lyrical Anna Livia Plurabelle in *Finnegan's Wake*. While Joyceans often scoff at Nora as an illiterate barmaid who failed to meet her husband's intellect and never read his work, the truth is that Nora was a literate, funny, and sharp-witted woman who read her husband's poems and short stories with great pleasure. Her bawdy, hilarious, and often insightful letters to her husband (he once told her, "You write like a queen") during their rare separations as well as her keen observations have made her one of the most fascinating women in twentieth-century literary history. As Brenda Maddox asserts in *Nora: A Biography of Nora Joyce,* her classic biography of James Joyce's lifelong companion, "Nora's life was shaken by the major political and social forces of the first half of the 20th century—two world wars, the struggles of Irish and Italian nationalism, the emancipation of women, even the anti-Semitism of New York society. With her strength, wit, and charm, she survived them, just as she survived thirty-seven years with James Joyce and taught him what life was about." Joyce called her his "portable Ireland" and it is plausible to argue that without Nora Barnacle, there could have been no James Joyce.

Nora Barnacle was born in Galway, Ireland, on March 21, 1884, to Thomas Barnacle, a baker, and Annie Healy, a dressmaker. One of six children, Nora got a taste of the nomadic existence she would lead with James Joyce later in life. The Barnacles were forever on the move, her father suffered from alcoholism, and at just twelve she was sent to live with her grandmother, Catherine Healy. As a child, she demonstrated independence, wit, and humor that would serve throughout her adulthood. She attended the Convent of Mercy and the National School before she left school for good at the age of twelve. While much is made of this fact by Joyce scholars, this was not unusual for a girl to complete her education at such a young age. Irish women were rarely educated, unless they were exceedingly wealthy. In 1896, Nora became a porter at a Presbyterian convent. Not yet thirteen, she was already a beauty and possessed a potent sexual allure. She had already gained her full height of five feet, ten inches and had beautiful red hair and a proud way of walking that would be the inspiration for all of Joyce's women. Later that year, Nora fell in love with Michael Feeney, who died of pneumonia. It was this incident in Nora's life that would become the inspiration for Joyce's masterpiece short story "The Dead." In the story, Greta Conroy tells her husband the tragic story of a boy she loved while she was living with her grandmother and attending a convent school in the west of Ireland. The boy, who Joyce renamed Michael Furey, dies while waiting in the cold outside young Greta's window. As Greta cries in the story, "I think he died from loving me." It is a beautiful story, and one that Joyce could not have told without Nora.

The next few years held more tragedy for Nora. Another boyfriend, Michael Bodkin, died of tuberculosis three years after Feeney met his own tragic end. Her grandmother died of bronchitis, and she was sent to live with her uncle Tommy, a gruff man who raised his niece with an iron fist. Years later when Nora fell in love with a young Protestant boy named

Willie Mulvagh, he beat her. Not one to take unfair punishment lightly, Nora packed up her belongings one week later and headed for Dublin. The year was 1904 and she was just sixteen years old.

She secured a position as a maid in Finn's Hotel on Leinster Street in Dublin. It was that summer that a young struggling writer saw a beautiful, stately young woman saunter up Nassau Street. The date was June 10, 1904, and the day would change both of their lives forever. Just six days later, on June 16, they had their first formal date, the date on which Joyce's *Ulysses* takes place and which will forever be known as Bloomsday. The couple began a mad love affair that began through a series of ardent letters. Deeply in love with Nora, but desperate to escape the stifling religious atmosphere of Ireland, Joyce began talking of leaving Ireland for Europe. Seeing no future in Dublin and estranged from her family, Nora asked to go with him. James said yes, responding, "No human being has ever stood so close to my soul as you stand." Joyce soon found a teaching job with the Berlitz School in Zürich. While Nora and James had more in common than one might suspect (both were from large families, with alcoholic fathers), Joyce's brother Stanislaus disapproved of Nora and would battle her for most of her life. Undeterred, Nora took the boat to Zürich, where James would meet her a few days later. She took an incredible risk in running away with a man who had made no promises to marry her, but she never looked back. It would be years before she returned to Ireland.

When they reached Zürich, they made love for the first time, and Joyce was delighted with Nora's enthusiasm and sexual appetite. It was the glue that would hold their relationship together for years to come, but Nora's sensuality would also fuel Joyce's own jealousies. While Joyce had no intention of marrying Nora, he pretended they were married and devoured every story in her short past, which would become the fodder for some of the greatest works in English literature. When Nora and Joyce discovered that the Berlitz job had fallen though, they moved to Poland, then onto Trieste in Austria, which became their home for sixteen years. While Joyce was awaiting the publication of his first collection of short stories, *Dubliners*, Nora discovered that she was pregnant. Unmarried, unable to speak the language, and lonely, Nora found it difficult to adjust to life in Trieste. Joyce drank heavily and Nora was shunned by many of the local townspeople for her burgeoning pregnancy. On July 26, 1905, Nora gave birth to their son, Giorgio, much to Joyce's delight. Joyce's brother, Stanislaus soon joined them, and the family moved in with a kind Italian couple called the Francinis. Although he was delighted with his young son and often sang to him in Italian, Joyce was about to face more disappointment. His collection of poems, *Chamber Music*, was declared "obscene" and was refused publication. The couple left for Rome so that James could finish his novel *Stephen Hero* (which would later become *A Portrait of the Artist As a Young Man*). Joyce was working in a bank, but money was still tight and they were often in debt and hungry. It was here that Joyce, starving and longing for Ireland, wrote the sumptuous dinner scene in "The Dead." The next year, Nora was pregnant again and *Chamber Music* was finally published. On July 26, 1907, Lucia Joyce was born. The next year, Nora became pregnant a third time but miscarried. In 1909, Joyce returned to Ireland to find a publisher for *Dubliners*, leaving Nora and their daughter behind. It was during this separation that the couple began the first in their series of famous love letters. Sensual, often salacious, and sometimes accusatory, these letters show Joyce's fierce love for Nora and his tendency toward possessiveness. In one letter, he accused her of infidelity with his close friend Vincent Cosgrove and asked her, "Is Giorgio our son?" Wisely, Nora did not respond to him for weeks. Joyce also praised her, saying, "You seem to turn me into a beast," and declared, "You are my bride, darling, and all I can give you of pleasure and joy in this life I wish to give you." Tired of being alone, Nora threatened to leave. Joyce begged her to stay and promised never to leave her again.

Over the next few years, Nora and James continued to struggle financially, but insisted on living in some luxury. Nora always dressed in the finest clothes and cared deeply about her appearance, and the couple had many friends. However, Joyce was still facing endless rejection from publishers and drinking more heavily than ever. Nora traveled to Ireland to meet with his publishers to investigate what was holding up the publication of *Dubliners*. James joined her, and the expatriates soon found that they were less than welcome. Catholic Ireland had not changed and Joyce left, vowing never too return. In 1913, *Dubliners* was finally published and Ezra Pound read part of *A Portrait of the Artist* and agreed to serialize it. Joyce was now a published and lauded author. Fueled by the acclaim, he finished his play *Exiles*, in which he once again used Nora as a model for the main female character, Bertha, who uses many of Nora's own words. And Nora, too, was feeling as though her life was taking shape. She was the "wife" of a writer who William Butler Yeats had proclaimed a "genius," with two beautiful, bright children. But the family was soon to be uprooted once again. In 1914, World War I was in full force and Trieste was heavily armed, so the family moved to Zürich, the city where Nora and James had first consummated their love. They soon made friends and Joyce received a grant from the Royal Literary Fund. Nora became a prominent figure, entertaining a cadre of Joyce's artist friends. She also became an actress, starring in a local production of John Synge's play *Riders to the Sea*, and, most important, serving as the inspiration for Molly Bloom in Joyce's next work, *Ulysses*.

In 1918, Joyce met Sylvia Beach, the owner of the Parisian bookstore Shakespeare and Company and one of Joyce's biggest fans. Joyce was now garnering the admiration of literary giants and Shakespeare and Co. had plans to publish *Ulysses* for 1,500 pounds. Finally, in 1922, *Ulysses* was published and became recognized as one of the great masterpieces of twentieth-century literature. Its heroine, Molly Bloom, became one of the most talked about, dissected, and overanalyzed characters in literature. Profane, loquacious, and deeply sensual, she seems to be the spitting image of Nora. Ironically, Nora, no prude herself, never finished *Ulysses* as she found it indecent. Joyce had become a star because of the book, but to Nora it became a cross to bear. One particular priest asked her one day, "Mrs. Joyce, cannot you stop your husband from writing those terrible books?"

Although James and Nora were becoming celebrities in Europe and spent time in Paris, their lives were taking a tumultuous turn. James had been diagnosed with glaucoma a few years earlier and was now nearly blind. Giorgio had begun an affair with Nora's friend, Helen Fleisch-mann, who was thirty-one years old (ten years older than he was) and al-ready a mother. Nora disapproved vehemently and believed that Helen was trying to steal her son from her. In 1929, doctors found a tumor near Nora's uterus and had to perform a full hysterectomy. To add to her trou-bles, Lucia was becoming more violent and out of control. She fell madly in love with Samuel Beckett, who was helping her father with his latest work, *Finnegans Wake*, and was crushed when her affections were not re-turned. Lucia was eventually diagnosed with schizophrenia, which was virtually untreatable. And the secret that James and Nora had tried to keep hidden so long had finally come out: they were still unmarried. Giorgio was intent on marrying Helen, but she was apprehensive about marrying an "illegitimate" man. To rectify the situation, Joyce agreed to marry Nora on July 4, 1931, in London. The press followed them every-where, but at last Nora felt like she had more stability being formally married to James. The next year, Giorgio took Lucia to an insane asylum. Never willing to admit that there was anything wrong with his daughter, Joyce was in agony. For the next several years, the Joyces lived in Paris and then returned to Switzerland at the beginning of World War II. James Joyce had already appeared on the cover of *Time* magazine, and in 1938 *Finnegans Wake* was published. But by the time the Joyces returned to Zürich, he was suffering from unbearable stomach pains and agoniz-ing eye problems. One month after their return, on January 13, 1941, Joyce died of a perforated ulcer. Nora's beloved James was gone and she paid tribute to him by having two death masks commissioned. At his fu-neral, she paid him the ultimate compliment when she said, "Jim how beautiful you are."

Now, without an income and her soul mate, Nora was in dire straits. After his death, she had to fight for years for access to his royalties, but she never stopped protecting his legacy. She tried to have her husband's body sent back to Ireland, but much as they did with his books, the Irish refused to let him in. She also approved the publication of Joyce's famed letters. By the late 1940s, Nora was suffering from acute arthritis that left her in severe pain. In 1951, she was hospitalized and died of a heart attack at the age of sixty-seven, with her cherished son by her side. Her death was reported in the international press, including *Time* magazine. In 1966, Nora was reburied next to her husband in Zürich and remains by his side in death just as she had for almost forty years. Although she would only return to Ireland a few times after she left with James in 1904, as Maddox observes, "She remains as much a part of Irish mythology as Queen Maeve."

22. GEORGIA O'KEEFFE

1887–1986

<small>ARTIST</small>

From the time I was small, I was always doing things that people don't do.
— Georgia O'Keeffe

When so few people ever think at all, isn't it all right for one to think for them and then get them to do what I want?
— Georgia O'Keeffe

Widely regarded as one of the greatest painters of the twentieth century, Georgia O'Keeffe was a major figure in American art since the 1920s, paving the way for female artists with her revolutionary vision, her sexual daring, and her powerful abstract images.

Georgia Totto O'Keeffe was born in 1887 on a farm in Sun Prairie, Wisconsin. She was the second child born to Frank O'Keeffe and Ida Totto. Her older brother, Frank, was born soon after their parents were married and Georgia followed a few years later. Her parents then had five more children. Georgia's father, Frank, was born in a log cabin on a farm in Sun Prairie to Irish Catholic farmers. His parents came to Wisconsin in 1848 during the Irish Potato Famine. When his father died, his mother, Kate, took over the farm. Kate was always a religious and frugal woman and ran the farm with the help of her sons. She was also a strong, independent woman who loaned money to others in the area. Frank tried to assert his independence by leaving the farm to homestead in the Dakota Territory. However, Kate convinced him to come back to Wisconsin by renting a neighboring farm for him. Kate also negotiated a business deal with the owner of the farm, Isabella Totto, which resulted in an arranged, loveless marriage between Frank and Ida, one of Isabella's daughters. Ida's mother was Dutch and English while her father was a Hungarian playboy who abandoned the family. Frank and Ida moved into the family mansion on the Totto farm, where they had seven children. Ida insisted that Frank leave the Catholic Church and raise the children as Protestants. It was a troubled marriage that would suffer many tragedies and have a profound effect on Georgia and her siblings.

Georgia was named "Totto" for her grandfather who had abandoned the family. This name would plague her for her entire childhood. Not only did she hate the name because it sounded like a boy's name but also her mother associated her with her father's name and his betrayal. As a result, Georgia's mother treated her badly. Georgia and her siblings recognized that her mother preferred her older brother Frank and all of her younger siblings. Her mother often made her stay in a back room when visitors came, which made Georgia feel that she was ugly. Because her mother did not show her any affection, she gravitated toward her father. He was an easygoing, affable man who often took her for rides into town so she could escape her mother. She became her father's favorite child. She was the only one to have her own room on the second floor and was afforded other privileges. Later, Georgia realized that her relationship with her father and mother was not just due to preference. Although she repressed the memories, it later came to light that her father had sexually abused her and that her brother had joined in the incest. Her sisters remember that she was "bossy" and always "running" the other girls. She also convinced them to break rules, take risks, and get into trouble. She later said, "From the time I was small, I was always doing things that people don't do." Like many victims of childhood incest, she was protective of her father and even maintained a highly inflated view of him. She could never admit all of her father's personal and business failures and embellished his accomplishments. She did not recognize that he was an alcoholic or that he had molested her. When he later did not protect her and even abandoned the family, she still made excuses for him and refused to criticize him. This relationship with her father affected her relationships with men for the rest of her life.

She attended several schools, including Sacred Heart Academy in

Madison, Wisconsin. At that school she took a drawing class taught by a nun who criticized her pencil drawing of a plaster cast of a baby's hand. The nun told her the drawing was too small. She later said she learned from this feedback and it made her think like an artist. She also made the decision to never draw anything small again. When she was nine years old, the family moved from Wisconsin to Williamsburg, Virginia, to escape the tuberculosis epidemic in Wisconsin. Her father had read erroneous information that Williamsburg was free of tuberculosis, so he insisted that they move. Ironically, the hot, humid climate in Williamsburg was actually more conducive to the spread of tuberculosis. Frank never admitted the mistake, so they stayed in Williamsburg. From most accounts, it appears that Frank was a hypochondriac who was afraid of germs. That fear caused him to make a costly decision to sell a successful farm and a beautiful house in Wisconsin to buy a lesser house with very little furniture. Frank and his family were regarded as "rough" by the people in Williamsburg, so her mother tried unsuccessfully to keep her previous status as an affluent woman. She sent the girls to a boarding school, Chatham Episcopal Institute. Georgia was considered "rough" by the other girls who dressed like southern belles in frilly dresses and wore their hair in ringlets. Georgia looked like a Quaker in her black dresses or men's clothes and straight, cropped hair. When others at the school saw this plain, dark-skinned, young girl, they thought she was a maid. The other girls tried to mold her into a southern belle but she refused to change. She dressed and looked like a boy—it was a pattern that continued the rest of her life, causing her to be mistaken for a man quite often.

At Chatham Episcopal Institute, she was soon noticed for her artistic ability. Her art teacher, Elizabeth May Willis, recognized her talent. Because Willis's face was partially paralyzed, she had experienced personal adversity and helped Georgia overcome her own challenges. Other students in the class remarked that in their art class Georgia "was queen." The art studio also helped her survive boarding school. She always had difficulty with academics, particularly in spelling and math computation, and she read very few books. She was as mischievous in school as she had been on the farm; she taught other girls how to play poker, cook in their rooms, eat dirt, and engage in many other rule-breaking behaviors. She also threw away many of her paintings and burned them. She told the other students, "One day I'm going to be famous and I don't want these paintings floating around to haunt me." In boarding school she knew she did not want to go to college and told everyone that she wanted to go to art school and become a famous artist.

She and her classmates engaged in lesbian relationships, which was common in boarding schools at the time. Most of the girls were heterosexuals who abandoned their lesbian affairs after they left boarding school, but Georgia never seemed attracted to men. Although some friends and family have denied she was a lesbian, evidence from letters, interviews, and other sources indicate that she had many lesbian relationships with women throughout her life. Her analyst said Georgia believed that she was a lesbian all her life but since homosexuality was not acceptable, she repressed it as much as possible and hid it from others. This repressed sexuality was evident in her work, but Georgia was always shocked that others saw female sexuality in her work.

Although it was unthinkable for a woman to become a famous artist, Willis convinced Georgia's parents to send her to art school. Her aunt and uncle lived in Chicago near the Chicago Art Institute, so her parents agreed to let her live with them while she attended school. Later, she said she was very lucky that these circumstances allowed her to attend art school. She attended the art institute from 1905 to 1906 and found that the school was very competitive. Because her aunt was very stern, she channeled all her energy into her work and had almost no social life. At the institute the excellent students sat near the front, which ensured continued excellence. She worked very hard and rose to the top quarter of the class. The instruction was conservative and the students' creativity and originality were discouraged; the students were required to copy masterpieces over and over in great detail. Georgia realized that she was really working hard but that she was less and less satisfied with her work. She also recognized that her work was increasingly similar to that of others. While she was in school that year, she contracted typhoid fever, forcing her to go home to recover for a year.

When she was ready to go back to school, Willis advised her to go to the Art Students' League in New York. Since her parents could not afford the expensive school, she earned money by modeling for other students. At a time when most of the female students became art teachers, Georgia stood out because she wanted to become a famous artist. She was influenced greatly by a class taught by William Merritt Chase. In his class, she discovered that art could be fun. He asked the students to create a small painting every day. Georgia created a series of small still lifes, which became a pattern for the rest of her life. He also gave her the idea that flowers were the most difficult subject to paint, more difficult that the human figure. His work, featuring soft colors and an oriental style, had an obvious influence on her work even though she denied this later. She discovered the importance of color and the technique that allowed her to create work that looked "as if it has been blown onto the canvas with one puff." Chase told his classes, "Great work comes from the heart. When only from the head, it is uninteresting." She learned much from imitating his work, but she started to feel that she was again not creating original work. "I saw that any idiot could come to copy another painting. I wanted to create a painting." She won first prize for the Chase still-life competition, winning a scholarship at the league summer school in Lake George. The men at the league did not accept women and actually persecuted them. Georgia joined them rather than fighting them. She endured their jibes and repressed her femininity. She became friends with George Dannenberg, often spending time with him, but she discouraged a romantic relationship. This year at the Art Students' League further shaped her work.

In 1908, she returned to Williamsburg to find that her family was in a severe financial crisis. During the crash of 1907, her family had lost most of the money they had earned from the sale of the farm and her father had invested most of the remaining money in a cement block business that failed. He was forced to sell their house and land. So he built a very badly constructed house out of the cement blocks, which was crooked and looked like a poorly built prison. The family had to take in boarders and their father was drinking heavily. Georgia had been out of touch with her family's declining financial state and was upset that her family could not afford her tuition to art school. She probably could have secured a scholarship, but instead went to live with her aunt and uncle in

Chicago. Unemployment was high throughout the country but in Chicago it was extremely high. So she worked in a series of menial jobs for two years and apparently did not paint for four years. She later said she did not even pick up a paintbrush during that time.

In 1910, she returned to Virginia with a terrible case of measles, which resulted in temporary blindness. She cooked and cleaned for her father and her two younger sisters, who still lived with their father. Her mother and two other sisters had moved to Charlottesville because her mother had tuberculosis. Her mother was illegally taking in boarders, which meant the family was keeping her tuberculosis a secret. In 1911, when Willis asked her to come to Chatham to teach art, she welcomed the escape. Her father was losing his mind and her mother was dying. She taught at Chatham for a year before returning to Williamsburg. By then, her family had reunited. Georgia's younger sisters, who were taking education classes at the University of Virginia, told her about an art class offered by Alon Bement. Bement, a student of Arthur Wesley Dow, used the Dow method to teach art. This method involved creating original art rather than copying it. Georgia was intrigued and enrolled in the summer class, which she enjoyed immensely. In this class there was no competition and no pressure, so she could paint the way she wanted. The Dow method, which was based on the oriental concept of beauty, emphasized that less is more. Bement went back to New York, but he asked her to help him teach the summer class when he returned to Virginia. She had to have a year of teaching in public schools, so she taught in Roanoke. This was the beginning of her teaching career.

In 1912, she accepted a teaching job in Amarillo, Texas. Although many people considered Amarillo a bleak part of the Texas panhandle, Georgia immediately loved it. She was amazed by the landscape and wrote to a friend, "and the SKY—you have never seen the SKY—it is wonderful." She always wanted to live in the West, remembering the stories from her childhood about Kit Carson, Billy the Kid, and the Indians in the Dakota Territory. Later she said, "This was my country. Terrible winds and wonderful emptiness." Amarillo was wealthy but still a rustic frontier town. Georgia drew attention because she lived an unconventional lifestyle, particularly for a teacher. She lived in a hotel next to a saloon rather than in the Methodist boardinghouse with the other teachers. She played poker with men, became friends with the cowboys, and dressed like a man. Although she was a gifted teacher, she was often in trouble. She had numerous conflicts because she refused to use the school's Prang drawing book, used the Dow method to teach art, allowed students to break rules (even allowing a boy to bring a horse into the classroom), and initiated arguments with many people in the town. Nevertheless, she taught students to look at the plains in a different way and to see the beauty of the plains. She was free to ride out into the plains and to develop her own artistic expression. On one of these trips, she discovered the Palo Duro Canyon, which is called the Grand Canyon of Texas. She struggled for a long time to paint the landscape with its range of sandstone colors and canyon architecture. She did not save the paintings from this period, but this experience affected her forever.

At the end of the year, when she went back to Charlottesville, her sister noticed that her work and approach had changed. She seemed to be creating work just for herself. From 1913 to 1916 she taught in South Carolina, then she went to New York to earn her bachelor's in education at Columbia University Teachers College and study with Dow. In addition, she again took art classes at the Art Students League. She wore long black dresses and lived in a tiny room with minimal possessions, which created an air of mystery. At the league, she was allowed to work in a curtained area of the room by herself at first, then later with two other students, Anita Politzer and Dorothy True. The two women admired Georgia and they all became very close. While Georgia and Anita were intellectual equals and friends, evidence indicates that Georgia was probably in love with Dorothy. Anita and Georgia remained friends and often wrote and sent work to each other. During this time, Georgia was introduced to feminism in several ways. She met Arthur Macmahon through Alon Bement, as well as many other male feminists who introduced her to the works of feminist authors, such as Floyd Dell. Dell's book about seven feminists, *Women As World Builders*, resonated with Georgia and she adopted Dell's ideas on living as an independent woman. As Dell said, "The woman who finds her work will find her love." Although she embraced some of the feminist ideas, she was not really a feminist. She dominated other women and revered men, often considering men superior. During this time, she also began a love affair with Macmahon. After she had sex with him, she began a series of landscapes that expressed her sexual feelings. These were the first of her psychosexual landscapes.

When Georgia sent her abstract drawings of Texas landscapes to Politzer, Politzer was so impressed that she showed the drawings to the photographer Alfred Steiglitz. Steiglitz was an art collector who owned the 291 Gallery that Georgia had visited when she was in art school. He was also amazed by her drawings and remarked, "Finally, a woman's feelings on paper." Georgia was very reluctant to show her work, so Anita did not tell her she was taking the drawings to Steiglitz. In 1916 when she returned to New York to complete her degree, she discovered that her work was being shown at 291 when a man told her that "Virginia" O'Keeffe's work was being shown there. Realizing that it could possibly be her work, she rushed over to see her sexual landscapes hanging in the gallery. She confronted Steiglitz but he refused to take her work down despite her angry protests. Although she should have been grateful to have her work displayed at 291 because it was the premier gallery for contemporary art, she felt terribly exposed. She had little confidence in her work and a tremendous fear of exposure after a lifetime of keeping secrets about her family. This fear of showing her work continued throughout most of her life, causing her great anxiety about public showings.

After she completed her degree, she returned to Texas to teach in a teachers' college and continued to paint west Texas landscapes. She returned to New York for her first solo show, which featured these landscapes. The reviews were generally favorable including one reviewer who said, "Now perhaps for the first time in art history, the style is woman." Steiglitz's acceptance of her work also gave her more freedom to be expressive and to even try sculpture. Her first sculpture was the *Bending Figure,* which was inspired by her mother Ida's death, which was very tragic and disturbing. Frank left the family again and the children who were still living at home did not make enough money to support themselves or Ida. As a result, they lived in abject poverty while Ida became sicker and sicker. One day when the landlord came to collect the overdue rent, Ida died a horrible death. When Georgia learned how her mother had died, she felt terrible and was ashamed for the rest of her life. She was so poor she could not afford to go home for the funeral or the burial. That summer when she and her older brother Frank went home to close the house, she became severely depressed. Her grief and depression prompted her to sculpt the *Bending Figure*. Later, when the abstract bent shape was compared to a penis, she was devastated.

Her return to Texas marked the beginning of one of her most creative periods. She became manic and eccentric, living and working alone, riding horses, shooting at cans with her rifle, and working for as many hours as she could stay awake. Her lifestyle and behaviors caused people to regard her as eccentric. She painted her rooms black, took down all her curtains so she could see the stars, and brought tree limbs into her house as decorative objects. She also invited young male students to her room and could not understand why it was unacceptable. While she was in Texas, Steiglitz wrote to her constantly saying that he loved her. He asked her to remain in New York but she refused. She was also keeping other men at a distance and refusing their proposals, including Macmahon and Paul Strand. She sent Strand passionate letters and then sent Steiglitz the same kind of letters. She wanted Steiglitz to be her mentor, patron, and father figure, but she did not want to be his wife. While she was in Texas, her sister Claudia came to live with her. They took a vacation in Colorado and also went through New Mexico. This was a dry period for her artistically and she became very unhappy with herself. Then, she became romantically involved with Leah Harris, a home economics professional. She completed a series of nude watercolors and wrote letters to Strand saying that she was finished with men. She again began many confrontations with people in the town and became known as an "angry woman." As her behavior became more and more rash, she was regarded as a "madwoman." Some sources have speculated that this rage might have sprung from her repressed homosexuality and her history of childhood abuse. She exhibited many of the signs of childhood incest.

In 1918, she took time off from her art to recover from an undisclosed illness, which seems to have been a combination of a nervous breakdown and the flu. She recuperated at Leah Harris's ranch, and was joined by

Strand, who was sent by Steiglitz to rescue her. Strand moved in with them until Georgia decided to leave Harris and return to New York. Her lengthy relationship with Steiglitz began when she returned. Although they were not having sex, Steiglitz photographed her in the nude frequently. She moved into Steiglitz's apartment while his wife was away on a shopping trip. While there, she walked around in the nude while Steiglitz took pictures. Eventually, his wife came home and found them. She was furious and gave Steiglitz an ultimatum. Steiglitz had had many affairs with women and men but not in front of his wife. At the same time, Georgia had entered into the world of Bohemian free love with Steiglitz's daughter, Elizabeth. When Steiglitz's wife gave him the ultimatum, he moved into Elizabeth's studio with Georgia. They began going to Steiglitz's mother's house in Lake George, New York. This began another productive period for both her and Steiglitz. Steiglitz had a showing of his photos, including the nude photos of a person titled *A Woman*. Georgia appeared briefly at the showing and then disappeared, adding to her mystery. Overnight, she became a celebrity and everyone knew her name after the exhibition.

Georgia continued to live in New York with Steiglitz for many years, spending most of her summers at the Lake George house. She was originally dependent on Steiglitz financially, but Steiglitz did not have much money of his own, so they were both dependent on relatives. Steiglitz was considerably older than Georgia but he had been infantilized by his mother. He was a hypochondriac who was always sick or thinking he was sick. Ironically, he acted like a father to Georgia, coddling and protecting her. He was a father figure at a time when her own father died accidentally from a fall. This relationship was ideal for someone who had been molested as a child. Living together was both socially and legally unacceptable at the time. Because it was illegal for them to cohabitate, they were able to live together only because they lived in a property owned by Steiglitz's brother.

Georgia began producing larger paintings on canvas using bright hues of yellow, red, and pink. The paintings caused controversy not only because the colors were not used at the time but also because the paintings looked like female genitalia. In 1921, she had her first major showing that featured still lifes and landscape paintings of Lake George and Texas. Steiglitz, who was obsessed with her, acted as a salesman for her work. They were married in New Jersey in 1924. Georgia was thirty-six and Steiglitz was sixty. Georgia dressed in black and refused to say the words "love, honor, and obey" as part of her vows. That same year, she began to make more money from her paintings and did not really need Steiglitz as much financially. When later asked why she married Steiglitz, she said it did not matter but that "I just know that I did not want to." Their relationship was more of a partnership than a real marriage. Despite the continual friction in their marriage, the pattern of winters in New York and summers in Lake George continued for many years. While Steiglitz and Georgia were married, Georgia was involved in the social life in New York. She met the Stettheimer sisters and participated in their salon with Gertrude Stein and other famous women, including Mabel Luhan, a patron of the arts. In 1929, she left Steiglitz to go to New Mexico at the invitation of Luhan, who owned a house in Santa Fe.

The trip to Santa Fe would change her life forever. Steiglitz, who was sick again, refused to go but insisted that their friend Beck accompany Georgia. The two women looked like lesbian lovers in a city that was a mecca for lesbians. They lived with Luhan while they toured the area, visiting Taos Indian reservations and other nearby areas. They met Ansel Adams and other artists at Luhan's home. Later, Luhan took credit for introducing Georgia to New Mexico. While Mabel left to have surgery, Georgia and Mabel's husband, Tony, began an intimate relationship. When Mabel returned home and discovered the affair, she did not believe that they did had not have sex. Mabel told Steiglitz what had happened and Steiglitz became despondent. Georgia returned to New York to be with him, but she was forever changed by New Mexico. She referred to the land of northern New Mexico, a place of stark beauty and infinite space, as "the faraway." She told others, "If you ever go to New Mexico, it will itch you the rest of your life."

After she returned to New York, she had a major exhibition and stayed with Steiglitz for a while. From 1930 to 1933 she traveled back and forth between New York and New Mexico. During this period, she painted her famous skull and bone paintings. She also began work on a mural for the World's Fair in New York. In 1933, she became completely over-whelmed by the job and suffered a breakdown. She had severe head-aches, eye problems, phobias, and crying episodes. She stayed with friends for a while but was eventually taken to a hospital, where she was diag-nosed as psychoneurotic. Her physical symptoms were caused by a men-tal breakdown. While she slowly recovered, Steiglitz was not allowed to see her for more than a few minutes each day and he became despondent.

She went back to New Mexico in 1934 to continue her recovery and she discovered Ghost Ranch. She knew immediately that she had to live there. She spent so much time there alone that the owners allowed her to live on the ranch. From 1934 to 1940 she spent her summers living in a small house on the property with a succession of women. She traveled the back roads in a Model A Ford. She removed the backseat, unbolted the front seat, and turned it around so that she could prop her canvas against the back wall of the car. Her art evolved continually during this period. Fascinated by the large wooden crosses that dotted the landscape and by the many churches of this region, she began a series of paintings featuring the crosses.

In 1940, she bought the house where she had been staying. The house had a view of the flat-topped mesa in the Jemez range, called the Peder-nal. She told others, "It's my private mountain. It belongs to me. God told me if I painted it enough, I could have it." In December 1945, she bought an abandoned hacienda in the village of Abiquiu, sixteen miles from Ghost Ranch. The five buildings on the property were renovated be-tween 1945 and 1948. While Georgia was spending the summer of 1946 in New Mexico, Steiglitz suffered a cerebral thrombosis. She quickly flew to New York and was by his side when he died on July 13, 1946. As both the inheritor and executor of his estate, Georgia found herself busy the next three winters in New York cataloging his works and finding suit-able institutions for his photographs and writings. Georgia had returned to "her land" each summer until Steiglitz's death in 1946. After she set-tled his estate, she moved permanently to her home in New Mexico.

Although she had a major retrospective at the Art Institute of Chicago in 1943 and later an exhibit at the Museum of Modern Art, she had only three solo shows during the 1950s. Her work was no longer considered avant-garde. She retreated from the limelight, spending time tending her garden at the Abiquiu home and traveling to Mexico, South America, Europe, and Asia. When asked why she traveled so much, she said that she wanted to see if she lived in the right place. In 1962, Georgia was elected to be the fiftieth member of the American Academy of Arts and Letters, the nation's highest honor society for people in the arts. In the 1970s there was a resurgence of interest in her work. She was invited to show at the Whitney Museum in New York City and her retrospective exhibit traveled to the Art Institute of Chicago and the San Francisco Museum of Art. This exhibit set records for attendance. In 1971, Georgia realized that her eyesight was failing. At the age of eighty-four, she was losing her central vision and only had peripheral sight—she was suffering from an irreversible eye-degeneration disease. She stopped painting in 1972. "When you get so that you can't see, you come to it gradually. And if you didn't come by it gradually, I guess you'd just kill yourself when you couldn't see."

In 1973, Juan Hamilton, a young potter, came to Georgia's ranch house looking for work. She hired him for a few odd jobs but soon hired him full time. For the rest of her life, he became her closest confidant, companion, and business manager. As she said, "He came just the moment I needed him." She later began making pottery herself. She had a large kiln installed at the ranch for firing pots. Hamilton inspired her to paint again. She hired a studio assistant to execute some of her ideas. During this time she agreed to accept interviews and other opportunities. In 1976, she wrote a book about her art with Juan's help and she allowed a film crew to do a documentary at Ghost Ranch. Her love for Ghost Ranch remained constant for the rest of her life. She remarked, "When I think of death, I only regret that I will not be able to see this beautiful country anymore . . . unless the Indians are right and my spirit will walk here after I'm gone."

In her late nineties, Georgia's health declined and she became quite frail. She moved to Santa Fe, where she died on March 6, 1986, at the age of ninety-eight. She had left instructions that she wanted to be cremated the next day. Hamilton walked to the top of the Pedernal Mountain and scattered her ashes to the wind over her beloved "faraway."

23. ROSE KENNEDY

1890–1995
MATRIARCH

She is the glue that has always held the family together.
—John F. Kennedy

I just made up my mind that I was not going to be vanquished by anything.
—Rose Kennedy

To this day, she remains America's most beloved matriarch. Called "the ageless colleen" and "the first Irish Brahmin," she became the head of a colossal political dynasty, but remained proud of her own Fitzgerald roots until the day she died. While friends said that her husband, Joseph Kennedy, provided the fire in the Kennedy family, Rose Kennedy provided the steel. Her long life held both agony and ecstasy. She had more and lost more in one lifetime than most women in history, and she saw her sons ascend to great heights only to lose three of them before their time. By her eightieth birthday, only four of her nine children were still living. Yet, she remained the epitome of grace under fire and lived by her favorite quote, "I know neither age nor defeat."

Rose Fitzgerald was born in 1890 in Boston. She was the first child born to John F. Fitzgerald and Mary Josephine ("Josie") Hannon Fitzgerald. Her grandfather left Ireland during the Potato Famine and settled in the Boston tenements. Her father was called Johnny Fitz or Honey Fitz and was well known as an athletic, talented leader. During Rose's childhood, he was elected to the Boston Common Council, the state senate, and then Congress. Johnny and Josie were like many other "shanty Irish" in Boston who wanted to rise to higher social and economic status, lose their accents, and buy lace curtains and cut glass. Her father was able to rise above the family's poor circumstances and owned a grocery and liquor store.

Honey Fitz was one of ten boys, so he was delighted to have a girl. Rose was always like her father and she was her father's favorite; she was enthusiastic, hard working, ambitious, self-disciplined, and charming. Rose's brothers and sisters were: Agnes, Thomas, John F., and Eunice. The family moved to Concord, Massachusetts, when she a young child. She attended Edward Everett Grammar School and earned all As. Always a mother figure, she also took care of the younger children in the family, who resented Rose because she was such a persistent taskmaster and her father was so devoted to her. Because Rose was the embodiment of all her father's hopes and dreams, he spent most of his time with her, took her on trips, and talked to her constantly. He told her stories about Ireland, talked about Irish history and culture, and discussed politics with her.

When Rose was in high school, the family moved to Dorchester, a Boston suburb. Her father had purchased *The Republic*, a Democratic newspaper. He turned the newspaper into a commercial success, which allowed the family to move into a large mansion. Rose's parents entertained local celebrities like Sir Thomas Lipton, the tea tycoon. Eventually, the income from the newspaper increased to the point that the Fitzgeralds could buy a house in Hull, an area that overlooked Boston Harbor. They were also able to take trips to Palm Beach in the winter. In 1905, during one of these trips to Palm Beach, her father announced his candidacy for mayor of Boston. Rose had begun to learn about how to campaign previously but she really became a master when she accompanied him during his mayoral race. Like her father, she loved politics but her mother and siblings did not. Rose was with him throughout his campaign and enjoyed the crowds, the speeches, and watching her father work the crowds. He won the race and was inaugurated as mayor in January 1906.

When Rose graduated from Dorchester High School in 1906 at the age of fifteen, she was the youngest student ever to graduate from the school. Her father, the new mayor, presented her graduation diploma to her. This was the first time in U.S. history a mayor had ever presented a diploma to a son or daughter. Rose had passed the entrance examinations to Wellesley College, so she expected to begin college there in the fall. However, her father decided she was too young and enrolled her in the Sacred Heart Convent in Boston. She continued to live at home and attended Sacred Heart classes during the day. Because she was still living with her family, she spent much of her time with her father attending parties, rallies, and meetings. In fact, Rose accompanied her father so much that she essentially replaced her mother at all events. One reporter said, "Rose displays depth and strength of mind rarely found in so young a woman. Undoubtedly her father's influence upon her life has broadened her outlook, so that she lives much more vividly than most girls of her age." During these years, she continued to learn all the nuts and bolts of politics, including the backroom strategy, fund-raising, speaking, getting out the vote, and connecting with people. At a time when women could not vote and politics was a man's world, Rose's passion for politics was remarkable.

At seventeen, Rose met Joseph Kennedy at Old Orchard Beach, Maine, and fell in love with him. Joe was the son of P. J. Kennedy, a powerful political leader in Boston. Although they occassionally argued, Rose's father and P. J. Kennedy often went to Maine for vacations or Democratic Club meetings and the children would sometimes join them at the beach. Rose's father did not approve of any of her suitors, but of all of them he favored Hugh Nawn. So Rose had to keep her feelings about Joe a secret. Eventually, her father began to suspect that Rose was interested in Joe and began plotting to keep them apart. In the summer of 1908, Rose and Agnes went abroad to study at the Convent of the Sacred Heart in Prussia. While she was there, she joined the Children of Mary of the Sacred Heart, a sodality that emphasizes the need to renew religious beliefs daily. That year in Prussia shaped her beliefs about being a Christian wife and mother; the principles of unselfishness, duty, and devotion became her guiding principles for the rest of her life.

When Rose returned to Boston, Boston society was changing. The Irish had begun to form their own society, the "high Irish." They went on vacations together, organized elaborate social events, and held their own debutante balls. Since she had completed her education, she spent her time engaged in cultural and charitable efforts. She worked for the Irish Catholic Cecilian Club, the Catholic counterpart to the Junior League. She started her own club, the Ace of Clubs, and kept herself busy with many projects. The Ace of Clubs began with eight members but eventually became a very important cultural club with hundreds of members. In this club she learned to speak to small, intimate audiences, which further honed her speaking skills. During this time, Rose was a member of a drama club, started a travel club, continued piano lessons at the New England Conservatory, attended lectures, played tennis, and still accompanied her father to social engagements.

In 1911, Rose had her debut and came out to Irish society. She was still in love with Joe and was secretly seeing him on the sly. However, her father thought his beloved daughter was too good for Joe and continued to try to put obstacles in their way. Joe had attended Harvard and worked as a bank examiner. Finally, when Joe was twenty-five, he became president of his father's bank, the Columbia Trust Company, making him the youngest bank president in the United States.

Rose's father was finally impressed, but he was still opposed to the marriage. Joe finally proposed to her and gave her an engagement ring. They were married in 1914 when Joe was twenty-five and Rose was twenty-four.

The newlyweds moved into their first home in Brookline. Joe was driven to be successful, and he continued to work long hours in the financial world. In 1915, their first child, Joseph Patrick Jr., was born. While Rose stayed home to care for the baby, Joe moved from one job to another, always trying to make more money. He owned several businesses including a movie studio. Although Joe was often gone, he was home enough to sire the Kennedy children who were born almost every year: John, 1917; Rosemary, 1919; and Kathleen ("Kick"), 1920. After they moved to a larger house, Eunice, Patricia, and Robert were born. Rose continued her social life in Boston but was always home in the evening to care for the children. She was a master of organization and made sure the children did their homework, studied their catechism, and worked hard. She admonished them to "work hard at everything in life." Rose remained very religious and took the children to church frequently. She also sent them to dancing classes, tennis and golf lessons, and baseball and football games. All the children learned to ski, swim, and sail. Grandfather Honey Fitz, Joe, and Rose all encouraged competition. Rose said, "We would try to instill into them the idea that no matter what you did, you should try to be first." Winning was everything and the children vied for their father's attention.

As Joe began working more on Wall Street, he spent the week in New York and came home for the weekends. He pressured Rose to move the whole family to New York, but she loved Boston. Finally, in 1926 he decided it was time to move to Riverdale, New York. The youngest two Kennedy children, Jean and Edward, were born in New York. During this time, they also began trips to Hyannis Port, which was where the whole family gathered and eventually became the real family home. Later, they moved to Bronxville, where the younger children attended school. Eventually, the children were sent to exclusive private schools throughout New England. No matter how much they were separated, they always came back to Hyannis Port. Rose taught them that the Kennedys were "a self-contained unit."

Although they were wealthy and seemed to have everything, life in the Kennedy family was not without problems. Rosemary, who had always been slower than the other children, was assessed by a number of doctors and professionals. Eventually, they found her IQ was between 60 and 70 and she was diagnosed with mental retardation. Over time, her behavior became more erratic and difficult to predict and control. John ("Jack") had scarlet fever and was continually ill throughout his childhood. While Rose was at home taking care of the children, her husband was often absent. He worked long hours and traveled for business, but he also had many affairs. When Rose realized he was sleeping with other women, she went home to her parents. Her father told her that she had made the decision to marry Joe and that she was married for life, so she would need to go back to her husband. He famously said, "You've made your bed now, Rosie. Go home to your family." These problems would only be the beginning of Rose's sorrows.

In 1937, Joe Sr. was appointed as the ambassador to England. So the family moved to England except for Joe and Jack, who were studying at Harvard, and Rosemary, who was at Marymount Convent. Rose served as a gracious hostess and gave her husband political advice when he would listen. They traveled throughout Europe and the younger children attended schools in England. In 1939, Joe gave a speech, the Trafalgar Day speech, which caused great controversy. He alleged that England and the United States were no longer real democracies and advocated that the democracies and dictatorships should not emphasize their differences. Rose had advised him not to give this speech, but he ignored this advice and endured the loss of faith of the British people. The incident cast a pall on the Kennedy name, which would continue until his sons were old enough to change public opinion. When war was declared in 1939, Rose took some of the children back to the United States. She moved into the Bronxville house while Joe Sr. remained in England. Joe continued to advocate isolationism, partly because he did not want his sons to go to war.

Joe Jr. was always his parents' favorite, particularly his father's, and he served as a surrogate father because Joe Sr. was gone so much. Joe Sr. groomed Joe Jr. to accomplish all the things he had wanted to do, including becoming president of the United States. As the Kennedy children grew up, they realized that Joe was not only the leader of the family but also the one who was destined to fulfill their father's dreams. The other children tried to live up to Joe but were always in his shadow.

In 1940, Joe Jr. left law school at Harvard to volunteer as a navy pilot. Jack also volunteered for service but was initially rejected by the army and the navy because of a back injury. Eventually, his father was able to get him accepted by the navy. Rose had two sons in the military when the country was on the brink of war. At the same time, Rosemary's condition continued to worsen and she became more difficult to control, so Joe and Rose made the difficult decision to send her to a private home. In 1943, Rose heard the news that Jack's PT boat was rammed by a Japanese destroyer but that he had saved himself and his crew. Shortly thereafter, Kathleen ("Kick") married Billy Cavendish, a Protestant, in England. Rose was completely opposed to the marriage and did not know that it had occurred until it was announced. Then the biggest tragedy happened: Joe Jr. was killed in action when his plane exploded in midair. Soon after, Kick's husband was killed in action. This was the beginning of what would be called the "Kennedy curse."

After Joe Jr. died, Joe Sr. and Rose decided that Jack would need to take his brother's place in fulfilling his father's political aspirations. Although Jack was not interested in politics and his parents really did not see him as a politician, Joe Sr. told Jack, "Your brother is dead. It is your responsibility to run for Congress." Rose also pushed her son to run for the congressional seat representing the Eleventh District in Boston, where her father, Honey Fitz, had served as congressman. Joe and Rose took a prominent role in their son's campaign. Rose understood precinct politics and had learned how to work these precincts when she campaigned for her father. All the experiences in Rose's life had prepared her for this campaign. Jack Kennedy won 40 percent of the vote and succeeded his grandfather as congressman. He referred to his mother as his "secret weapon."

Jack won the congressional races in 1948 and 1950. During this time, tragedy struck again. In 1948, Kick was flying from London to Cannes, France, and was killed in a plane crash. Rose's father died in 1950. In 1952, the family decided that Jack should campaign against Henry Cabot Lodge for the Senate seat in Massachusetts. Again, Joe and Rose threw themselves into the campaign and the rest of the family jumped in with Bobby as Jack's campaign manager. It seemed that the Kennedys were everywhere, going door to door to get out the vote. As in previous campaigns, Rose was invaluable. She stumped tirelessly, speaking at meetings all day and attending events in the evening. When the family discovered the proportion of women was greater than men, she held numerous ladies teas. Dave Powers said, "She was the greatest campaigner of them all." When Jack won the Senate seat, Henry Cabot Lodge complained, "It was all those damned tea parties!"

In 1960, Jack decided to run for president. All the Kennedys campaigned hard and long. Rose again played a vital role. Although she was near seventy, she worked day and night, traveling all over the United States during the primaries and the election races. When Jack was elected president, Joe and Rose attended the inauguration and were there to celebrate Jack's fulfillment of the family dream. She became the Queen Mother of Camelot, often serving as a hostess to dignitaries at the White House.

A year after their son became president, Joe suffered a stroke. He made some progress for a while but then declined over the next seven years. Although she was always concerned about her husband, she traveled extensively throughout Europe, spending as much time as possible in Paris. She loved to shop and always wore designer clothes. When she was in the United States, she attended social events in New York, Palm Beach, and Hyannis Port. She attended many parties, many of which were benefit charities. She gave lectures, including "An Evening with Rose Kennedy." She also campaigned for Ted when he successfully ran for Senate.

In November 1963, Rose was in Hyannis Port with Joe preparing for Thanksgiving with the family when she heard the news about her son. She had played golf and was taking a nap when she was awakened by the shrieking sounds of her maid. She watched in horror as the news unfolded. When Bobby called, she said, "I can't stand it. I have to keep moving." She walked the rest of the day. At her son's funeral she told the emperor Haile Selassie, "It's wrong for parents to bury their children—it should be the other way around."

This was the first of another series of tragedies that Rose would endure. Her son, Bobby, was assassinated in 1968. Teddy was involved in the Chappaquiddick scandal, which would cloud his political career throughout his life. Joe died shortly thereafter. Rose had lost four of her children and her husband. The media called these tragedies "the Kennedy curse." But in her inimitable way, she told reporters, "God does not send us a cross any heavier than we can bear." Although in many ways Rose faded from the spotlight after Teddy's political defeat in 1980, when he lost the bid for president she remained the anchor of the family until her death.

Rose Kennedy died in 1995 at the age of 105. She is buried next to her husband in Brookline, Massachusetts.

24. ELIZABETH GURLEY FLYNN

1890–1964
LABOR ACTIVIST

History has a long-range perspective. It ultimately passes stern judgment on tyrants and vindicates those who fought, suffered, were imprisoned, and died for human freedom, against political oppression and economic slavery.
—Elizabeth Gurley Flynn

She was one of the founding members of the American Civil Liberties Union, who dedicated her life to the socialist and feminist movement in the United States. The writer Theodore Dreiser called her "an East Side Joan of Arc," but in life, Elizabeth Gurley Flynn was a true egalitarian—modest, humble, and dedicated to her beliefs. At the tender age of sixteen, she was already a full-fledged activist and was expelled from school for being "too political." The daughter of an Irish nationalist and the descendant of Irish rebels who fought in the 1798 Rebellion, Elizabeth experienced a passion for activism that began when she was just five years old.

Elizabeth Gurley Flynn was born on August 7, 1890, in Concord, New Hampshire. During her childhood, the family was surrounded by poverty, a reality she was made keenly aware of by her socialist parents. Her father was an organizer for the Industrial Workers of the World (IWW) and often took his daughter along to his meetings at Union Square, where she would often speak on behalf of socialism. In 1900, her family moved to the Bronx, New York, where Elizabeth attended public school. As a child, she would often attend meetings at the Harlem Socialist

Club on 125th Street, and by sixteen, she had made her first public speech, called *What Socialism Will Do for Women*. She had already been arrested for the first time, with her father, at the age of fifteen—it would be the first of many. As a teen, Elizabeth was also a member of IWW Local Chapter 179, which, she recalls, "blazed a trail like a great comet across the American labor scene from 1905 to 1920."

She attended her first IWW Convention as a delegate from Local 177 in Chicago in 1907. Around this time, she also befriended James Connolly, the Irish revolutionary leader and IWW organizer, who was living in New York at the time. In 1908, Elizabeth attained real notoriety when she was arrested in Missoula, Montana, for exercising her right to free speech. Now a full time worker for the IWW, she was defying a city ordinance that made street speech unlawful. It was also at this time that she met Jack Jones, a miner, whom she married that same year. In 1912, Elizabeth attended the Lawrence, Massachusetts, mill strike in which fourteen thousand mill workers walked out of work and the mills remained empty for three months. The original leaders of the strike, Joe Ettor and Arturo Giovannitti, had been arrested. Elizabeth and IWW National Leader Bill Haywood were brought into the strike. They addressed more than ten meetings a day, and the strike ultimately marked a huge victory for the IWW and put Elizabeth firmly in the public eye.

Elizabeth was in charge of the evacuation of the children of the strikers. When the police tried to arrest the children, Elizabeth made sure that the press covered their ill-treatment. The mill workers won the strike by mid-March and secured wage increases of from five to twenty-five percent.

For the next few years, Elizabeth was a force to be reckoned with. She came to the defense of labor leaders and political prisoners, and was the foremost champion for Joe Hill, a union organizer who had been falsely arrested and charged with the murder of a grocery store owner in Salt Lake City. Elizabeth began visiting him in jail and took his case to the IWW, pleading with them to offer support. "Can we afford to give up our Joe Hill without a struggle?" she asked. Despite her efforts, Joe Hill was executed on November 19, 1915. Before his death, he wrote a song for Elizabeth called, "Rebel Girl."

Now the mother of a five-year-old son, Fred, who was born in 1910, Elizabeth was traveling all over the country on IWW business, which forced her to leave her son with her mother and sister. By 1920, her marriage to Jack was beginning to dissolve and the couple soon separated. Despite the upheaval in her personal life, Elizabeth continued to fight for birth control and women's rights. Her deep concern for civil liberties led her to found the American Civil Liberties Union in 1920, and she soon became a member of its national board.

During the 1920s, Elizabeth took up her most passionate cause to date—the case of Italian anarchists, Nicola Sacco and Bartolemeo Vanzetti, which would become one of the most famous cases in history. Because of their radical leanings, they two men had been accused of a brutal robbery and murder in Braintree, Massachusetts. Unfortunately, the men were politically radical during the "Red Scare," the period after World War I when any American with communist leanings was being targeted.

Elizabeth was one of the first to investigate the case and became the head of their defense league. She and the rest of the labor movement fought tirelessly, but the men were executed on August 23, 1927.

For the next few decades, Elizabeth continued her work with a number of causes, including women's rights. In the 1930s, Elizabeth joined the Communist Party, and the next year, she made her first speech as a Communist at Madison Square Garden. Twelve years later, she ran for Congress in New York on a platform of women's rights and received fifty thousand votes. In 1951, she became a victim of McCarthyism and was charged with conspiracy to overthrow the government. She was arrested, but before she went to jail, she ran for Congress from the Bronx on the Communist Party ticket under the slogan "Vote— No! to McCarthyism. For Peace and Jobs! Amnesty for All." On January 24, 1951, she began a two-year prison term in Alderson Women's Federal Prison in West Virginia.

In 1964, Elizabeth traveled to the Soviet Union. Almost immediately she was hospitalized for a stomach disorder and died suddenly on

September 5. Symbolically, she had died in Moscow, and was given a full state funeral in Red Square. The *New York Times* ran a full-page story on the funeral, featuring one of Elizabeth's most famous quotes: "I believe in a socialist America. What a May Day that will be to celebrate. Hail to it."

25. NORA CONNOLLY

1893–1891
MILITARY STRATEGIST

You took me to meetings as your daughter, now I come to them myself, as a worker.

—Nora Connolly O'Brien, to her father ,
James Connolly

My father was once asked how he would describe a free Ireland, and he replied, 'All Ireland free and independent from the centre to the sea, and flying its own flag out over all the oceans.' It is this vision which has inspired fighters for Irish freedom for centuries. The Easter rising was just one link in the unbroken tradition of struggle for this goal. But in the North we have another enemy besides the British—the renegade Irishmen, I call them. They want to be part of Britain and not part of the nation where God placed them.

—Nora Connolly

When history remembers the heroes of the 1916 Easter Rebellion in Ireland, the name James Connolly is among the most revered. But it his daughter, Nora, who helped to organize the uprising, and as James Connolly himself asserted, "Were it not for her bravery, the revolution may never have happened." Nora Connolly was not only a revolutionary but also a visionary feminist who helped pave the way for female union organizers in Ireland and the United States.

Nora Connolly was born in 1893 in Scotland. In the late 1890s, the Connolly family arrived in Ireland from Scotland, where James Connolly founded the Irish Nora Connolly O'Brien Socialist Republican Party. Irish Republicanism, which was essentially a struggle of the working class for their economic independence and freedom from imperialistic colonialism, nearly mirrored the principles of socialism. The socialism of Connolly professed that freedom would not be won by establishing a quasi-independent Irish parliament (as first Daniel O'Donnell, then later Sinn Féin) purported. He felt that such an arrangement would not be viable considering the extreme poverty and persecution under which most nationalists lived.

In 1903, the Connolly family moved to New York, and it was in America that Nora became politically active. During the day she worked as a milliner, and at night she attended labor union meetings with her father. While in New York, James and Nora met John DeVoy, the head of the American faction of the Irish Republican Brotherhood, Clan na Gael. Clan na Gael would later send money to Connolly in Ireland to pay for the Easter Rising. With his daughter's help, James Connolly also founded the Irish Socialist Federation in 1907 and *The Harp* newspaper, which Nora helped edit. In 1908, James moved his family to Belfast, where he worked at the Irish Transport and General Workers Union. Nora also went to work at a clothing factory, which would later play a pivotal role in the Easter Rising.

Immediately, Nora became active in Cumann na mBan and the Gaelic League, and often held "rifle practice" on Sunday mornings at 11 A.M. According to Margaret Ward in *Unmanageable Revolutionaries*, "Nora Connolly was the principle organizer of the branch, and she was determined to ensure that the women were given the same opportunities as the men." She also joined the girls' branch of Fianna Éireann, an organization that taught military drills and the use of firearms. Nora and her sister Ina also became friends with Countess Markiewicz, and together they petitioned the *Fianna,* a republican boy scouts organization that the countess had founded, arguing for the admittance of girls.

In 1914, after James Connolly became leader of the Irish Citizen Army (a precursor to the IRA), Nora began recruiting volunteers for the Citizen Army on her father's behalf. As she recalls in her memoir, *Portrait of a Rebel Father*, "They came, their faces black with coal dust, some powdered with cement or grain, up from the ships, out from the dockyards, machine shops, factories, deserting carts, lorries, vans." Nora and her father were already being targeted for their political involvement, and in 1914, the British authorities closed down a newspaper they had started together, *The Irish Worker*. Undeterred, the next year they started a new paper, *The Worker's Republic*. By this time, the nationalist movement and the labor movement were beginning to unite, much to the chagrin of the British government. James Connolly's union alone, the ITGWU, already had three thousand members.

To dissuade strikers, many companies began to institute lock-outs, in which employers literally locked the doors on their employees, allowing many of them to go without work for months at a time. Poverty and starvation were already rampant in Dublin, and this practice only made conditions more unbearable within the city's tenements. Again, Nora was at the forefront right along with her father during the strikes and often traveled back and forth from Belfast to Dublin to deliver messages to the union organizers. It was also during these trips that Nora began running guns for Constance Markiewicz. During her stay, she succeeded in organizing hundreds of volunteers to move thousands of guns from the countess's house outside Dublin to safer haven in Belfast. According to Anne Marreco in her book *The Rebel Countess*, "Nora Connolly and some of the girls had to sit on the rifles in order to hide them."

The "Howth gun-running" as it was later known, would become good practice for Nora. By 1916, her father entrusted her with organizing the Easter Rising. She re-formed her friendship with John DeVoy in New York, who was also helping with the funding of the rebellion, and helped Liam Mellowes (the republican Na Fianna leader who had just escaped from Redding Gaol) return to Ireland by disguising him as a priest. On Easter Sunday, April 23, 1916, the date of the Rising, Nora returned to Belfast to join Cumman na mBan and the Citizens Army. Upon arrival, she was told that there would be no fighting in the North, and Nora and eight other women traveled to Dublin. There James sent Nora to alert Sean MacDermott, the Irish Volunteer leader who was stationed at the GPO (the General Post Office that would become the Rising's headquarters), and she also smuggled messages to Pádraig Pearse, another leader of the Rising.

Nora trusted her instincts that the Rising would still happen in Dublin, so when she returned to Belfast she organized the other women in Cumann na mBan, and together, they traveled back to Dublin to take part in the fight. Because of Nora's competence and leadership, they became the only organized group from the North to take part in the Rising. When she arrived in Dublin, she then told her father about the rumors that were causing so much of the confusion. James Connolly would remark afterward that because of his daughter's foresight, much of the miscommunication that surrounded the Rising was contained. As Margaret Ward affirms, "If it had not been for the invaluable work of carrying messages that was undertaken by women, the Rising would have been an even more confused venture than it was." More than ninety women took part in the Rising, most of them delivering messages, food, first-aid supplies, and ammunition.

The Rising lasted six days, with a little more than two hundred Irish volunteers fighting to stave off twelve thousand British soldiers. Eventually, the men were forced to surrender. James Connolly was badly wounded, and all sixteen leaders of the Rising, including Eamon De Valera, Pádraig Pearse, and Sean MacDermott were imprisoned and sentenced to be executed. De Valera's life was spared because he was born in the United States and had dual citizenship.

James Connolly was shot on May 12, 1916, at Kilmainham Jail. He had to be strapped to a chair because his wounds were so severe that he was unable to stand. The spot of his execution is still marked today with a white cross in the yard of the jail. The night before he died, he told his daughter just how invaluable her work during the Rising had been. Now grief-stricken over the death of her father and his friends, Nora hoped to find a way to earn money for her family at the age of twenty-three. Instead, she found herself being co-opted by leaders of the republican movement in the United States to give lectures on the Easter Rising.

After the lecture tour was over, she decided to move back to Ireland and continue the work that she and her father had started. In 1918, she began working in the Irish Transport Union in Dublin and campaigned on behalf of Sinn Féin. The next year, she married fellow activist Seamus O'Brien and became paymaster of the IRA. In 1926, she was elected to the Dáil and served three terms. Like many others who opposed the 1921 treaty, she was imprisoned, along with her husband, in Kilmainham Jail. By the time she was released, her husband was imprisoned in Mountjoy. Shortly after her release, she began a friendship with Leon Trotsky, who was interested in the Irish nationalist struggle. In the following passage, from a letter dated April 8, 1936, she expresses an interest seeking his help for the cause:

The Labour Party recently adopted a new programme and constitution, the first step towards achieving the leading role in the revolutionary movement in Ireland. The new programme is not yet a correct revolutionary one, but it is such an enormous advance on the previous one, that we are not indulging in any carping or cavilling criticism. Through it they can supply an alternative to Fianna Fáil (the majority Republican party in the Irish parliament, An Dáil) as by adopting James Connolly's doctrine of the twin ideals of national and social independence they have ended the divorce between the national and Labour movements. This programme will be ready shortly. I could also send you a copy.

Although she is best known for her heroic role in the Easter Rising, Nora Connolly remained a lifelong nationalist. Shortly before her death on June 17, 1981, she attended rallies in support of Bobby Sands and his fellow hunger strikers, and she remains a revered figure in Irish history. Perhaps the ultimate tribute came from her father, who told her the night before he died, "You have done all you can."

26. DOROTHY DAY

1897–1980
REFORMER

Women think with their whole bodies and they see things as a whole more than men do.

—Dorothy Day

Women especially are social beings who are not content with just husband and family, but who must have a community . . . even in the busiest of our lives, we women are the victims of the long loneliness.

—Dorothy Day

Often called a modern-day saint, Dorothy Day was the first woman to reconcile the tenets of Catholicism with the radical politics of socialism. She started her life as a journalist but became the patron saint of the poor and dispossessed in the U.S. One of the few who practiced what she preached Dorothy lived as humbly and modestly as those she dedicated her life to helping. As she would later comment, "I offered up a special prayer, a prayer which came with tears and anguish, that some way would open up for me to use what talents I possessed for my fellow workers, for the poor."

Dorothy Day was born in Brooklyn, New York, November 8, 1897, the third of five children, to John Day and Grace Saterlee. Her father was a prominent journalist of Scots-Irish ancestry. The family moved to San Francisco in 1904, then lost everything in the San Francisco earthquake of 1906. Her father's office burned to the ground, and the Day family moved into a tenement flat on Chicago's South Side. John Day was frequently unemployed, and the family often survived on potato soup and bread. It was experience that would foster Dorothy's compassion toward the poor. It was in Chicago that Day began to form positive impressions of Catholicism. Later in life she would recall her discovery of a friend's mother, a devout Catholic, praying at the side of her bed. Without embarrassment, she looked up at Day, told her where to find her daughter, and returned to her prayers. "I felt a burst of love toward [her] that I have never forgotten," Day recalled.

Despite their frequent poverty, John encouraged his daughter to read the classics, and in 1914, at the age of sixteen, Dorothy entered an essay competition sponsored by the *Chicago Examiner*. She won a scholarship to the University of Illinois at Urbana.

Despite her brilliance, she was more interested in becoming a socialist and a writer than being a student. As she later recalled, "I was sixteen and filled with a sense of great independence." Two years later, she left college and moved to New York, where her father had taken a job as a reporter at the *Morning Telegraph*. She found a job as a reporter for *The Call*, a socialist newspaper that covered labor unions, and she also worked for *The Masses*, a magazine that opposed American involvement in the European war. While in New York, she was often poor and took in laundry to earn extra money. She also joined the Socialist Party.

It was on the streets on New York that she began to see the abject poverty and homelessness that would become the focus of the rest of her life. She recalled, "The sight of homelessness and workless men lounging on street corners and sleeping in doorways in broad sunlight appalled me. There is a smell in the walls of such tenements, a damp ooze coming from them in the halls. . . . It is not the smell of life, but the smell of the grave." During her time at *The Call*, she was earning five dollars a day and working until two in the morning.

She began to mingle in intellectual and artistic circles, and also began protesting World War I. In November 1917, Dorothy traveled to Washington, D.C., where she protested in support of women's suffrage. The police arrested thirty-five demonstrators, including Dorothy. She was sentenced to thirty days in Occoquan Prison in Virginia, where the women were treated brutally. They eventually went on hunger strike for their right to political status. After ten days, the women were given the right to wear their own clothes. After she returned to New York City, she decided to give up journalism in favor of nursing. Because of the war, there was a severe shortage of nurses, and Dorothy believed she could be of more use this way.

In the spring of 1918, she signed up for a nurse's training program at King's County (Brooklyn) Hospital. As a nurse, she worked grueling twelve-hour days and witnessed death firsthand. She also met and fell in love with Lionel Morse. Against the mores of the time, she moved in with him and soon found that he was an alcoholic with a violent temper. In 1919, she became pregnant and underwent an illegal abortion on the Lower East Side (the kind Margaret Sanger would fight so hard to eradicate). It was a haunting experience that stayed with her forever. Morse eventually left her. The next year, she married a man who was twenty years older than she was, Barkley Toby, a business promoter who traveled constantly; the marriage soon fell apart. During her separation, she wrote *The Eleventh Virgin,* a study of one woman's search to find her own place and her conflicted relationship with God. She reunited with Morse briefly, going to Chicago to be with him. There she also began a friendship with Mae Kramer, who was staying at an International Workers of the World flophouse at the time. Police raided and arrested both women for prostitution, and Dorothy was imprisoned for the second time. Again she saw how brutally women prisoners were treated. "I have never seen such anguish, such unspeakable suffering," she said.

In 1922, in Chicago working as a reporter, she roomed with three young women who went to Mass every Sunday, and holy day, and set aside time each day for prayer. It was clear to her that "worship, adoration, thanksgiving, supplication . . . were the noblest acts of which we are capable in this life."

Sick of Chicago, Dorothy traveled to New Orleans in 1923 and took a job with the *New Orleans Item.* She lived near St. Louis Cathedral and often attended evening benediction services. In 1924, *The Eleventh Virgin* was published. She sold the movie rights for five thousand dollars and moved back to New York, where she bought a beach cottage on Staten Island. She became involved with Forster Batterham, an English botanist and socialist she had met through friends in Manhattan. Batterham was a social reformer who did not believe in marriage or God. Dorothy was becoming more and more tied to the Catholic church by this time and found his lack of faith disturbing. "How can there be no God," she asked, "when there are all these beautiful things?" Despite their religious differences, they moved in together in 1925 and Dorothy soon became pregnant, much to her delight. "For a long time I had thought I could not bear a child, and the longing in my heart for a baby had been growing," she remembers in her autobiography, *The Long Loneliness*. "My home, I felt, was not a home without one." Forster was less excited about the news.

On March 5, 1926, Tamar Theresa Day was born. Immediately, the couple began to battle over religious differences. Dorothy wanted her child to be baptized in the Catholic Church. "I did not want my child to flounder as I had often floundered. I wanted to believe, and I wanted my child to believe, and if belonging to a Church would give her so inestimable a grace as faith in God, and the companionable love of the Saints, then the thing to do was to have her baptized a Catholic." After Dorothy converted to Catholicism in 1927, Batterham left her for good. Now alone, Dorothy was also struggling to find a way to reconcile her religious views and radical beliefs. She traveled to Mexico City, where the Catholic Church was in trouble, and began writing for *Commonweal*.

In 1932, she covered the Hunger March in Washington, D.C., and after seeing the poor and unemployed, she decided to dedicate her life to working for them. She said, "I offered up a special prayer, a prayer which came with tears and anguish, that some way would open up for me to use what talents I possessed for my fellow workers, for the poor."

Back in New York the next day, Dorothy met Peter Maurin, a French reformer who believed that the common good could be found in the teachings of Jesus Christ. He was also looking to found a radical Catholic newspaper in the city. George Schuster, who was editor of *Commonweal* at the time, told him to contact Dorothy, and the two began a lifelong friendship. Maurin educated her about Catholicism and scripture, and also told her of his desire to start centers for the poor and homeless throughout the city. Dorothy paid the Paulist Press fifty-seven dollars to print twenty-five hundred copies of an eight-page tabloid paper. She named it *The Catholic Worker* and sold the paper for a penny a copy, "so

cheap that anyone could afford to buy it." On May 1, 1933, the first issue
was published, and focused on the plight of coal miners and child labor.

By December, ten thousand copies were being printed each month
and were sold at Communist rallies throughout the city. Dorothy and
Maurin also realized another dream and set up a house on Charles Street
to feed the homeless and the unemployed in the area. They eventually
served more than one thousand men a day, and no one was every turned
away. Dorothy described these men, many of whom were drug addicted
and ill, as "grey men, the color of lifeless trees and bushes and winter soil,
who had in them as yet none of the green of hope, the rising sap of faith."
They opened a second house on Mott Street, and by 1941, there were
thirty homes of hospitality all over the country.

Starting in 1935, Peter and Dorothy had also experimented with
farming communes and rented a house with a garden on Staten Island.
They then bought Mary Farm in Easton, Pennsylvania, and the Mary
Farm retreat in Newburgh, New York. Many visitors to the farm were
children from the slums who were seeking a better life than they had in
the city. Dorothy continued to give public lectures and gave her donations
back to *The Catholic Worker*. In 1938, she published *House of Hospitality*
and *From Union Square to Rome*.

Dorothy strongly opposed World War II, and this unpopular view,
particularly among fellow Catholics who had never subscribed to paci-
fism, caused many of her workers to leave the movement. Dorothy was
beginning to suffer from stress-related illness, and would suffer an even
greater loss when her beloved friend Peter Maurin died in 1949. Dorothy
became increasingly ill because of the poor conditions and sanitation at
the house in Mott Street. In the 1950s, she became a victim of anti-
Communist hysteria, and the FBI came to her door daily. At the end of
the decade, she had a huge FBI file, and not much else to show for her
struggle. But despite her hardships, she published her autobiography, and
joined the civil rights movement in the South, which put her in even
more danger. One night, when she was visiting a multi-racial commune
in Georgia, a member of the KKK pumped bullets into her window.

In the 1960s and '70s, she became involved in the anti-war movement
along with the Berrigan Brothers, and she campaigned with Cesar

Chavez for workers' rights. In 1973, at the age of 75, she was imprisoned for taking part in a banned picket line in support of farm workers. Despite recurring heart problems, she continued her speaking engagements, and in 1976 she opened a women's homeless shelter on the Lower East Side.

Dorothy died peacefully in her sleep on November 29, 1980, with her daughter by her side. Although she was a friend of Mother Teresa and was acknowledged by many to be a saint, she often said, "Don't call me a saint. I don't want to be dismissed so easily." Today, the Catholic Worker movement still offers aid to the homeless and dispossessed and has one hundred working farms across the country.

27. MARGARET MITCHELL

1900–1949
AUTHOR

Until you've lost your reputation, you never realize what a burden it was.
—Margaret Mitchell

Life's under no obligation to give us what we expect.
—Margaret Mitchell

In the 1930s, the United States was still reeling from the Great Depression. Unemployment was at a record high, and nowhere was poverty and desperation more dire than in the American South. And nowhere was racism more blatant. In 1936, a young Irish American novelist would transform the way Americans and the rest of the world viewed race relations in the United States with *Gone with the Wind*, one of the most popular books of all time. In the first six months that it was published, it sold more than a million copies. To this day, more than 30 million copies have been sold worldwide in thirty-eight countries, and both the novel and movie version of *Gone with the Wind* continue to captivate readers and audiences worldwide. With her epic novel, Margaret Mitchell cast new light on one of the most complicated periods in U.S. history and introduced millions to an Irish American heroine who continues to be one of the most fascinating character in literary history. Margaret Mitchell remains the most successful historical novelist of the mid-twentieth century, even though her work was confined to a single book.

Margaret Munnerlyn Mitchell was born in Atlanta, Georgia, on November 8, 1900. Her mother, Mary Isabelle "Maybelle" Stephens, was of Irish Catholic ancestry. Her father, Eugene Muse Mitchell, an Atlanta attorney, was Scotch Irish and a French Huguenot. The Mitchells were quintessential southerners. The family included farmers, planters, soldiers, preachers, patriots, and politicians. Many members of the family fought in the American Revolution and the Civil War. The Mitchells lived in Atlanta before it was Atlanta. Margaret's great-grandfather was a fire-and-brimstone Methodist preacher and her grandfather was a lawyer who became an officer during the Civil War. After the war ended, he came back to Atlanta and became a city councilman and wealthy attorney.

Margaret's father, Eugene, was a brilliant student and poet who also became an attorney and joined his father's law firm. Maybelle and Eugene had three children, Russell, who died in infancy, Alexander Stephens, and Margaret Munnerlyn. Over the years, the family lived in several homes in Atlanta, including a stately home on Peachtree Street. When Margaret was about two years old, the family moved to the home where she spent most of her childhood. Soon after they moved, she was playing too near the fireplace when her skirt and petticoat caught fire. Although her brother was able to put out the fire before Margaret was injured, she and her family were upset by the accident. Her mother decided to put all of her dresses and skirts away and dress Margaret in boy's pants and shirts and a tweed cap. Because she looked like a boy and was a tomboy, other children started calling her "Jimmy," the name of a boy in a newspaper cartoon. She played baseball and tennis, rode horses, and kept a huge menagerie of animals. The family often visited relatives at the Fitzgerald homestead outside Atlanta and went on vacations in North Carolina, New Jersey, and other states on the East Coast. On these trips, Margaret had the opportunity to engage in her favorite activities, including playing outdoors, exploring the woods, playing with the animals, and spending time with family.

When she began school, she had to leave her tomboy Jimmy persona behind. Her mother insisted that she dress like a girl again and that her friends call her Peggy. Margaret attended private schools, but she was not an exceptional student. One day she told her mother that she could not understand math and did not want to return to school. Maybelle dragged Margaret to a rural road where plantation houses had fallen into ruin.

She pointed to the houses and said, "It's happened before and it will happen again. And when it does happen, everyone loses everything and everyone is equal. They all start again with nothing at all except the cunning of their brain and the strength of their hands." Although she did not like school, she loved reading. Her family remembers that she was always absorbed in a book. Her parents insisted that she read the classics despite her desire to read what she wanted to read. Her parents alternated between bribing her and punishing her to encourage her to read good literature. Learning to write also had a profound effect on her life. Her brother recalls that she wrote hundreds of stories when she was young. The stories that survived indicate that she was a natural storyteller.

As Margaret grew up, her family had a great influence on her. Maybelle was a suffragette who influenced her daughter's thinking, which then clashed with her father's conservative ideas. Her relatives told her stories about the Civil War and she grew up listening to stories about old Atlanta and the battles the Confederate army had fought there during the war. When she was fifteen, she wrote in her journal: "If I were a boy, I would try for West Point, if I could make it, or well I'd be a prize fighter—anything for the thrills." At her mother's insistence, she attended a private finishing school and graduated from the local Washington Seminary. Always rebellious, Margaret battled with her mother about school and almost every other element of her life. Despite this penchant for more male pursuits, she continued writing and became involved in drama. When she was in high school, she wrote and directed many plays. She was also courted by many prominent young men in Atlanta, including many soldiers. She finally settled on a New York aristocrat, Lieutenant Clifford Henry.

She entered Smith College to study psychology in 1918. She said she wanted to study medicine and possibly become a psychiatrist, but most accounts propose that she fabricated those aspirations. The great flu epidemic interrupted her freshman year when students were quarantined and then sent home at the end of the fall semester. After her fiancé was killed in action in World War I and her mother contracted the flu and died, Margaret left college to take care of her brother and father in Atlanta. Although she was relieved to leave college, she was deeply affected by her mother's death. She defied her mother's dying wishes that she stay in school instead of coming home to take care of her family. She found taking care of her mother's home very daunting and grueling and quickly hated the responsibility.

As a single young woman during the jazz age, she was anxious to get back into the social scene. She worked diligently to plan her own debut. In 1920, she was presented as a debutante to Atlanta society. She later wrote about her society experiences in nonfiction, like her article "Dancers Now Drown out Even the Cowbell" in the *Atlanta Journal Sunday Magazine*. Like other debutantes, she soon joined the Junior League. She insisted on doing her charity work in black and "social disease" wards. This kind of charity work, which was considered scandalous by the league, and her "wild behavior" ensured that she never became a full member of the league. Margaret was too free-spirited and intelligent to be satisfied with life as a debutante. She argued with her fellow debutantes over how to distribute the money they had raised for charity and she shocked society with a provocative dance she performed with one of her suitors.

During this time, she had a series of accidents and illnesses, including appendicitis, flu, a hip injury, and several riding accidents that resulted in intestinal problems and many broken bones. She also fought increasingly severe depression and insomnia. Despite all her injuries and health problems, she continued to write, but very little of what she wrote during this period survived. She was also very popular with the Atlanta men. As the Atlanta gossip columnist wrote, "She has in her brief life, perhaps, had many more men really, truly 'dead in love' with her, more honest-to-goodness suitors than almost any other girl in Atlanta."

In 1922, she married Berrien Kinnard Upshaw. Even though he had been one of her suitors, he had not been at the top of the list. Some speculate that she decided to marry because all her friends were getting married. Their marriage was a disaster from the beginning. After their honeymoon, the couple went to live in her father's house, which did not work well. Berrien was erratic and descriptions of his mood swings indicate that he may have been bipolar. He did not complete college, and he held a series of odd jobs. So Margaret decided to begin working as a writer, using the name "Peggy Mitchell," which threatened her husband's self-esteem. Some accounts report that Berrien physically abused her and may have even raped her. The combination of all these factors created so much stress on their marriage that Margaret filed for divorce in 1923.

Before the divorce, Margaret started her career as a journalist under the name Peggy Mitchell, writing articles, interviews, sketches, and book reviews for the *Atlanta Journal*. The job was tough and the conditions were less than ideal, but she really enjoyed the work. At the *Journal* she met John Robert Marsh, an advertising manager, who encouraged Margaret in her writing aspirations. She married Marsh in 1924 and continued to work as a reporter until 1926, when an ankle injury required her to leave her job.

While she was home convalescing, she began working on the novel *Gone with the Wind*. She typed on a portable typewriter balanced on her lap. She did not tell anyone except her husband that she was writing a novel, and she never expected it to be published. She put the finished chapters in manila envelopes and hid them where no one could see them. By 1935, word had leaked out about the book and was widely discussed in Atlanta because of her social connections. Finally, Lois Cole, a friend who worked for Macmillan Publishing in New York, told her boss, Harold Latham, about Margaret's book. Latham went to Atlanta and met with her, but she denied that she was writing a book. Just before Latham was to return to New York, she changed her mind. She stuffed the envelopes into a suitcase, went to his hotel, and gave the suitcase to him, saying, "Take it before I change my mind." The thousand-page novel, which was later compared to Leo Tolstoy's *War and Peace*, was published by Macmillan in 1936. The retail price of the book was $3.

Although the reviews at the time were mixed, half a million copies of the novel were sold in the six months after its publication. It broke sales records and was also a featured selection of the Book of the Month Club in July 1936. In May 1937, Margaret was awarded the Pulitzer Prize. In 1939, the book was adapted into one of the most popular films of all time, starring Clark Gable and Vivien Leigh. Margaret sold the film rights to the producer David O. Selznick for $50,000, and later received another $50,000. The film premiered on December 15, 1939. Margaret did not take any part in the motion picture adaptation but attended the premiere in

Atlanta, overcoming her shyness. The film won ten Academy Awards, including best picture.

Gone with the Wind brought her fame and a tremendous fortune. Nevertheless, it did not bring her much happiness. The book brought intense scrutiny and attention from the press and the public. Critics questioned the book's contribution to literature because of the historical view and depiction of racism and the Klu Klux Klan. Margaret and her husband lived modestly and quietly and traveled rarely.

During World War II, Margaret helped sell war bonds and volunteered for the American Red Cross. She was named honorary citizen of Vimoutiers, France, in 1949, for helping the city obtain U.S. aid after the war. On August 16, 1949, she and her husband left their home to go to a movie when they were struck by a drunk driver. Margaret died in Atlanta five days later.

Gone with the Wind became the most talked about novel in American popular culture from a time predating its actual publication, and its screen adaptation was the biggest "event" movie of the twentieth century. In a time long before modern feminism was even thought of, Margaret Mitchell and the sensibilities that she brought to the book helped push two generations of upper-middle- and middle-class southern women into the twentieth century, describing the conflict between their proper upbringings and their need for independence.

28. HELEN HAYES

1900–1993
ACTRESS

*Every human being on this earth is born with a tragedy, and it isn't origi-
nal sin. He's born with the tragedy that he has to grow up. That he has to
leave the nest, the security, and go out to do battle. He has to lose everything that is lovely and fight for a new loveliness of his own making, and it's
a tragedy. A lot of people don't have the courage to do it.*

—Helen Hayes

The hardest years in life are those between ten and seventy.

—Helen Hayes

*My mother drew a distinction between achievement and success. She said
that "achievement is the knowledge that you have studied and worked hard
and done the best that is in you. Success is being praised by others, and that's
nice, too, but not as important or satisfying. Always aim for achievement
and forget about success."*

—Helen Hayes

Named the "first lady of the American theater," Helen Hayes was
not just the consummate actress, she was also the consummate
professional and philanthropist. The two-time Academy Award–winning American actress had boasted a career that spanned almost eighty
years and was one of the few performers who has won an Emmy, a
Grammy, an Oscar, and a Tony Award. Her establishment of the Mary
MacArthur Fund, with the March of Dimes, helped children who suffered from polio, and the Helen Hayes MacArthur Hospital, which she
helped establish, became the first hospital in the United States to help

paralyzed survivors of polio. While Helen spent her life honing her craft, she also spent it developing her character.

Helen Hayes Brown was born in 1900 in Washington, D.C., to an Irish American Catholic family. Her mother, Catherine Estelle ("Essie") Hayes, was an actress who traveled with a stock company, the Liberty Belles. Her father, Frank Van Arnum Brown, was a salesman for a wholesale meat company and also traveled extensively. While her parents traveled, Helen lived with her grandmother, Graddy Hayes, in Brightwood, a suburb of Washington. Her grandmother played a prominent role in her life. Her grandfather, Pat Hayes, was a religious fanatic who became an angry, abusive man. In her autobiography, Helen explains that the Hayes family was "scamp Irish," as most of the family was poor. Her grandmother grew up in Liverpool, England, during the time of Queen Victoria and Prince Albert, which had a profound effect on her life.

Helen's mother was determined to get out of her father's house and rise above her family's situation; she always dreamed of another life. As Helen says, "Life was a drawing-room comedy to my mother, and she felt she had been relegated to the kitchen." Essie was obsessed with high society, reading the society pages and soaking up any information she could find about the elite. She even named Helen for Helen Gould, a leading socialite of the time. Acting allowed her to escape her ordinary life and to become someone else. She was enthralled with her acting career despite the fact that she performed with a third-rate company. Essie was happiest when she was acting, but Helen remembers that she and her father were happiest when her mother came home. In her autobiography, Helen recalls that her mother's "returns were the high spots of my childhood." Her mother was funny and "found humor everywhere except in the tiny world where her drab marriage and dreary motherhood had trapped her." From Helen's description, it appears that her mother might have been bipolar: she was at times hysterically funny but then she had tantrums and became sullen and angry. She also drank heavily to escape the boredom. Her father and Helen were constantly baffled and troubled by her mother's erratic behavior and mood swings.

Frank, Helen's father, was completely the opposite of Essie. He was jolly and laid-back. In her autobiography, Helen describes him as "fat and jolly, adored by all children." He was satisfied easily and was happy to be married. He had married Essie because he loved her and put up with her mood swings. Helen wrote about her father in *On Reflection*: "In harmony with the world, he was in perpetual discord with his restless wife. He was dear and I adored him, but I can quite understand how enraging his passivity must have been to the seething woman who was my mother."

Essie became a "stage mother" to compensate for her own lack of success as an actress. She pushed Helen toward a career that would make her famous. Her decisions about Helen were often based on her own vanity rather than on what was best for Helen. For example, Essie decided that her daughter would go to Holy Cross Academy, not because she was a devout Catholic or because Helen would get a good education, but because they did not require her daughter to have the smallpox vaccination that would "mutilate" her. Fortunately, Helen did get a good education and the nuns at the school appreciated theater. Helen's first role was Peaseblossom in the school's production of *A Midsummer Night's Dream*. Essie had her take dance and violin lessons and took her to the theater to see all the great actors and to concerts to see great musicians.

She began a stage career when she was very young. Her professional career really began when she was five years old. Lew Fields, of the comedy team Weber and Fields, saw her at the May Ball, a charity event at the Belasco Theater. After he saw her impersonation of the Gibson Girl from Ziegfeld Follies, he wrote to the theater manager that if she would like a career when she was older, he "wanted to be the first in line." During the summer, Fred Berger, the producer of the Liberty Belles, was looking for a child actor; Essie made a deal with him to allow Helen to perform if he gave Essie the lead role. So Helen made her professional debut with her mother. She continued to perform in the summer stock plays that Berger produced for several years.

During this time, Essie insisted that Helen take French lessons so that she would become a "lady." Finally, her mother decided it was time to go to New York to see Lew Fields. She waited until Fields came out of his office and showed him a photograph of Helen in her Gibson Girl outfit. Fields remembered Helen and signed her to be in the play *Old Dutch* at the age of eight. Helen and her mother moved to New York while her father stayed in Washington and sent half of his salary to them. Although she missed her father, she remembered that she and her mother had "a marvelous time" exploring New York and then touring with many plays. Essie, who became known as "Stage Mother Brown," was resented by the directors, producers, and actors because of her close relationship with her daughter. However, Helen became the favorite little star of Broadway actors and producers like Fields, John Drew, and George Tyler. Helen later attributed much of her success to her early mentors.

Between the ages of five and twenty, Helen appeared in dozens of plays including *Midsummer Night's Dream* (1905), *Babe in the Woods* (1908), *Jack the Giant Killer* (1909), *A Royal Family* (1909), *Children's Dancing Kerrness* (1909), *Mrs. Wiggs of the Cabbage Patch* (1917), *Within the Law* (1917), *Pollyanna* (1917), *Penrod* (1918), *Dear Brutus* (1918), *On the Hiring Line* (1919), *Clarence* (1919), *The Golden Age* (1919), and *Báb* (1920). When she was ten years old, she was in the short film *Jean and the Calico Doll*. She received excellent reviews in the fantasy play *Dear Brutus*. A review in the *New York Times* called Helen's performance "a wonderful blending of dream beauty and girlish actuality." Helen received her first widespread media attention for the play *Pollyanna*. She was actually seventeen years old when she played the young girl, but she earned respect as a leading lady. From that moment on, she was called the "great Miss Hayes."

Until her mid-twenties, George Tyler, who had become her producer, ran her life. He was very protective as was her mother. So she was not allowed to socialize and attend parties with the other actors and actresses. This made it difficult for her to meet new friends and date men. Then in 1924, Tyler wanted her to join the Fidelity League, a union largely loyal to producers. Helen chose the Actors' Equity Union, however, a rival union that represented actors and lobbied to raise stage actors' salaries. When Helen stood up to him, she was able to break his hold on her and become more independent.

When she began attending parties, she met Charlie MacArthur, a Chicago journalist and playwright. At one party in particular, she did not enjoy the boisterous crowd, so she sat in a corner. Just as she was considering leaving, a handsome man approached her and offered her some peanuts. As he put them in her hand, he said, "I wish they were emeralds." Helen instantly fell in love with him. Although many people told her that their relationship wouldn't work, they both possessed a childlike charm and were happily married until MacArthur's death in 1956.

Helen moved to Hollywood when her husband signed a Hollywood contract. Her sound film debut was *The Sin of Madelon Claudet*, for which she won the Academy Award for Best Actress. She followed that with starring roles in *Arrowsmith* (with Myrna Loy), *A Farewell to Arms* (with Gary Cooper, whom Hayes admitted finding extremely attractive), *The White Sister*, *What Every Woman Knows* (a reprise from her Broadway hit), and *Vanessa: Her Love Story*. However, she never became a box-office favorite.

Helen's first child was born amid a somewhat humorous controversy. While she was pregnant, Helen was the main character in the play *Coquette*. She became very sick and was forced to quit the production, leaving the director to close the play altogether. The other actors were owed severance pay, but the producer Jed Harris attempted to get out of it by saying Helen's reason for leaving was an "act of God" that he couldn't control. Eventually, he had to pay the actors, but Mary MacArthur would always be remembered as the "Act of God Baby." Helen and Charlie adopted a son, James, in 1939. Jamie, as Helen sometimes called him, went on to star in the long-running television series *Hawaii Five-O*. Tragically, just ten years later in 1949, Mary contracted polio while on a summer stock tour with her mother. She died soon after, leaving Helen devastated; she vowed then to give her life to helping polio victims and their parents.

Helen and Charlie eventually returned to Broadway, and she starred for three years in *Victoria Regina*. In 1953, she was the first-ever recipient of the Sarah Siddons Award for her work in Chicago theater, and was selected again in 1969. She returned to Hollywood in the 1950s, and her film career began to rise. She starred in *My Son John* and *Anastasia*, and won the Academy Award for Best Supporting Actress in 1970 for *Airport*. She followed that up with several roles in Disney films such as *Herbie Rides Again*, *One of Our Dinosaurs Is Missing,* and *Candleshoe*. In 1983, the Helen Hayes Theater was named in her honor.

Unlike many of her Irish colleagues, Hayes was a pro-business Republican who attended the last Republican National Convention before her death, which was held in Colorado, but she was not as far-right as others (e.g., Adolphe Menjou, Ginger Rogers, and John Wayne) in the Hollywood community of that time. She was also the recipient of a star on the Hollywood Walk of Fame. Helen Hayes died on (St. Patrick's Day) March 17, 1993, of congestive heart failure at the age of ninety-two, not long after the death of her friend Lillian Gish, with whom she had been friends for many decades. She was buried in the Oak Hill Cemetery, Nyack, New York. The lights on Broadway were dimmed for one minute on the day she died.

29. RACHEL LOUISE CARSON

1907–1964

ENVIRONMENTALIST, BIOLOGIST

Those who dwell, as scientists or laymen, among the beauties and mysteries of the earth are never alone or weary of life.

—Rachel Carson

In 1962, a young biologist published the book *Silent Spring,* which chronicled the horrors of toxic chemicals in drinking water and the presence of a deadly pesticide called DDT. While the book was dismissed by some as alarmist and misleading, it exposed millions of Americans to the dangers of man-made chemicals, including President John F. Kennedy. As soon as he finished *Silent Spring*, he immediately appointed a presidential advisory committee to investigate the hazards of pesticides and herbicides on animals, plant life, and humans. Within the next decade, Rachel Carson's research led to the establishment of the Environmental Protection Agency and the eradication of DDT. It also sparked a new term and a new movement: environmentalism. As Peter Matthiessen observed in *Time* magazine's Top 100 of the Century, "Before there was an environmental movement, there was one very brave woman and her very brave book."

Rachel Louise Carson was born in 1907 on a small family farm in the Pittsburgh suburb of Springdale. As a child, she spent many hours learning about ponds, fields, and forests from her mother. When she was just ten years old, she had her first poem published in the *St. Nicholas Literary Magazine.* Always fascinated by writing, she originally went to school to study English and creative writing, but switched her major to zoology. Her talent for writing would help her in her new field, as she resolved to "make animals in the woods or waters, where they live, as alive to others as they are to me." She graduated from the Pennsylvania College for Women, today known as Chatham College, in 1929 with magna cum laude honors. Despite financial difficulties, she continued her studies in zoology and genetics at Johns Hopkins University, earning a master's degree in zoology in 1932.

Carson taught zoology at Johns Hopkins and at the University of Maryland for several years. She continued to study toward her doctoral degree, particularly at the Marine Biological Laboratory in Woods Hole, Massachusetts. Her financial situation, never satisfactory, became worse in 1932 when her father died, leaving Rachel to care for her aging mother; this burden made continued doctoral studies impossible. She took on a part-time position at the U.S. Bureau of Fisheries as a science writer working on radio scripts. In the process, she had to overcome resistance to the then-radical idea of having a woman sit for the civil service exam. In spite of the odds, she outscored all the other applicants on the exam and in 1936 became only the second woman to be hired by the Bureau of Fisheries for a full-time, professional position, as a junior aquatic biologist. She also wrote radio scripts for the Bureau of Fisheries.

At the U.S. Bureau of Fisheries, Rachel worked on everything from cookbooks to scientific journals and became known for her ruthless insistence on high standards of writing. Early in her career, the head of the bureau's Division of Scientific Inquiry, who had been instrumental in finding a position for her in the first place, rejected one of Carson's radio scripts because it was "too literary." He suggested that she submit it to the *Atlantic Monthly*. To Carson's astonishment and delight, it was accepted and published as "Undersea" in 1937. Carson's family responsibilities further increased that year when her older sister died at the age of forty, and she had to care for her two nieces.

The publishing house Simon and Schuster, impressed by "Undersea," contacted Carson and suggested that she expand it into book form. Several years of working in the evenings resulted in *Under the Sea-Wind*

(1941), which received excellent reviews but was a commercial flop. It had the misfortune to be released just a month before the Pearl Harbor raid catapulted the United States into World War II.

Carson rose within the bureau (by then transformed into the Fish and Wildlife Service), becoming chief editor of publications in 1949. For some time she had been working on material for a second book: it was rejected by fifteen different magazines before *The Katie* serialized parts of it as "A Profile of the Sea" in 1951. Other parts soon appeared in *Nature*, and Oxford University Press published it in book form as *The Sea around Us*. It remained on the *New York Times* bestseller list for eighty-six weeks, was abridged by *Reader's Digest*, won the 1952 National Book Award, and resulted in Carson being awarded two honorary doctorates.

Carson's success allowed her to give up her job in 1952 to concentrate on writing full time. In 1955, she completed the third volume of her sea trilogy, *The Edge of the Sea*. It, too, was a best seller, winning further awards, and was made into an Oscar-winning documentary film. This documentary severely embarrassed Carson: appalled by the film's sensational style and the distortion of facts, she disassociated herself from it. Through 1956 and 1957, Carson worked on a number of projects and wrote articles for popular magazines.

Family tragedy struck a third time when one of the nieces she had cared for in the 1940s died at the age of thirty-six, leaving a five-year-old orphan son. Carson took on that responsibility alongside the continuing one of caring for her mother, who was almost ninety by this time. She adopted the boy and, needing a suitable place to raise him, bought a rural property in Maryland. This environment was to be a major factor in the choice of her next topic.

Starting in the mid-1940s, Carson became concerned about the use of newly invented pesticides, especially DDT. "The more I learned about the use of pesticides, the more appalled I became," she wrote later, explaining her decision to start researching what would eventually become her most famous work, *Silent Spring*. "What I discovered was that everything which meant most to me as a naturalist was being threatened, and that nothing I could do would be more important."

Silent Spring was Carson's first book focused on the environment, and pesticides in particular. Carson explored the theme of environmental connectedness: although a pesticide is aimed at eliminating one organism, its effects are felt throughout the food chain, and what was intended to poison an insect ends up poisoning larger animals and humans.

The four-year task of writing *Silent Spring* began with a letter from the custodian of a Massachusetts bird sanctuary that had been destroyed by aerial spraying of DDT. The letter asked Carson to use her influence with government authorities to begin an investigation into pesticide use. Carson decided it would be more effective to raise the issue in a popular magazine; however, publishers were uninterested, and eventually the project became a book instead.

Now, as a renowned author, she was able to ask for (and receive) the aid of prominent biologists, chemists, pathologists, and entomologists. She used *Silent Spring* to create a mental association in the public's mind between wildlife mortality and overuse of pesticides like dieldrin, toxaphene, and heptachlor. Her cautions regarding the previously little-remarked practices of introducing an enormous variety of industrial products and wastes into wilderness, waterways, and human habitats with little concern for possible toxicity struck the general public as common sense, as much as good science: "We are subjecting whole populations to exposure to chemicals which animal experiments have proved to be extremely poisonous and in many cases cumulative in their effects. These exposures now begin at or before birth and—unless we change our methods—will continue through the lifetime of those now living."

Even before *Silent Spring* was published by Houghton Mifflin in 1962, there was strong opposition to it. As *Time* magazine recounted in 1999: "Carson was violently assailed by threats of lawsuits and derision, including suggestions that this meticulous scientist was a 'hysterical woman' unqualified to write such a book." A huge counterattack was organized and led by Monsanto, Velsicol, American Cyanamid—indeed, the whole chemical industry—duly supported by the Agriculture Department as well as the more cautious in the media.

Some went so far as to characterize her as a mere birdwatcher with more spare time than scientific background, calling her unprofessional, and a fringe of her critics accused her of being a communist. In addition, many critics repeatedly asserted that she was calling for the elimination of all pesticides, despite the fact that Carson had made it clear she was not advocating the banning or complete withdrawal of helpful pesticides, but was instead encouraging responsible and carefully managed use, with an awareness of the chemicals' impact on the entire ecosystem.

Houghton Mifflin was pressured to suppress the book, but it did not succumb. *Silent Spring* was positively reviewed by many outside of the agricultural and chemical science fields, and it became a runaway best seller both in the United States and overseas. Again, *Time* magazine claims that, within a year or so of publication, "all but the most self-serving of Carson's attackers were backing rapidly toward safer ground. In their ugly campaign to reduce a brave scientist's protest to a matter of public relations, the chemical interests had only increased public awareness."

However, her claims on DDT still remain controversial because so far DDT has failed to yield direct evidence demonstrating that it causes cancer in humans.

Pesticide use became a major public issue that was helped by Carson's April 1963 appearance on a CBS television debate between her and a chemical company spokesman. Later that year, she was elected to the American Academy of Arts and Sciences and received many other honors and awards, including the Audubon Medal and the Cullen Medal of the American Geographical Society.

Carson received hundreds of speaking invitations, but was unable to accept the great majority of them. Her health had been steadily declining since she had been diagnosed with breast cancer halfway through the writing of *Silent Spring*. In one of her last public appearances, Carson testified before President Kennedy's Science Advisory Committee, which later thoroughly vindicated both *Silent Spring* and Carson. However, she never did live to see the banning of DDT in the United States. She died on April 14, 1964, at the age of fifty-six. In 1980, she was posthumously awarded the Presidential Medal of Freedom, the highest civilian honor in the United States.

30. MARY MCCARTHY

1912–1989
AUTHOR

Her life has been a sad one for so young a girl. One needs to know something about her history in order to understand her.
> —Adelaide Preston, principal of Annie Wright
> High School (the high school that
> Mary McCarthy attended)

We all live in suspense from day to day; in other words, you are the hero of your own story.
> —Mary McCarthy

Life isn't about finding yourself, life is about creating yourself.
> —Mary McCarthy

Mary Therese McCarthy may be one of the most misunderstood authors in recent time. Her early life was markedly different from the life of privilege depicted in her well-known novel about young women at Vassar, *The Group*. Born in 1912 in Seattle, Washington, Mary was the first of four children born to Roy Winfield and Therese ("Tess") Preston McCarthy. The McCarthy family had originally immigrated from Ireland before the Potato Famine to Illinois and then later to Minneapolis. The Prestons, Mary's mother's family, were eastern European Jews who settled in Seattle.

After Mary was born, her parents had three sons within five years: Kevin, Preston, and Sheridan. Roy and Tess, Mary's young parents, struggled financially because they had four small children and Roy did not have the job skills to support them. When Roy grew up in Minneapolis, he became an alcoholic and his family often had to pull him out of bars. He was hospitalized for alcoholism in Oregon and then met Tess at a hotel in Oregon. After they married, they moved to Minneapolis and Roy began drinking again. Tess convinced him to move back to Seattle, but they struggled financially and Roy's family had to support them. Roy quit drinking when Mary was born, but their financial struggles continued. In an effort to help them, Roy's parents bought a house for them in Minneapolis. In 1918, the family was traveling from Seattle to Minneapolis by train when Roy and Tess experienced flu symptoms. They had contracted the influenza that killed more people in the United States than any other epidemic. Both parents died, leaving Mary and her brothers orphans at the ages of six, four, three, and one.

When they arrived in Minneapolis, the children were taken in by their great-aunt Margaret Sheridan McCarthy and her new husband, Myers Shriver. The Shrivers, who did not have any experience with children, were not only extremely frugal and religiously conservative but also physically and psychologically abusive. They beat the children with a hairbrush and a razor strop, fed them badly cooked food, and deprived them of stimulation. Mary had read books before her parents died, but the Shrivers would not allow the children to read books. They said they wanted to save electricity and further explained that books would give the children too many ideas. For the same reasons, they denied the children the opportunity to listen to records, see movies, or engage in any activities outside events at the Catholic Church or the parochial school they attended. At the parochial school, the nuns taught reading through readers that included stories but did not allow the children to read entire books. Mary later said, "For a child afflicted with book hunger, it was a deprivation of fiendish cruelty."

In her books *Memories of a Catholic Girlhood* (1957) and *How I Grew* (1987), Mary recalls others examples of how the Shrivers withheld "cultural sustenance" as well as physical and emotional sustenance. The Shrivers expected "perfect behavior" and enforced very strict rules. The children were not allowed to be friends with other children, could not leave the yard except for school, or play with toys. Mary reports that she only saw one movie, *The Seal of the Confessional*, in the church basement. The only music the children heard consisted of band concerts, the church organ, and her grandmother's player piano. Uncle Myers listened to the radio with headphones so that the children could not hear it. The children were given boiled, tasteless foods while he ate foods that the children were not allowed to eat, including bananas and other fresh fruits. He required the children to shell peanuts for the candy he made but they were not allowed to taste it. Eventually, Mary grew tired of being deprived, so she found her uncle's bananas and ate thirteen in one sitting. This gorging not only made her very sick but also earned her a beating. The Shrivers' punishments were often arbitrary. The children were locked outside all day no matter how cold or hot it was. Mary was also beaten or punished for her accomplishments. When she won a citywide essay writing contest, her uncle beat her to "keep her from getting stuck up" and also took her $25 prize money. She was also punished when she performed in a play at church and could mouth all the parts in the play. Even though Mary complained to her grandparents and cousins about the Shrivers' treatment, this pattern of abuse continued for six years.

Finally, in 1923 her maternal grandparents, Harold and Augusta ("Gussie") Morganstern Preston, rescued the children and took them back to Seattle. Her brothers were sent to boarding school, while Mary moved in with her grandparents in their upper-class home. Harold was a well-known and successful attorney, and Gussie was known for her beauty and elegance. The Prestons wanted Mary to have an excellent education, so they enrolled her in the Forest Ridge Convent School for her primary education. Now, Mary could use the school library as well as the extensive library in her grandparents' home. She recalls that she "gobbled" books the way she had gobbled the bananas in her uncle's pantry. She always liked "boy's" books better than "girl's" books. She later described this experience of being rescued and reintroduced to the world by saying, "I was born as a mind in 1925, my bodily birth having taken place in 1912."

However, the cultural and social deprivation she had suffered made the social aspects of school more difficult for Mary. She had missed many parts of childhood that other children had experienced, including movies, music, and books, so she could not easily converse with other children. She later remarked that she had missed so much she could not ever really catch up. She reports that she really had no friends and she also felt alone in her grandparents' house. Her grandparents, who were very reserved, lived upstairs in the house while Mary's room was downstairs. Although Mary's life had improved greatly in some respects, she was still deprived emotionally and socially.

When Mary completed primary school, she asked her grandparents to allow her to go to a public school. Against their better judgment, they allowed her to attend Garfield High School in the central district of Seattle. After she completed her freshman year her grandparents withdrew her because they felt the school was not challenging enough and not the "right school" for her. Mary also remembers this as the time she "lost her faith" and discovered "intellectuals." Her grandparents sent her to the Annie Wright Seminary, a Protestant boarding school, for the remainder of high school. Mary later said that attending Annie Wright really determined her fate. Although the school was essentially a finishing school, she was influenced by a teacher, Dorothy Atkinson, who taught journalism. Academically, she was at the top of her class and wrote articles for the school newspaper and short stories. Nevertheless, Mary describes herself as "wild" and "in trouble" all the time. She lost her virginity when she was fourteen with a man who was probably about twenty-six years old. Although they only had sex one time, they wrote letters to each other for years. Despite the fact that she was in trouble in school for smoking, leaving the grounds, and making sarcastic remarks, she graduated as the class valedictorian. If they went on to college, most Annie Wright graduates attended the University of Washington; however, many got married immediately after high school. Having been influenced by Atkinson, who had attended Vassar College in Poughkeepsie, New York, Mary decided to apply to Vassar.

She was admitted to Vassar in 1929. Before her freshman year, she attended a play in Seattle with her grandfather and met Harold Johnsrud, an actor from New York. She saw him in several other plays and met up with him while she was taking summer drama classes. They began an affair during Mary's freshman year that continued throughout her college years. Mary had intended to pursue drama at Vassar because she had always been interested in acting. However, an incident during a play ended that pursuit. Mary's character was supposed to be dead but she pulled her tunic down and the audience laughed. She realized she would never be an actress and began concentrating her efforts on her true talent: writing.

Although she found Vassar intellectually stimulating, she described it in letters to Johnsrud as "brittle, smart, and a little empty." She also later realized that the students at Vassar were isolated from the rest of the world. It was 1929 but Mary recalls that they did not know about the stock market crash until long after it happened. Mary really learned about the effects of the crash during her trips to see Johnsrud, who was out of work and living in a cheap apartment in New York. Despite the isolation from the world, Mary said Vassar "remade" her. She was introduced to new ideas and people from different ethnic and cultural groups. She belonged to the "smoking room set," a group of young women who smoked and engaged in intellectual conversation. The young women in this group were the inspiration for the characters she created in her book about young women at Vassar, *The Group*. Like a character in the book, she started a rebel literary magazine. She became engaged to Johnsrud during her sophomore year and they married in 1933. The wedding is also described in *The Group*. Mary graduated, Phi Beta Kappa, with her bachelor's degree in 1933.

After she graduated and married Johnsrud, Mary wrote short stories while Johnsrud directed, wrote, and acted in plays. They also wrote a movie together but could not sell it. Because Mary's short stories were rejected, she began writing book reviews, which were published. She wrote a successful series of articles for *The Nation*, titled "Our Critics, Right or Wrong." These articles made her some enemies but also made her famous at the age of twenty-two. *The Nation* asked her to write another series of articles about theater critics and to write critiques of detective fiction. Despite this success, the young couple struggled financially and Mary needed to work to earn additional money. She worked as a secretary for an art dealer who she had worked for while in college, and she also worked for a journalist. In 1936, she met John Porter at a dance while Johnsrud was touring in a play. She had an affair with Porter and asked Johnsrud for a divorce so that she could marry Porter. While she was in Reno waiting for the divorce, she decided she did not love Porter. She wrote to Porter who was in Mexico but received no response. She later learned that he had died in Mexico. Her marriage to Johnsrud had ended and she was a single woman again.

Politically, Mary had been progressively moving to the left since college. Like most college students, she was influenced by books and discussions at Vassar, but she was also greatly influenced by Johnsrud's political beliefs. She became an editorial assistant at the publisher Covici-Friede, where most of the employees were communists. As the result of a conversation at a party, her name was added to the letterhead of the American Committee for the Defense of Leon Trotsky. She was harassed by phone and criticized in a Stalinist magazine. During this time, the Moscow show trials had split American intellectuals into pro-Stalin and anti-Stalin camps. The debate resulted in Mary becoming more solidly anti-Stalin. Mary recalls that this period was when she became a true intellectual, a literary person who is concerned with public affairs. She became a theater critic for the *Partisan Review* and began living with one of the coeditors, Phillip Rahv, a Marxist Russian. She then wrote a book with Robert Craig about H. V. Kaltenborn, a well-known radio commentator. While she was working for Covici-Friede and writing for the *Partisan Review*, she met Edmund Wilson, a literary critic who had been asked to contribute to the magazine. While she was living with Rahv, she began seeing Wilson.

In 1938, she married her best-known spouse, Edmund Wilson. She resigned from Covici-Friede and moved to Connecticut to live with Wilson. The marriage was a surprise to most of their friends and later Mary said she did not really love him. Not only were they not compatible but also Mary reported that Wilson was abusive. Even when Mary was pregnant, he physically abused her, throwing her out of bed and beating her. Mary began psychoanalysis soon after their marriage and continued therapy throughout the marriage. After Wilson beat her badly, a doctor advised her to go to a hospital to recover. Although Mary thought she was going to New York Hospital, through a series of events that has never been fully explained, Mary found herself confined in a mental hospital.

While she was there, Wilson encouraged her to get an abortion. Mary considered having an abortion but eventually decided against it. She and Wilson had a son, Reuel Kimball Wilson, Mary's only child.

Throughout their marriage, they had struggled financially because neither of them had a regular job. After the baby was born, they moved to Chicago when Wilson accepted a teaching position at the University of Chicago. Their relationship continued to be tumultuous; at times their fighting was so loud that the police were called to intervene. After a year in Chicago, they moved to Cape Cod but also maintained a place in New York. Mary wrote several short stories, which were published, convincing her that she could write fiction. She also wrote her first novel, *The Company She Keeps*, published in 1942. By the summer of 1945, Mary could no longer endure the combative marriage and left Wilson. They were divorced in 1945.

Following their divorce, Mary accepted a teaching position for a year at Bard College in Annandale-on-Hudson, New York, just north of Vassar. While at Bard, she met a member of the staff of the *New Yorker*, Bowden Broadwater, whom she married in 1946. For a semester in 1948, Mary taught English at Sarah Lawrence College in Bronxville, New York. During her marriage to Broadwater, Mary wrote prolifically, publishing eight books between 1949 and 1961, including *The Oasis* (1949), *The Groves of Academe* (1952), *Venice Observed* (1956), *Memories of a Catholic Girlhood* (1957), and *The Stones of Florence* (1959). She also began a close friendship with the philosopher Hannah Arendt that continued throughout their lives. When Arendt, who was a German-born Jew, was attacked by the Jewish community for her book on Adolf Eichmann, Mary defended her views. They wrote to each other often and their correspondence was later collected in the book *Between Friends* (1995). In addition, she contributed numerous articles to such periodicals as *Atlantic Monthly*, *The New Yorker*, and *Harper's*, as well as *Partisan Review*.

While she was on a lecture tour in Poland for the U.S. Information Agency (USIA) in late 1959 and early 1960, she met and fell in love with James West. West was working for the USIA and planned their itinerary for the four weeks they spent in Poland. Mary and West divorced their spouses and were married in April 1961. Mary also became stepmother to

West's three children. Beginning in 1963, the novel *The Group* remained on the *New York Times* bestseller list for almost two years. The book was made into a movie with the same name in 1966. The Wests traveled between their two homes, an apartment in Paris and a house in Castine, Maine, and maintained an active social life.

During the 1960s, Mary, who had opposed World War II, also protested the Vietnam War. She offered shelter to draft resisters and AWOL soldiers, visited Hanoi and Saigon, and wrote against the war. She proposed that "Vietnam was a symbol of the right of U.S. capital to flow freely throughout the globe" and the Vietnamese resistance had made Vietnam "a neo-imperialist proving ground." Mary wrote several books during this period, including *Vietnam* (1967), *The Writing on the Wall* (1970), *Birds of America* (1971), *The Mask of State: Watergate Portraits* (1974), *Cannibals and Missionaries* (1979), and *Ideas and the Novel* (1980).

In 1980, Mary started a controversy when she was a guest on the *Dick Cavett Show*. Cavett asked her which writers she considered to be overrated. Mary responded that she could not think of any "overpraised" writers except for Lillian Hellman. She accused Hellman of being "overrated," a "bad writer," and a "dishonest" writer. When pressed to explain how she was dishonest, Mary said, "every word [Hellman] writes is a lie, including 'and' and 'the.'" Hellman was furious and responded by filing a $2.5 million libel suit against McCarthy. During the 1980s, Mary McCarthy became a celebrity, not so much for her "twenty-two books of fiction, criticism, art history, political journalism and memoirs" as for Hellman's $2.5 million lawsuit. It appeared that the lawsuit would end when Hellman died, but it did not end until Mary died. This feud was the basis for the play *Imaginary Friends* by Nora Ephron

On October 25, 1989, Mary died of cancer at New York Hospital at the age of seventy-seven. Before she died, she was working on the second volume of her autobiography, which was published posthumously in 1992 as *Intellectual Memoirs: New York, 1936–1938*.

Mary McCarthy's contribution to the world is difficult to pinpoint. Best known for her intellect and acerbic wit, she is acknowledged as an excellent critic and writer of fiction and nonfiction. As Elizabeth Hardwick said, it is "hard to think of any writer in America more interesting and unusual than Mary McCarthy." Morris Dickstein wrote in *The New Yorker* that Mary's "sharp style made her the most feared and forthright writer in New York." However, much of her writing did not receive widespread public acclaim. She is often recognized as a progressive woman who contributed to the feminist cause, but she criticized feminists and was criticized by them. In addition, she is celebrated as an intellectual known for her political beliefs and her interest in social justice. Her life spanned the rapidly changing twentieth century and throughout her life she questioned the norms of society. Probably, Mary would be most proud of her distinction as an intellectual.

Regardless of which contributions are judged to be most important, Mary's triumph over her early life was a major accomplishment. When they were adults, Mary's brother asked her if the course of their lives had been the result of adjusting to the death of their parents. Mary's reply was that she felt that orphan children are often looked down on by the rest of the family and therefore, "try to distinguish themselves—usually favorably." Mary certainly distinguished herself favorably.

31. PAT NIXON

1912–1993
FIRST LADY

I have sacrificed everything in my life that I consider precious in order to advance the political career of my husband.

—Pat Nixon

Of all the Irish women who are chronicled in the *Daughters of Maeve*, there may be none more misunderstood than Pat Nixon. While many may see her as a shrinking violet who sacrificed her entire life to her husband, the former first lady was a strong, resilient woman who overcame insurmountable obstacles and became a silent partner in one of the most unforgettable political duos in presidential history. Known as "Buddy" to her husband, she called the position of First Lady "the hardest unpaid job in the world."

Pat Nixon, born Thelma Catherine Ryan, came into the world on March 16, 1912, in Ely, Nevada, a small mining town in eastern Nevada. Because her parents, Will Ryan and Kate Halberstadt, were poor miners, Thelma was born in a miner's shack. Her father, who had been a sailor on a whaling vessel, was a prospector hoping to make his fortune mining a claim. To make a meager living, he worked as a timekeeper for one of the mining companies. His family had come from County Mayo, Ireland, and part of the family had settled in New England. Always seeking adventure, Will had traveled throughout the world and finally arrived in Ely.

He married Pat's mother, German-born Kate Halberstadt, after her husband died in a flood. Kate had two children from her first marriage, Matthew and Neva. Matthew had been sent to live with his wealthy

184

grandparents in California but Neva lived with the Ryans. Kate and Will had two sons before Thelma was born, Bill and Tom. In her biography of her mother, *Pat Nixon: The Untold Story*, Julie Nixon Eisenhower writes about how her mother's name changed throughout her life. Although she was born Thelma, her father never liked that name. Since she was his baby girl, he and her brothers always called her "Babe." He also insisted that her birthday be celebrated one day after her true birthday, March 16, because March 17 was St. Patrick's Day. When her brother Bill asked his father why they celebrated her birthday a day late, he answered, "Well, she was there in the morning—my St. Patrick's Babe in the morning." (Pat would later be called "Babe" by her family, "Buddy" by her classmates, and finally "Pat" after she changed her name to Patricia in honor of her father's insistence that she was his St. Patrick's baby.)

Ely was a boomtown and modern in some ways. The town had a new school, a water system, and other amenities. However, it was a frontier town and the Ryans were barely scraping by on Will's salary at the mine. After Babe was born, Kate begged Will to move to southern California. He was reluctant to give up his dream of striking it rich prospecting, but he finally relented. He agreed to give up mining to become a farmer in California. The family traveled by train to look for land near Los Angeles. They finally found a ten-acre "ranch" in Artesia, a town about twenty miles outside of Los Angeles. The ranch house on the property had no electricity or running water and was barely big enough for the family of six.

The entire family worked to run the small "truck farm," which barely supported them. Will, who learned to run the farm by reading agricultural journals, became a local expert in farming and was often asked for advice. He was called "the cabbage king" because his cabbages were the biggest and best in the area. He was also known as a highly ethical and honest man. Although he was a successful farmer, he never really acted or looked like a farmer and never lost his spirit of adventure. As Tom Ryan said, "my dad was always chasing rainbows." He continued to take risks in an attempt to make his fortune, speculating in oil wells and mines. He also read books, newspapers, and journals voraciously, often trading reading materials with neighbors. Significantly, he read to Babe who often fell asleep on his lap while he was reading to her. In addition, he told his children stories about his life—stories about the adventure of whaling and prospecting. In her biography of her mother, Eisenhower explains, "His stories made a particularly strong impression on Babe. The escape through books, the love of travel and adventure, and the fierce independence became as much as part of her as they were of her father."

Babe was a beautiful child who frequently received attention from strangers. She had shining red-gold hair and almond-shaped hazel eyes that changed from brown to green to gray-blue. As she told her daughter Julie, one of her earliest memories was traveling to Los Angeles in the "electric car" when she was about three years old. A couple was taken by her beauty and offered her peppermint candies. This was the first time she had ever seen or tasted candy.

She and her mother made frequent trips to Los Angeles so that her mother could visit her son, Matthew, who lived with his grandparents. Babe learned that these trips were very important to her mother not only because she could visit her son but also because she could escape from the farm. As Pat Nixon later told her daughter Julie, "We lived in the country . . . my mother longed for something more." These trips also taught Babe that there was something more beyond life on the farm.

In 1917 when the United States entered World War I, anti-German hysteria grew to the point that it affected Germans living in the United States. Because she was born in Germany, Kate made her children promise that they would not tell anyone that she was German. She also stopped speaking German to her neighbors and did not ever speak about her family in Germany. Kate secretly sent her "egg" money to her family but no one else contacted the family in Germany or knew anything about them. She hid her contacts from her husband because he was ironically fanatically anti-German. Later, Pat and her brothers regretted that her mother had to keep her family a secret and that they knew so little about their German heritage.

The family struggled to make a living on the farm. Daily life on the farm was typical of farm families of that era. The children were expected to do chores before school every day, help with the planting and harvest, feed the animals, and generally help run the farm. Babe and her siblings learned not to expect much and not to express their feelings. Their father discouraged public displays of emotion and affection, so there was little physical or verbal expression of affection in the family. Her father's method of expressing affection was teasing, which Babe took seriously. The children were also taught to hide any signs of disappointment. If they had extra money, her father would buy her an ice cream cone while they were in town, but often he could not. She learned not to show her feelings. As she told Julie, "In our family we held our disappointment."

Because he routinely held his emotions in check, Will also exploded periodically, particularly when he had been drinking. He would pick fights with Kate and become so verbally abusive that the children would beg him to stop. Pat later admitted to Julie that she had repressed many of those memories. Confessing that her father's temper and the fights had really affected her, she explained, "I detest temper. I detest scenes. I just can't be that way. I saw it with my father." She admitted, "To avoid scenes or unhappiness, I suppose I accommodated to others." All three of the Ryan children became "even-tempered adults who preferred silence to confrontations."

Babe was an excellent student. She learned to read by reading her older brothers' schoolbooks, so she was a reader when she entered school. Her teacher would often show her off for visitors by asking her to read. She always impressed her teachers by being calm, mature, and tenacious. She became the embodiment of her father's adage, "If it's worth doing, it's worth doing right." She skipped second grade and became a perfectionist who demanded much of herself. She also performed frequently at her school, reciting prose pieces. She was so effective that local clubs began asking her to perform for their events. Her escape was always reading. As she later said, "It gave me a horizon beyond the small town we were living in. Somehow I always knew that there was more in the world than what we were experiencing then." She also loved being outdoors gardening and playing with her friends who lived on the neighboring farm. She and her friends often engaged in mischief such as raiding beehives, rolling and smoking cigarettes with the boys, and other activities that were not acceptable for girls at that time. She and her half sister Neva were not close, partly due to the age difference but also due to Neva's constant complaining and bad temper. Neva, who was jealous of her brother who lived with his wealthy grandparents, caused her mother constant grief. Babe tried to be as good as possible to cause her mother less trouble and unhappiness.

In the summer of 1925, Kate contracted Bright's disease (a kidney disease) and was diagnosed with cancer of the liver. The children realized their mother was in pain but did not know she was so ill until she finally saw a doctor. By that time, they learned that her illness was advanced and untreatable. Because there was no hospital in town, Kate had to move into the doctor's house and was never able to go home again. Babe and her brothers became even closer during this time as they supported each other and their parents. Since Babe skipped a grade, she was in the same freshman class as Tom. At the age of thirteen, she took over most of her mother's responsibilities besides her usual chores. She did almost all the cleaning and cooking for the family and also cooked for the hired help during harvest. The cooking often affected her own appetite so that she ate almost nothing. Her brothers helped her with some of the cleanings but they lowered the shades in the house so that no one would see them doing "women's work." Between all the work and school, there was no time for play. In addition, the family went to the doctor's house every night to care for Kate. Babe often stayed through the night to take care of her mother. Kate died in January 1926 about six months after she was diagnosed. When her mother died, Babe realized that she knew very little about her mother; life on the farm was so busy that they did not have time to talk or ask questions about their mother.

Her mother's death really affected Babe. She had to grow up immediately. As she later told Julie, "When my mother died, I just took responsibility for my life." She had to learn how to complete multiple tasks simultaneously, completing her school work while she was caring for the family. For example, she would study while she was ironing and set her hair in waves while the steam came off the stove when she was cooking breakfast. Due to all the work, she could not stay long after school, which meant that she could not participate in sports. Her brother Tom later said she inherited her mother's personality, "She had a big heart. She sacrificed and did things without complaining."

Despite her workload, Babe did participate in debate, oratory, and drama. She loved performing in plays because it provided an escape from her difficult life. She was also active in student government and well liked and respected by her peers and teachers. For years after she graduated, the principal used her life as an example when he was speaking to other students. He told them about this remarkable young woman who was able to take care of the household, complete her studies with excellent grades, and still participate in extracurricular activities.

While she was trying to keep the family together, no one realized that her father was slowly dying of tuberculosis. He was a stubborn man who never saw a doctor. When he was finally diagnosed, Babe and her brothers were in such shock that they later could not remember how they learned that their father was dying. Besides the emotional stress her father's illness placed on the family, it also meant more work for Babe. Beyond caring for another ill parent, she also had to sterilize all his eating utensils and clothes to protect the rest of the family. She boiled everything in pans with disinfectant that was so foul smelling that she again had no appetite. She finally wrote to her father's family in Connecticut to tell them that her father was dying. One of his sisters came to stay with the family before he died and helped while she was there. However, the burden of caring for the family continued to fall on Babe for several years.

By the time Babe and her brothers graduated from high school, they were really already on their own. They made the decision that when their father died, they would not settle his estate until after Bill was twenty-one. That would mean that they could stay together and would not need a guardian. Even though they all received scholarships for college, they could not afford for all of them to go. They decided that Tom had the best chance of earning a large athletic scholarship so he should go first. Bill would stay home to run the farm and Babe would care for their father. Tom promised that he would ensure that Babe could go to college later. She took care of her father until his condition became so bad that he had to go to a sanatorium. She took shorthand classes and got a job at Artesia's First National Bank to pay for her father's hospitalization. Before he died, Will, who had always been protective of his attractive daughter, asked his son to continue to protect her. Although he promised his father he would honor his request, Bill knew that his sister did not need protecting because she was like her father. As Bill later said, "My dad was determined to get things done and she had his determination and grit, grit, grit. She had grit. Life didn't stop there; things went on. She fought for everything she got."

After their father died, Babe enrolled in Fullerton College in 1931 as "Patricia" Ryan. She had never really been called Thelma by anyone except teachers and no one other than her mother had ever liked the name. Since she had always been her father's "St. Pat's Babe," she changed her name to her father's favorite name: Patricia. The Great Depression had hit everyone in the United States very hard, but farmers were particularly affected. Bill and Pat decided to rent the farm to a Japanese man who wanted to grow strawberries. Bill worked as an electrician while Pat worked at the bank as the bookkeeper and janitor. Bill helped her scrub the floors in the evening because she was still running the house, working part time, and attending college part time.

She left California for the first time when friends of her aunt in Connecticut hired her to drive them from California to Connecticut. She spent time with her family in the Northeast and became close to her aunt, who had become Sister Thomas Anne. Her aunt became a major influence in her life from that time on. She helped her find a job at a tuberculosis hospital in Seton, New York, which also influenced her later life. She loved hospital work and wrote to Bill, "Sometimes I feel that I should like to spend my life just working with the afflicted unfortunates—helping them to be happy." While she was in New York, several significant events happened in her life. She became involved in a romance with one of the doctors at the hospital and dated several other men, but dating was difficult because she lived with the nuns. In 1933, while Franklin and Eleanor Roosevelt were in office, she traveled to Washington, D.C., where she took the White House tour. Later, she went to a hospital conference that Al Smith, governor of New York, and the Roosevelts attended. She was eventually given responsibility for the hospital pharmacy and x-ray departments. At the end of two years there, she had saved little money because the pay was so low and she often gave money to the patients. She was offered the opportunity to perform in a Paramount Pictures movie but she turned it down because there was no job security. Finally, in 1934 Tom had saved enough money to keep his promise to send her to college.

In 1934, she and her brothers moved into an apartment together and she enrolled in the University of Southern California (USC) on a research fellowship. She worked for a psychology professor and carried a full load. She stood out at USC as an excellent student and a hard-working, mature young woman. Dr. Frank Baxter, her English professor, later commented that she always looked tired because she worked so much, but she was always a good student. He said, "She stood out from the empty-headed, overdressed little sorority girls of that era like a good piece of literature on a shelf of cheap paperbacks." She and her brothers all worked and attended classes, so they did not see each other much. She still had most of the responsibilities for taking care of the house and she also continually scrambled for part-time jobs. One of her best jobs was working as a movie extra and she even had a speaking role in one film. She was offered the opportunity to sign a contract as an actress but the contract was only for one film, so she turned it down. In addition, she also did not want to be under the control of a director and the studio. Later, she worked at Bullock's department store as a model, salesperson, and then eventually as the assistant buyer. She enjoyed many aspects of the job, particularly the opportunity to meet movie stars who shopped there. She considered a career there but the job paid poorly and she had taken enough hours in education in college to become a teacher. She graduated cum laude with a teaching certificate and began searching for a teaching position.

Teaching jobs were scarce at that time and at twenty-five years old she was considered too young by many districts for a teaching position. Because of her excellent recommendations and the influence of her high school principal (who was now the superintendent of the school district), she managed to secure a position as a commercial teacher for Whittier High School in Whittier, California. She moved to the little Quaker town of Whittier, which was just eight miles from Artesia, where she had grown up. More than half of Whittier was Quaker and the town was home to Whittier College, which had a profound influence on the town. She found that there were many unwritten mores in the town that came from the Quaker influence. As a young, attractive teacher, she initially had some difficulty establishing discipline in the classroom but soon she was respected by her students and the other teachers. She became friends with another young teacher at the school and they moved into an apartment in town together. Many of her male students had a crush on her and would often hang out near her apartment, which was just across the street from the bowling alley. She usually went into Los Angeles to date men to avoid the town gossip. As a teacher, she connected with her students. She was understanding of those who had to work part time and who were tired or dozing in her classes. She also kept her door open to students when she stayed after school every day for several hours. One student wrote a letter to Ann Landers years later about how this young teacher had helped her, calling her "a saint."

While she was teaching at Whittier High School, a young man named Richard Nixon was the Whittier deputy city attorney. He had graduated from Whittier College and went on to law school. Pat met Richard when she auditioned for the Whittier Community Players, the local community theater. She did not want to try out for a part but the school district strongly encouraged community service and the superintendent had asked her to audition for the lead role. During the audition, she was given the lead role while Richard secured a supporting part. He fell in love with her at first sight and even told her as they were leaving, "You may not believe this, but I am going to marry you someday." She was shocked and looked at him to see if he was teasing, but she realized he was serious. Later that evening, she told her roommate, "I met this guy tonight who says he is going to marry me." She learned that Richard had been a brilliant student, was a member of the Wingert and Bewley law firm, was the Whittier deputy city attorney, and was an active member of local service organizations. He was considered "a darling bachelor" by the women in the town. They also had much in common. Richard's family was Irish and his father had a hot temper. As a result, he also hated scenes and avoided conflict whenever possible. They both escaped by reading, enjoyed oratory, and wanted to travel. Richard's family had endured tragedy similar to Pat's family; one brother died from tuberculosis and another became chronically ill from the disease and died in his early twenties. His illness had placed a huge financial strain on his parents, who owned a small grocery store. Pat and Richard became close during the play rehearsals and by the end of the play, Richard took Pat home to meet his parents. Her fondness for him continued to grow. When her friends asked about him, she prophetically announced, "He is going to be president someday."

Richard persistently pursued her for the next two years. He proposed to her many times, although she indicated to him that she was not as in love with him and not yet ready for marriage. Richard was not deterred and finally she accepted his proposal in 1939, when she was twenty-eight years old. They were married in a small family ceremony later that year. She taught one more year and they lived frugally so that they could save money to travel. After that school year, Richard received a letter from the general counsel of the Office of Price Administration offering him a job in the agency in Washington, D.C. They moved to Washington in 1942, where Richard worked as an attorney for the agency while Pat first volunteered for the Red Cross and then secured a job in the same agency.

During that year, Richard decided he did not like being another attorney among many in Washington and applied for active duty in the navy in 1942. His Quaker family did not support his desire to serve in a war, but Pat supported his decision. He was sent to the Naval Air Station in Ottumna, Iowa, where Pat secured a job in a bank as a bookkeeper for the stamp-rationing program. However, Richard still wanted active duty in the war. He was sent to San Francisco and then finally to the South Pacific. Pat stayed in San Francisco while he was away and they wrote to each other constantly. In 1944, he returned to the base in San Francisco and then they were sent to Philadelphia, New York, and finally Baltimore. While they were in New York, Pat discovered that she was pregnant. Although he was offered the opportunity to become a commander in the navy, Richard was considering running for a political office. He and Pat had discussed the idea for several years and in 1945 the opportunity was presented to him.

Richard Nixon's first political opportunity came when a group from

Whittier was looking for a candidate to run as the Republican candidate for Congress. When he was selected as the candidate, he and Pat moved back to Whittier to launch his campaign. They moved in with his parents in January, and their daughter was born in February. They decided to name her Patricia because that was Pat's favorite name and her nickname became "Tricia." Soon after Tricia was born, Pat began campaigning for Richard. Richard's mother took care of Tricia during the day while Pat worked on the campaign. Pat and Richard invested most of the money they had saved during their marriage and even invested Pat's small inheritance from the sale of her parents' ranch. They had no experience running a campaign but they successfully organized house meetings and coffees that became an effective strategy. Ironically, during the campaign some Democrats broke into their campaign office and stole their expensive campaign brochures. During Watergate, Pat remembered the incident and wondered how the Watergate break-in was so different from this break-in during their first campaign. In the end, Richard and Pat won the hard-fought election. In 1946, when he was thirty-three and Pat was thirty-four, Richard became a newly elected congressman.

In December 1946, Richard, Pat, and Tricia moved to Washington, D.C., to begin his first congressional term. Because the war had just ended, there was a housing shortage in Washington, which made finding a place to live very difficult. In addition, there was virtually no orientation for new representatives. Pat found that the congressional club for wives was really just a social club to organize social events. She was accustomed to an active role in her husband's life and most recently his political life, so this was a difficult transition for her. Although she was a mother and helped with mail in the office, she worked less during this time than she ever had in her life. During this term in office, Richard gained some national attention when he worked on the Marshall Plan. In 1948 when his term was to expire, the Nixons just assumed he would run again. Later, when Julie asked her mother if they had discussed whether he would run again, Pat said, "Oh, no. You run until you cannot run anymore."

In 1948, the Nixons began their second campaign for Congress. Pat was pregnant with their second child, Julie, and caring for their family as well as helping Richard's ailing parents, who had moved to Pennsylvania. For the first time in her life, Pat began to resent the burdens of her life. She rarely saw her husband and took care of all the household responsibilities so that her husband could devote all his time to his office. In July 1948, Julie was born during a particularly hot week. Richard's mother came to take care of Tricia but she became ill, so when Pat came home from the hospital, she took care of the two children and her mother-in-law. Although Richard had promised to spend more time with the family, he went to the Republican National Convention, where Thomas Dewey was nominated, and then spent the fall campaigning for Dewey. He also became involved in the famous Hiss case. Alger Hiss, who had served in the government in several capacities, was accused of being a communist infiltrator. He denied the allegations and denied knowing an avowed communist who had testified before the Committee on Un-American Activities. Nixon did not believe Hiss and made his views known. When the Committee on Un-American Activities was attacked, Nixon was at the center of the controversy. Although Hiss was found guilty, the case took a toll on the Nixons. Later, Pat told Julie that the reason that people often went after her father was "that no one could control him—not the press, not the lobbyists, not the politicians. He did what he thought was right, and from the time this became apparent in the Hiss case, he was a target." As a result, the Nixons were subjected to a very ugly campaign against them in 1948, in which Richard was accused of many false charges including attacks on his character.

Despite the controversy and the attacks during his congressional campaign, Richard maintained his seat and then decided to run for the U.S. Senate. In 1949, he began his campaign and Pat traveled with him throughout California in an old station wagon, bringing their grassroots campaign to as many people as possible. Not only was the pace exhausting but also she had to arrange for the care of Tricia and Julie, who were two and four at the time. She often had to leave them with babysitters because her in-laws lived on the East Coast and they were not able to care for them. After a long and grueling campaign, Richard won the Senate seat in 1950.

When Richard became a senator, he and Pat were finally able to buy a house and settle into a more stable life in Washington. Richard still traveled frequently, but he was home for major family events. By 1952, there were rumors that Richard was a possible candidate for vice president. At first, Richard and Pat did not take the rumors seriously, but by the time they went to the Republican National Convention, they discovered that his nomination was likely. After Dwight Eisenhower won the nomination for president, they learned he had selected Richard and the rumors became a reality. During the campaign, the Nixons were again subjected to controversy and accusations, this time about campaign contributions. Richard offered to step aside and allow Eisenhower to choose another candidate, but Eisenhower stood by Richard. In his famous "Checkers" speech, Nixon denied the charges that he had accepted any contributions that were not legal. He explained that Pat did not have a mink coat but instead had a "respectable Republican cloth coat" and that the only gift they had accepted was a dog they had received from a contributor from Texas, who had heard the Nixons mention they wanted to get a dog for their daughters. The dog, a black and white cocker spaniel, was named Checkers by Tricia. The media, who focused on that element of the speech, dubbed his speech the "Checkers" speech. Despite all the turmoil and the emotional effect on the Nixons, they survived the experience. The Eisenhower-Nixon ticket won the race and Richard Nixon became the vice president of the United States.

In 1952, the role of the vice president was vague and the role of the wife of the vice president was even more vague. She had to learn the strict protocol for every event in Washington and at first she made naive mistakes. She shared her husband's journeys abroad in his vice presidential years.

John F. Kennedy interrupted Nixon's assent in 1960, winning the presidency by the narrowest margin of the twentieth century. After losing a 1962 race for governor of California and holding his "last press conference," Nixon patiently laid the groundwork for a comeback. In 1964, he campaigned for the Republican presidential candidate Barry Goldwater at a time when other prominent Republicans were keeping their distance from the leader of the budding conservative movement. The Republican Party lost in a landslide that year, but Nixon won the gratitude of conservatives, the growing power within the party. The Republican Party's huge losses in 1964 were offset in 1966 when two years of the Vietnam War and urban riots led to huge Republican gains in congressional elections. In 1968, Nixon won a presidential election almost as narrow as the one he had lost in 1960. He was then reelected in 1972 with a larger percentage of the votes than any other Republican during the cold war.

One of Pat Nixon's major causes in the years that she lived at the White House was "volunteerism," as she called it. She used her position as First Lady to encourage volunteer service—"the spirit of people helping people." She spent hours answering all her mail personally. Like Jacqueline Kennedy, she had an interest in adding artifacts to the Executive Mansion. In the end, Pat's work brought in over 600 paintings and furnishings into the White House Collection. She also instituted a series of performances by artists at the White House in varied American traditions—from opera to bluegrass. She also continued to travel with her husband during his presidency. Her travels included the historic visit to the People's Republic of China and the summit meetings in the Soviet Union. Her first solo trip was a journey of compassion to take relief supplies to earthquake victims in Peru. Later, she visited Africa and South America with the unique diplomatic standing of Personal Representative of the President. She was always considered a charming envoy.

Pat met the troubled days of Watergate with dignity. "I love my husband," she said, "I believe in him, and I am proud of his accomplishments." In August 1974, President Nixon resigned from office. As he made his resignation speech, Pat was upstairs in the residence packing for California. They left the White House on August 9, 1974, for San Clemente, California. Pat was in failing health in retirement and suffered a stroke in 1976, and again in 1982. A longtime heavy smoker, she also battled mouth cancer, emphysema, and a degenerative spinal condition. In December 1992, while hospitalized with respiratory problems, the former first lady was diagnosed with lung cancer. She died at her home in Park Ridge, New Jersey, at 5:45 A.M. on June 22, 1993, at the age of eighty-one with her daughters and husband by her side, the day after her fifty-third wedding anniversary. Her husband followed her in death ten months later. She and the former president are buried at the Richard Nixon Library and Birthplace in Yorba Linda, California. Her epitaph reads: "Even when people can't speak your language, they can tell if you have love in your heart."

3 2. BILLIE HOLIDAY

1915–1959
SINGER

Anything I do, I sing, it's part of my life.

—Billie Holiday

She was the best jazz singer I had ever heard.

—John Hammond, producer and promoter

She was one of the jazz world's most gifted singers and one of its most tragic figures. "Lady Day" as she would later be called, was born into a time when discrimination against African Americans was at its peak, and she suffered mightily for it. While many music aficionados think they know the real story of Billie Holiday—the drugs, the abusive childhood, and the tragic death—few realize that this icon of the music world was the granddaughter of an Irish slave owner. While she has been identified as one of the music world's great black singers, she also identified with her Irish roots and would come to embrace them throughout her life. Blessed with impeccable phrasing and a cornet-like voice, Billie would go on to change the world of jazz for female vocalists forever. She also redefined what it means to be African American and Irish.

Billie Holiday was born Elinore Harris (later changed to Fagan) on April 7, 1915, in Baltimore. Her parents were Sarah Harris, who called herself Sadie Fagan, and Clarence Holiday. Because her parents were not married when she was born, she was given her mother's preferred maiden name, Fagan. Her birth certificate reads "Elinore Harris," but the doctor's notes read "Elinoir" while the hospital records read "Eleanor." Her name was spelled various ways throughout her life but "Eleanora" seems to be

199

the most common spelling. Because she changed her name to Billie Holiday later, it is not commonly known that her birth name was some variation of Elinore. Although it is accepted that Clarence Holiday was her father, the father's name listed on her birth certificate is one of Sadie's friends, Frank DeViese.

When she was born, her parents were mere teenagers. Her father had seduced her mother when she was working as a maid for a white family. As teenagers, Clarence Holiday studied the trumpet and other instruments and her mother worked as a maid. Biographers vary widely in their accounts of the relationship between Sadie and Clarence. Some say that her parents married and she took the name Holiday. More reliable sources argue that Clarence married several other women but never married Sadie.

Clarence was drafted in World War I and was sent to Europe. He suffered lung damage during the war and had to take up the guitar. He became so good that he toured with big bands and was always on the road. Most accounts say that Clarence seldom visited Sadie and the baby Eleanora and did not provide any financial support. To make a living, Sadie had to travel to take jobs out of town. Eleanora was forced to live with her cousin Ida, who she says was physically and verbally abusive to her. She found comfort in her grandparents and great-grandmother, who spoke of Charles Fagan, the white Irish plantation owner who was the great-grandmother's master and father of her sixteen children.

Eleanora went to school in Baltimore and some reports indicate that she went to school until about fifth grade. But she would cut class to sneak into the movies to see her favorite actress, Billie Dove. She loved the actress so much that she later took her name. She attended public schools in Baltimore but played hooky so much that she was sent to juvenile court. The judge ordered that she attend the House of Good Shepherd for Colored Girls. While she was in elementary school, she worked for Alice Dean, a local brothel owner. She worked for free just to listen to Dean's jazz collection.

Because her mother often took transportation jobs that required her to travel, Eleanora was left with a variety of people. During this time, her great-grandmother died and Eleanora was so devastated that she was confined to a hospital for a month. Billie later told the story that when she was ten years old, a forty-year-old neighbor tried to rape her when she was coming home from school one day but she fought him off. He was arrested and sentenced to five years in prison, but Billie was sentenced to an institution until she reached the age of twenty-one. Billie's mother, with the help of a wealthy family, got her released at the age of twelve. Some sources argue that this story is false and that Billie was confined to the House of Good Shepherd for playing hooky. Billie was released to her mother's custody when she returned to Baltimore in 1925 and married a dockworker named Philip Gough. They lived with Gough until he died three years later.

After she was released from the institution, she moved to Harlem, where she worked as a "20 dollar" call girl. One day a client almost killed her for something sexual that she refused to do. Because of his influence, she was arrested and spent four months in a correctional facility. Upon release, she again became a prostitute. Times became difficult because of the Great Depression, and Billie was forced to find a real job. One day while looking for a job, she wandered into a speakeasy named Pod and Jerry's. She said she needed work and could dance, but in fact she could not dance. They asked if she could sing. When she finished singing a song called "Trav'ln All Alone," the place was in tears. She was hired that night. Some accounts indicate that by this time she was calling herself Billie.

Harlem was just reaching its peak in 1930 as a musical and theatrical center when Billie started her career. The great music styles that originated in St. Louis, New Orleans, and Chicago all seemed to meet in New York. The repeal of Prohibition made speakeasies legal clubs and Billie decided to remain at Pod and Jerry's. She became an "ups" girl—girls who would get up and sing for tips. Most of the girls would pick up their tips by grabbing the money between their thighs but Billie was too dignified and refused.

Billie's singing style gained in popularity. She just didn't sing a song, but communicated it. Each song became a story from a segment of her life, and the crowds loved it. She built her style on elements from her culture, the "field holler" and church hymn. The field holler was used by slaves to pass messages to other slaves. It was incomprehensible to the white slave owners, and the church hymn was transformed by American blacks into spirituals. Although she was considered a jazz singer, all her songs still had a bluesy sound.

In 1935, Billie made her first appearance at the Apollo, which was considered the mecca of music in Harlem. Although struck with stage fright, she more than impressed the audience. She was on her way, not only on stage but also in recording studios. Billie's career in the mid-1930s was growing when she sang in Harlem, but outside of Harlem, people thought she sang too slow and not jazzy enough. Because of criticisms like these, and her extreme sensitivity to criticism, she was having a rough time professionally. Personally, life became a little better when she met the sax player Lester Young. They took an immediate liking to each other and eventually became soul mates. However, on March 1, 1937, she received the tragic news that her father died of pneumonia in a Dallas hospital, which sent her into a deep depression. In 1938, she joined the Count Basie Band, but only lasted eight months because of the extensive travel.

During the period between 1940 and 1945, Billie became one of the most desired singers on Fifty-second Street, an area called "swing street." The small intimate size of these clubs was ideal for her. She totally captivated the audiences. She was making $1,000 a week. One of her best-known songs was "God Bless the Child," which she helped to write. Her inspiration for the song came from a visit to her mother's restaurant Mom Holiday's on Ninety-ninth and Columbus Avenue. One day when she asked her mother for some money and was refused, her mother said "God bless the child that's got his own."

The man most important in launching her career was the promoter John Hammond, who thought she was the best jazz singer he had ever heard. A legend in the music business, Hammond was also responsible for the careers of Benny Goodman, Aretha Franklin, Bob Dylan, and Bruce Springsteen, and many others.

Although her career was successful, it did not last long because of her addiction to drugs. On August 25, 1941, she married Jimmy Monroe. As they were both opium users, their marriage started falling apart in the first year. This is when she started using heroin. They divorced and she became involved with the trumpeter Joe Guy, another heroin addict. After three weeks in a rehabilitation center, she thought she kicked the habit, but her addiction to heroin resurfaced. In 1947, she was sentenced to one year in a women's prison in West Virginia after the federal agents found narcotics in her hotel room. She said, "The case was called 'The United States vs. Billie Holiday.' And that's just the way it felt."

Billie's life after her release from prison was a roller-coaster ride of singing appearances and narcotics. A highlight came in 1954 when she went on her first tour in Europe and sang in Germany, Holland, Belgium, France, Switzerland, and Scandinavia. The audiences were so enthusiastic and receptive that she said they brought a new meaning to her life. She said, "The stuff they wrote about me in Europe made me feel alive." She mused that if she had this kind of encouragement years earlier, she might have had more left of her morale and voice.

In 1956, Billie married Louis McKay, whom she had known for twenty years. He went with her on her tours in the United States and Europe and gave her a sense of security that she never had before. In 1956, her autobiography *Lady Sings the Blues* (written with William Duffy) was published. She later admitted that she did not write any of her "autobiography" and claimed that she had never even read it. Regardless, the account of her life was brutally honest. Biographers still doubt all the facts in the book, but the majority of those that read it got the main message.

In 1958, she filed for divorce from McKay. At 3:20 A.M., on July 17, 1959, she died at the age of forty-four. The medical report listed her cause of death as congestion of the lungs, complicated by heart failure. As one jazz writer put it, "She had been dying by inches for years." Billie Holiday may have died all too young, but her legacy lives on. Recordings like *Lady in Satin* and the recording she made with Lester Young and Columbia Records remain the very epitome of great jazz and pop singing and continue to sell in the millions. In 1973, the movie based on her autobiography, *Lady Sings the Blues*, starring Diana Ross opened to wide critical acclaim.

33. MAUREEN FITZSIMONS O'HARA

B.1920
ACTRESS

As a woman I am proud to say that I stood toe-to-toe with the best of them and made my mark on my own terms.

—Maureen O'Hara

Above all else, deep in my soul, I'm a tough Irishwoman.

—Maureen O'Hara

I prefer the company of men, except for Maureen O'Hara. She's the greatest guy I ever met.

—John Wayne

The best effin' actress in Hollywood.

—John Ford

Perhaps no other woman has come to embody the image of the fiery, formidable Irish colleen more than Maureen O'Hara. From the moment she graced the screen as Mary Kate Danaher in John Ford's tour-de-force *The Quiet Man*, she embodied the kind of brassy, brainy woman that every woman wanted to be—and every man wanted to spar with. To the public, she was a host of superlatives: the ultimate screen siren, "a woman who gave as good as she got with the Duke," the "first woman swashbuckler," the "Pirate Queen," "Frozen Champagne," "Window Dressing," "Big Red," "The Queen of Technicolor," and in her own words "the toughest Irish lass who ever took on Hollywood." But behind the scenes, Maureen O'Hara's journey from Ranelagh, County Dublin, in Ireland to the silver screen was hard won and filled with prejudice, troubled marriages, and the pervasive belief that it really is a man's world. Despite seemingly insurmountable obstacles, this was one woman who managed to prove them wrong—and forge a remarkable sixty-year career in "an absurdly masculine profession."

Maureen Fitzsimons O'Hara was born the second of six children on August 17, 1920, in Ranelagh, a middle-class suburb of Dublin, to Marguerita Lilburn Fitzsimons, considered one of the most beautiful women in Ireland, and the businessman Charles Fitzsimons from County Meath. It is no surprise that this gifted woman would come from such a successful family. Maureen's mother was an accomplished contralto, her father was part owner of the renowned Irish soccer team the Shamrock Rovers, and her older sister Peggy was a talented soprano who was invited to sing all over the country at state and diplomatic affairs. Her younger siblings Florrie, Charles, Margot, and James also possessed the same star quality, rounding out one of the most beautiful and gifted families in the Dublin area.

Even from her childhood years, signs of her greatness were already being foretold. Much like Brigid before her, Maureen received a prophecy that would color the rest of her life. When she was five years old, a gypsy woman came to the Fitzsimons's house and told her, "You will leave Ireland one day and become a very famous woman known all around the world. You are going to make a fortune and be very, very rich." Maureen countered, "I will never leave Ireland," but her fate was sealed. She knew her destiny and that she would "set the world on fire."

As a child, Maureen was every inch the tough competitor that she would remain her entire life. She excelled at all sports including Irish field hockey, and she begged her father to form a women's soccer team so she could play, but she also loved to sing and perform in the organized stage shows in the Fitzsimons's backyard starring her brothers and sisters. At the age of six, she gave her first dramatic performance (a poetry recital) and began to take singing and acting lessons. By that time, she knew she wanted to become a great actress and joined the Rathmines Theatre Company, working after school and into the evenings. While

Maureen realized that pursuing an acting career would leave little time for a normal childhood, she chased her dream ardently.

When she was twelve years old, a cruel but life-changing incident at the Irish Sisters of Charity School in Milltown, Ireland, made Maureen more resolute than ever. Two teachers at the school tormented her relentlessly. Perhaps it was jealousy, and perhaps they realized the same truth that the gypsy woman knew years before—that Maureen was destined for greatness. Whatever their motivations, they made fun of her when she and her sister walked down the hall in new sweaters, taunted her when she won an acting competition at a festival, and made her stand in front of her class and told her to show what she had done to win the prize. She refused and stood in front of the class defiantly while the teachers and class laughed. True to form, she promised herself that the "two old biddies would never beat me" and that she would win. It was on that day that she vowed to stand up to everyone and "take it on the chin." And she promised herself she would be a famous actress and that the class would brag that she was in their class. She would also tell the world how much they had hurt her.

Fortunately, Maureen's mother realized she was serious about acting and sent her to elocution school, and her career began to gather steam. She won national acting Feis awards for drama and theater as a teenager and was contacted by Radio Telefis Eireann (RTE) and promptly hired to act in classical plays on the radio. The RTE was the only radio station in Ireland, so the entire country heard her performances. By the age of thirteen, she was one of Ireland's most famous actresses. Despite her phenomenal achievements, Maureen's mother and father were practical, which is why they insisted that Maureen enroll in secretarial and bookkeeping classes. She became a trained stenographer and bookkeeper, which would later boost her film career when taking dictation for the script of *The Quiet Man* from the director John Ford.

In 1934, just barely shy of her fourteenth birthday, Maureen realized another dream: she was accepted into the prestigious Abbey Theatre in Dublin. Even though she was hired to do mostly manual labor, it was an opportunity that would change her life. While at the Abbey, Maureen was offered a screen test in London at Elstree Studios, which required that she dress in a "gold lamé dress with flapping sleeves like wings." The entire scene called for her to walk repeatedly to a ringing telephone, pick up the receiver, and then slam it down.

She hated the heavy makeup and ornate costume, and she thought the whole experience was ridiculous. The screen test gave her a bad feeling about movies, and she quickly returned to the Abbey. It was there that she had her first leading stage role and where an agent introduced her to the actor Charles Laughton.

Laughton and his partner, Eric Pommer, owned the film company Mayflower Pictures and were looking for a young woman who could fill the leading role in their new picture *Jamaica Inn,* which was directed by Alfred Hitchcock. Laughton asked her to read from a script but she politely declined, stating that she could not read a script she had not read all the way through beforehand. When Laughton asked her if there was any film footage of her, she told him about the screen test. While his reaction to the test was similar to Maureen's, he couldn't forget Maureen's hauntingly beautiful eyes and her obvious acting talent. The next day he called his partner and showed him Maureen's test. Pommer found that her eyes were so haunting that he wanted to sign her immediately. When Maureen went back to Dublin, she found an offer of a seven-year contract waiting for her from Mayflower Pictures. Because she was only seventeen years old, the contract was signed not only by Maureen but also by her parents.

Her movie career had officially begun—she would be costarring in *Jamaica Inn*, opposite Charles Laughton. Before filming, Pommer and Laughton decided that Maureen's last name Fitzsimons was a bit too long for the marquee and changed it to O'Hara.

Jamaica Inn was a great success and made Maureen a star. Then glowing reviews called her the "girl with the black cherry eyes." *Jamaica Inn* would not only change Maureen's professional life but her personal life as well. She met George Brown, a member of the production crew on set and began dating him. Maureen was not really interested, but he pursued her during and after the filming so fervently that she relented. Because her parents were so strict and her acting career took so much of her time, she had never really dated. Ironically, one of the most beautiful women in the world had no experience with men. Maureen was so young that when Laughton offered her the female lead of Esmeralda in *The Hunchback of Notre Dame*, her mother went with her to Hollywood.

But George continued his relentless courtship, calling her even when she was on set. She finally gave in to his persistence and agreed to meet him at an address he gave her; a house where he had arranged for an official to marry them. Maureen was so stunned that she went through the ceremony as if in a dream, and she was married before she realized what had happened. Still in shock and only eighteen years old, she did not tell her mother, but Marguerita found the wedding ring in her purse and confronted her. She told her mother that she did not know why she had married Brown

Although her romantic life was already in turmoil, *The Hunchback of Notre Dame* was a major success. At nineteen, Maureen had already starred in two major motion pictures with Laughton, establishing her as one of Hollywood's premiere leading ladies, and she remained so throughout her career. Maureen's contract was then bought by RKO, which disconcerted her because it would mean she was owned by a studio and trapped in Hollywood. More important, it meant that she would not be able to go home to her beloved Ireland. It was 1939, and the war was beginning in Europe, making travel almost impossible. RKO was also insistent on casting her in "dud" movies because it believed that she could save them. But Maureen had even larger obstacles to overcome. Turning to Laughton for help with her troubled marriage to George Brown, she finally got an annulment in 1941, forever severing at least one bad relationship in her life.

She married William Houston Price in 1941, seventy-five days after her divorce from Brown. Maureen had met Price when he was the dialogue coach on *Hunchback*, and much like Brown, he had pursued her since then and pressured her to end her marriage. Already burned by one marriage, she was hesitant to marry him but eventually gave in. Immediately after the wedding, she realized that he had a serious drinking problem and was often gone for days. She would later lament that she could not believe that she made the same mistake twice, allowing two men to pressure her into relationships she did not want. She and Price were officially divorced in July 1952.

While the stunning movie star seemed destined for misfortune in love, she was poised for superstardom in Hollywood. In 1941, the same year as her ill-fated marriage to Price, the director John Ford cast Maureen as the lovely Anghared in the 20th Century-Fox film *How Green Was My Valley*, beginning a lifelong friendship between them. Ford and O'Hara made five memorable movies together: *How Green Was My Valley*, *Rio Grande*, *The Quiet Man*, *Wings of Eagles*, and *The Long Gray Line*. Ford later described Maureen as "the best bloody actress in Hollywood." In a stroke of genius, Ford paired her with John Wayne—the perfect match to the equally powerful Maureen O'Hara. While she stood five feet, eight inches tall, Wayne was a strapping six foot, four inches, and her sensual, yet fiery appeal gave Wayne even more sex appeal. Suddenly, audiences became intoxicated by the Wayne and O'Hara chemistry on screen, and she went on to make five pictures with him.

As her star was constantly on the rise, Maureen made numerous television appearances in the 1950s, '60s and '70s, which gave her the opportunity to pursue her love of singing on variety shows starring Perry Como, Andy Williams, Ernie Ford, George Gobel, Bob Hope, and Garry Moore. She also starred in several dramas on television and was acclaimed for her performance in *Mrs. Miniver*. Her performance in the Broadway musical *Christine*, based on a story by Pearl Buck, was equally lauded by critics.

Throughout her career, she remained the consummate professional, respected by those who worked with her and adored by directors. Unlike many actresses of her day, she was no prima donna, and she always came to the set prepared, with her lines learned, and ready to deliver her best performance. Leading men like Jimmy Stewart, Henry Fonda, Brian Keith, and John Wayne always looked forward to working with her, and she captivated some of the most respected directors in Hollywood, including Alfred Hitchcock, Walter Lang, John M. Stahl, and Carol Reed.

In 1968, she enjoyed her first happy marriage to Charles Blair, the famous aviator who had been a friend of her family for many years. Blair had been a brigadier general in the air force, a senior pilot with Pan American, and was famous for his incredible record-breaking aeronautic achievements. It was then that she decided to become a full-time wife and retired from films in 1973 after making the TV movie *The Red Pony* with Henry Fonda. Blair and Maureen soon bought and managed a commuter seaplane service in the Caribbean called Antilles Airboats and also published the magazine on the Virgin Islands called *The Virgin Islander*, for which she began writing the monthly column Maureen O'Hara Says. . . . As the wife of Charles Blair, Maureen said, "I got to live the adventures I'd only acted out on the Fox and Universal lots." Tragically, Blair was killed in a plane crash in 1978. Maureen was devastated; she called her years with Blair ten of the happiest years of her life. In spite of her grief, she remained strong and vital and was elected chief executive officer and president of Antilles Airboats. She was the first woman president of a scheduled airline in the United States. In the 1990s, she became president of a golf club in Ireland, before retiring to St. Croix in the Virgin Islands. She also spends time in New York, Los Angeles, and Ireland.

She comes out of retirement on occasion to make a few select movies. In 1991, she starred with John Candy in *Only the Lonely,* and in 1995 she starred in a made-for-TV movie called *The Christmas Box* on CBS. Her most recent movie, *Last Dance,* aired on CBS in October 2001. Although she has made fewer movies in the last decade, she remains every inch the movie star. Two of her Web sites still receive more than 250,000 hits per day. Her memoir *'Tis Herself,* which was published by Simon and Schuster in 2004, received critical acclaim and her promotional tour in Los Angeles, New York City, and later in Ireland drew thousands of fans. That same year, she was honored in Galway by the Galway Film Festival and by the Irish Film Institute with its prestigious Lifetime Achievement Award. Maureen has also received numerous awards from cities and countries around the world, including Boston, Los Angeles, Fort Worth, Miami, New York, and Mexico, as well as many awards for her service to charities and to the military, such as the Variety Boys Club Heart Award, the Military Order of the Purple Heart Award "for meritorious and conspicuous service," and the John F. Kennedy Memorial Award (she is the first and only woman to receive this award to date) as an "Outstanding

American of Irish descent for service to God and Country." Throughout her career, she has won professional accolades and awards such as the *Irish America Magazine* Lifetime Achievement Award, the Producer's Guild of America Award, the Irish Heritage Award, the Helen Hayes Lifetime Achievement Award, and Woman of the Year from *Irish America Magazine* in 2004. She will always be remembered for her incredible beauty, her lovely, lyric soprano voice, her athletic ability that allowed her to perform physical feats that most actresses couldn't begin to attempt, but still remain totally feminine and elegant, and, most important, her ability to create an equality to her male costars.

Above all, she became the epitome of what she so famously thought being an Irishwoman should mean: "Strong and feisty, has guts, stands up for what she believes, believes she is the best at what she does, face any hazard, loyal to her kinsmen, accepting of others, will sock you in the jaw if you have it coming, only on her knees before God."

34. FLANNERY O'CONNOR

1925–1964

AUTHOR

It is better to be young in your failures than old in your successes.

—Flannery O'Connor

Although she wrote only thirty-one short stories and two novels, some critics consider Flannery O'Connor the finest short story writer of the twentieth century. With her brilliant use of foreshadowing, brutal imagery, and unerring ear for lyrical dialogue, she helped reshape the American Gothic tradition in literature, and gave new voice to American women writers.

Mary Flannery O'Connor was born in Savannah, Georgia, on March 25, 1925, the only child of Edward and Regina O'Connor. The region, which would pervade Flannery's work for the rest of her life, was completely segregated and economically depressed. Flannery enjoyed a stable family life in the parochial Catholic community. She attended St. Vincent's Grammar School for Girls, which was almost exclusively Irish. As she recalls, "I was brought up where there was a colony of the over Irish." Her father, who had roots in County Tipperary, had been a successful real estate agent but began showing signs of illness at a young age. It is more that probable, as Jean Cash observes *in Flannery O'Connor: A Life,* that he may have been suffering from lupus, the same disease that would later plague his daughter.

When Flannery was thirteen, her family moved to Milledgeville, Georgia, where her mother's father had been mayor for several years. Regina O'Connor came from a family of strong women, and the strong sense of matriarchy that Flannery experienced as a child would later become one of the great themes of her fiction. Soon after the move, her father became gravely ill and died suddenly at the age of forty-one. Flannery attended the Peabody School and became art editor of the *Peabody Palladium*. By this time, she had already written three books, *Mistaken Identity*, *Elmo*, and *Gertrude*. Flannery was also dealing with social issues at this time. In a world of Southern belles, she was somewhat homely, and this feeling of inadequacy would often influence her work.

In 1942, she enrolled at the Georgia State College for Women, where she began publishing in *Continuum*, the campus literary magazine. One of her most notable stories of this period was the grim "Elegance Is Its Own Reward." Flannery was already beginning to make a name for herself. In 1945, she was listed in the *Who's Who in American Colleges and Universities*, and exhibited art at the university of Georgia. She was then accepted at Iowa State University, which featured the premiere creative-writing program in the country; she was one of just three women in the program. In 1947, she won a scholarship that would allow for one of her works to be published with Rinehart publishers. The novel was *Wise Blood*, her masterpiece. The same year she received her M.F.A., and spent time at Yaddo, an artist's colony in Saratoga Springs, New York, where she could finish her novel. Yaddo had been home to such well-known American writers as Dorothy Parker, Eudora Welty, and Carson McCullers, and Flannery was certain she could find inspiration there. But Yaddo was not what she expected. Instead of a dedication to a higher calling, she found that the writers there were, not surprisingly, more interested in (in her words) "sex, drugs and godlessness." As her biographer Jean Cash recalls, "She was really shocked to find that many of these gifted fellows appointed to do critical work at Yaddo were unwilling or unable to believe in God."

She left Yaddo and went to live in New York, where she met Mary McCarthy, who shared her growing interest in communism, as well as Robert Giroux, the famed publisher. It was 1949, and Flannery was already ill—she had already undergone kidney surgery. By 1950, she was diagnosed with lupus. After her diagnosis, she decided to return to Milledgeville, and the authoritarian Regina. Perhaps more than the disease itself, acclimating to life with her controlling mother after being so independent was extremely difficult. They moved to Andalusia, a farm out-side of Milledgeville, where Flannery was dependent on Regina for al-most all of her needs. Back in Georgia, she was surrounded by racial tensions, and this fueled her sympathetic treatment of African American characters, although her public statements often seemed ingrained in racism. She was also now surrounded by farm families, and they would have a profound influence on her characters in *Country People* and *The Displaced Person*.

In 1952, *Wise Blood* was published, and the residents of Milledgeville hated the book. They saw it as an indictment of their community. The novel, which deals with a young religious fanatic who tries to start his own "Church Without Christ" was aptly described in advertisements as "a searching novel of sin and redemption." Her second novel, *The Violent Bear It Away,* written in 1960, also explores the life of a young minister who falls from grace. As Flannery would later explain her infatuation with characters of the Protestant faith, "I can write about Protestant be-lievers better than Catholic believers—because they express their belief in diverse kinds of dramatic action which is obvious enough for me to catch. I can't write about anything subtle."

With all her success, Flannery was so ill by this time that she could barely type. Her immune system was seriously compromised and doctors knew very little about the disease. "I write every day for at least two hours," she said in an interview in 1952, "and I spend the rest of my time largely in the society of ducks." She continued to make public appear-ances, however, and between the years of 1953 and 1964, she gave more than sixty lectures and readings. And she kept writing. In 1954, she won the O. Henry contest with her story "Greenleaf." In spite of her brilliance and wide recognition, Flannery could never seem to impress her mother. Regina reportedly fell asleep while reading *Wise Blood*. As Flannery once recalled, "The other day, she asked me why I didn't write something that people liked instead of the kind of thing I do write." She often described her relationship with her mother as "the enduring chill."

Because of her illness, Flannery never married and took a vow of celibacy. In 1953, she did fall in love with Erik Langkjaer, a textbook salesman who worked with Harcourt, but the love was unrequited. From

1955, Flannery was using crutches and suffered chronic hip problems. She also underwent an operation to remove an ovarian tumor, which re-activated the lupus. Flannery died at the age of thirty-nine on August 3, 1964, of kidney failure. Her second collection of short stories, *Everything That Rises Must Converge*, was published posthumously in 1965. In 1978, John Huston directed a movie based on *Wise Blood*. Although Flannery died before she was forty, she is considered to be one of the masters of the short story in American literature, and her work has gone on to influence the work of Louise Erdrich, Sue Miller, and Larry Brown, among others.

35. JACQUELINE LEE BOUVIER KENNEDY

1929–1994

FIRST LADY, ICON

She was a blessing to us and to the Nation, and a lesson to the world on how to do things right, how to be a mother, how to appreciate history, how to be courageous. No one else looked like her, spoke like her, wrote like her, or was so original in the way she did things. No one we knew ever had a better sense of self. She made a rare and noble contribution to the American spirit. But for us, most of all she was a magnificent wife, mother, grandmother, sister, aunt, and friend. . . . She graced our history. And for those of us who knew and loved her, she graced our lives.

—Senator Edward Kennedy at
Jacqueline Kennedy's funeral

To the outside world, she was grace, style, and dignity personified. Behind closed doors, she was the strong-willed, irreverent, and rapier-witted woman who despised the title First Lady, "It sounds like a saddle horse." The brightest light in John F. Kennedy's Camelot, Jacqueline Bouvier was born into wealth and privilege in New York's exclusive Southampton on July 29, 1929, to John "Black Jack" Bouvier, a handsome, rakish stockbroker of French extraction and Janet Lee, a beautiful socialite who hailed from the prestigious Lee family of Virginia. While her childhood was financially secure, it was also marked by disappointments that would later form Jackie's character. Her parents divorced when she was just six, separating her for long periods of time from her beloved father. As a result, young Jackie began to withdraw from the world, pouring her energy into reading, writing, and art. Her solitude made her fiercely independent and private, two qualities that later became her trademarks.

Although most of the world fell in love with her when she became First Lady in 1960, Jackie was a star well before she laid eyes on Jack Kennedy. By the time she was twenty-four, Jackie had been named "Debutante of the Year," attended Vassar College and the Sorbonne, been featured in *Vogue* for winning the prestigious Prix de Paris competition, and earned a degree in French literature from George Washington University. In 1952, Jackie landed her first job at the *Washington Times-Herald* as inquiring photographer and sealed her fate. Her new position entailed roaming the streets of Washington, D.C., and asking its citizens questions that betrayed her classical education: "Chaucer said that what women desire most is power over men. What do you think women desire most?" Although she spent most of her time interviewing people on the street, her new job enabled her to rub shoulders with Washington's power elite. In May 1952, she attended a dinner part hosted by Charlie and Martha Bartlett. One of the guests was John F. Kennedy, a senator from Massachusetts. After a whirlwind romance, Jack Kennedy took her home to meet his father, Ambassador Joseph P. Kennedy.

Although she was about to become a member of the most recognized Irish family in America, Jacqueline Lee Bouvier could claim Irish roots that rivaled those of her husband. Janet Lee's maternal grandfather came to the United States from Ireland during the Potato Famine and was superintendent of New York City Public Schools. This part of family history was later buried when Janet began telling everyone that he was a Civil War veteran from Maryland. While she portrayed herself as being 100 percent French, Jackie was half-Irish and only one-eighth French. While it seems logical that this part of Jackie's family tree would be celebrated and publicized by the most famous Irish Catholic family in the country, it remains the least-known part of her life. Joseph P. Kennedy, being the shrewd politician and clan chieftain that he was, knew how to use her background, and he used it for maximum effect. The Kennedy clan had money, power, fame, and brains. What it needed now for a successful political legacy was cache, and Jackie had that in spades. She had an aristocratic French background, an impressive Vassar education, and the necessary Catholic pedigree that JFK would need for a wife. In Joe's estimation, Jackie's French bloodline added elegance to the Kennedy family. That Jackie was the granddaughter of a Potato Famine immigrant somehow took the glamour out of her impeccable background. Kennedy was also all too familiar with the anti-Irish discrimination that still pervaded the country. He had experienced "the no Irish need apply" philosophy that was still prevalent when he tried to join exclusive clubs in his native Boston. For this reason, he chose to downplay Jackie's Irishness, and it remains a little-acknowledged fact to this day. And it was not the first time that Jackie would prove to be an invaluable asset in Jack's political life.

John and Jacqueline were married on September 12, 1953, in a lavish ceremony that did not include her father—Black Jack had been slighted by Janet Bouvier and was told that he could give the bride away but couldn't attend the reception. Jackie's father headed straight for the nearest bar and never made it to the ceremony. It would be the first of many disappointments for Jackie during her marriage. Despite her incredible strength, she found the first years of married life incredibly difficult. As a political wife, she had to learn to share her husband with his demanding family and most of Washington's movers and shakers. Jack Kennedy was also suffering from Addison's disease, the debilitating disease that attacks the adrenal glands, and Jackie was his constant nursemaid. She changed his bandages, read to him for hours, and never left his side. Ironically, she was experiencing her own health problems, as she suffered from a series of miscarriages. In 1956, after helping her husband campaign during his bid for vice president on Adlai Stevenson's ticket, she gave birth to a stillborn baby girl. In 1957, Jackie suffered an even greater tragedy when Black Jack was diagnosed with liver cancer. He died quickly after and Jackie found out too late to see him.

The following year, life began to look more promising for Jackie. She gave birth to Caroline (a remarkable Irish woman in her own right) on November 27, "the happiest day of her life," and Jack Kennedy was becoming a serious contender for the presidency. The new family was being celebrated everywhere, and Jackie's gift for public relations was beginning to reach its peak. Her glamour, sophistication, beauty, and keen intellect dazzled the public and offered a new and vibrant presence. Jackie soon became Jack's deadliest weapon. From holding press teas to speaking fluent Spanish in front of a crowd in New York, Jackie used all her skills to help Jack's campaign. Though heavily pregnant again, she was a tireless worker for his presidency.

John F. Kennedy was elected in November 1960 as the thirty-fifth president of the United States. At the age of thirty-one, Jackie was one of the youngest First Ladies in history, and her mission was clear from the first moment she set foot in the White House. After a thoroughly depressing tour given by Mamie Eisenhower, Jackie discovered that the White House had become a dismal, dire place in which there was no central heating, abysmal food, and worst of all, a shocking lack of alcohol. Jackie was determined to restore it to its former glory and to bring arts and culture back to the forefront of American life. After being told that the White House budget was too small to accommodate such changes, she took matters into her own hands. Over the next three years, she set out to make the White House "a showcase for great American artists and creative talent" and literally changed it forever. Jack and Jackie began inviting luminaries from the arts and literature like Pablo Casals, Leonard Bernstein, and William Styron. True to her promise to make the White House the grandest house in the United States, Jackie immediately founded the Fine Arts Committee for the White House, an organization dedicated to finding and funding authentic furniture, and she created the White House Historical Association, an umbrella organization dedicated to preserving presidential history. In a stroke of genius, she conceived and single-handedly oversaw the production of the *White House Guidebook*, which has sold 8 million copies over the years and continues to help fund art, furniture, and portraits for the White House to this day. Always a dedicated mother, she built a nursery and kindergarten for the children of White House employees, which she personally directed. And in 1961, she initiated the appointment of a Special Consultant to the President on the Arts. Over the years, Jackie became a practiced diplomat, charming Nikita Khrushchev and captivating Charles de Gaulle and the whole of France with her Chanel couture and flawless French accent. As First Lady, she showed the American public how to dress, how to act, and how to raise their children. And in November 1963, she showed the country how to grieve. As de Gaulle observed, "She gave the world an example of how to behave."

After JFK's assassination on November 22, 1963, Jackie helped give birth to his legacy, exhibiting a strength and dignity that gave the American public the courage to move on. She planned the state funeral according to the ceremony for President Abraham Lincoln, and she oversaw every detail. Jackie made the unprecedented and very brave decision to walk behind her husband's coffin during the funeral procession, and even though it was a security nightmare, she refused to be swayed. Shortly after the funeral, Jackie made another characteristically brilliant move. She invited Theodore White, the author of *The Making of a President,* to the Kennedy Compound in Hyannis Port, and created one of the lasting myths in history—JFK's Camelot—thereby sealing her husband's place in history.

In the following years, Jackie's will and strength never waivered. She remained a fiercely devoted mother to her children and a tireless and loyal friend to her brother-in-law, Robert F. Kennedy, until his assassination in 1968. (She was the only one who had the courage to turn off the machines in the hospital when it was clear Bobby had been rendered brain dead.) She survived an arduous marriage to Aristotle Onassis, moved to New York, and acquired a prestigious job at Viking Press as an editor—for $10,000 a year. In 1979, she continued to build Jack's legacy when she opened the John F. Kennedy Public Library, a beautiful and moving tribute to her husband's life and presidency.

Through it all, she remained very much her own woman. In her final years, she became a respected editor at Doubleday, found a worthy companion in the diamond merchant Maurice Tempelsman, and enjoyed her new role as a grandmother. In 1993, at the height of her happiness, Jackie was diagnosed with non-Hodgkins lymphoma. It was her final life event and she handled it with her signature grace. As Edna O'Brien observed, "She was secretive about her life and she was secretive about her death." She died on May 19, 1994, and was buried in Arlington Cemetery, next to her husband. She remains a part of Camelot's legacy forever.

36. GRACE KELLY

1929–1982
ACTRESS

Emancipation of women has made them lose their mystery.

—Grace Kelly

The freedom of the press works in such a way that there is not much freedom from it.

—Grace Kelly

Hollywood amuses me. Holier-than-thou for the public and unholier-than-the-devil in reality.

—Grace Kelly

I've worked with many fine actresses, but in my opinion the best actress I ever worked with was Grace Kelly. Ingrid, Audrey, Deborah Kerr were splendid, splendid actresses, but Grace was utterly relaxed—the most extraordinary actress ever.

—Cary Grant

If you've ever played a love scene with her, you'd know she's not cold . . . besides, Grace has that twinkle and touch of larceny in her eye.

—James Stewart

Hailed as "America's fairytale princess," her beauty, elegance, and sophistication continue to captivate fans all over the world, and more than twenty years after her death she ranks among the top 100 Hollywood stars of all time. The ultimate "Hitchcock Blonde," Grace Kelly's cool icy looks would come to symbolize patrician elegance, but this grand-daughter of Irish immigrants was so much more than another beautiful face. Her steely determination, sophistication, and sly intelligence would enable her to survive and excel in the movie business, a world previously dominated by men. And while she fought to shake off the aloof image she cultivated both on and off screen, she was in reality a sensual and passion-ate woman whose life ended far too soon.

Grace Patricia Kelly was born in Philadelphia on November 12, 1929, to John and Margaret Kelly. Of Irish German descent, Grace was the third oldest of four children in the Kelly family: Peggy (b. 1925), John Jr. (b. 1927), Grace (b. 1929), and Elizabeth Anne (b. 1933). Her father's fam-ily was exceedingly accomplished—one of Grace's uncles was the Pulitzer Prize playwright George Kelly, while another was the famous vaudeville comedian Walter Kelly. Grace's father was a wealthy building contractor, and "Kelly for Brickwork" was a familiar sign at area job sites in Phila-delphia.

Jack Kelly was also a famous sculler in a city that revered water rac-ing. The first American to win an Olympic sculling race, he was voted the greatest oarsman in U.S. history. Despite his ability, he was eliminated as an entry in the Diamond Sculls at England's Henley Royal Regatta on the grounds that he had performed manual labor. The Regatta had a code that allowed only "gentlemen" to race. He reared his only son, John Jr. ("Kell"), to be a famous sculler who would someday avenge his father's rejection. Because Jack was so focused on Kell and Grace was female, she eluded her father's attention and he was unimpressed by her accomplish-ments. While many believe that she was born to the role of princess, she was never a debutante and never applied for admission nor was received in mainline Philadelphia society. The Kelly family was Roman Catholic and newly rich, two strikes against admission to the highly restrictive so-cial registry of that day.

The Kellys were strict with their children, particularly the girls. They were raised in the Catholic Church and Grace's mother was extremely re-ligious. The children were expected to do chores and spend time with the family, and much of the family life was focused around Kell's athletic ca-reer. While her brother trained for rowing, Grace spent her time at school, at home doing homework and reading, and at the Old Academy Players acting in plays.

Influenced by her aunt and uncle's careers in the theater, Grace wanted to become an actress from an early age. Those who believe in fate might also attribute Grace's acting career to her name. Grace was named for her aunt Grace, her father's late sister, who had been an actress. When her sister Peggy was christened, her grandmother Kelly told the parents that she wished that they had named the baby Grace. Her grandmother said, "It's an old Irish belief that if you name a baby after a talented relative, sometimes the talent rubs off on the namesake."

As a young girl, Grace was overshadowed by her famous uncles and her brother. After her high school graduation in 1947, she went to New York. She applied for college but was denied admission to Bennington College in Vermont. She was really only interested in studying acting at the American Academy of Dramatic Arts. Her father warned her about the "dangerous profession" that her famous uncles had pursued but grudgingly gave his permission.

Set on stardom, she moved into the Barbizon Hotel for Women in New York, where many other soon-to-be famous actresses lived, including Candice Bergen, Liza Minnelli, Cloris Leachman, and Ali MacGraw. She was admitted to the American Academy of Dramatic Arts but the admissions officers described Grace's voice as "nasal" and "improperly placed." She took speech classes while studying acting, during which her teacher told her she had to lose her Philadelphia accent. When she went home, she no longer talked like her father, mother, brother, or sisters. Her family teased her mercilessly and called her new manner of speaking "Gracie's new voice." Some of her friends said she was actually speaking in a "British accent." Grace defended herself, saying frostily, "I must talk this way for my work."

Soon after she moved to New York, she became a successful model. She promoted Old Gold cigarettes and appeared on the covers of magazines such as *Cosmopolitan* and *Redbook*. Then she made several television commercials, which she thought were terrible. She quipped, "Anyone watching me give the pitch for Old Golds would have switched to Camels." She also performed in several television dramas. Implausibly, even Grace Kelly suffered major rejection. When she auditioned for summer stock and Broadway plays, many casting directors found her to be too tall (she was reportedly five feet, six or seven inches), too leggy, too intelligent looking, or too mature.

Finally, she made her debut on Broadway in 1949. Her first Broadway role was playing Raymond Massey's daughter in August Strindberg's *The Father*. The reviewer Brooks Atkinson of the *New York Times* wrote, "Grace Kelly gives a charming, pliable performance of the bewildered and brokenhearted daughter." In 1950, Grace received a plaque from the publication *Theatre World* proclaiming her one of twelve of the most promising personalities of the Broadway stage for 1950.

While many believe that Grace was as lucky as she was talented, she actually had to overcome major obstacles when she moved to southern California to work in movies. Despite her deadly good looks, she was not regarded as the "Hollywood type." While she was poised and well bred, she was also shy and serious. In addition, many directors and casting agents still found Grace's voice extremely unusual. While in New York, Grace had turned down small movie roles because she did not want to be "another starlet."

Nevertheless, in 1951 she appeared in her first film, *Fourteen Hours*, when she was twenty-two. The role was a small part, but she was offered a contract after the picture was completed. In 1952, she was offered the role of Amy Kane in *High Noon* (1952), a well-received but controversial western starring Gary Cooper and Lloyd Bridges. In spite of good reviews, Grace was very critical of her performance. She compared her ability to convey emotion to Gary Cooper's expressiveness and began to doubt whether she should continue her movie career. The director John Ford, however, disagreed with this assessment. When he saw a test that Grace made for another movie, he commented, "This is no mere beauty. This girl can act. I want her for *Mogambo*." MGM wouldn't take her unless she signed a seven-year contract—the first major one that Grace signed. She made *Mogambo* in 1953 with Clark Gable and Ava Gardner. This role won her an Academy Award nomination and a Golden Globe for Best Supporting Actress. Most enviably, she also had an affair with

Gable. When she was asked to defend her behavior, she retorted, "What else is there to do if you're alone in a tent in Africa with Clark Gable?"

Her role in *High Noon* and a screen test for the film *Taxi* attracted the interest of the director Alfred Hitchcock. Hitchcock enlisted Edith Head to transform Grace into his ideal of the elegant, beautiful blonde. In 1954, Hitchcock featured her in *Dial M for Murder*, which made her a star, and in *Rear Window* with James Stewart. She was extremely busy that year appearing in three other films, including *The Country Girl* with Bing Crosby. She won both an Academy Award and a Golden Globe for Best Actress for *The Country Girl*. When she came home with an Academy Award for Best Actress, Grace Kelly was now a movie star. Finally, her father had to accept that his daughter was successful and had fulfilled a greater dream than his own. His daughter, who had received the least of his attention and devotion, was now *the* "Grace Kelly."

Until this time of her life, very little is mentioned about her relationships with men. She dated several of her handsome costars, including Gary Cooper, William Holden, and Bing Crosby, as well as Oleg Cassini. Despite her later reputation for promiscuity, many actors thought she was cold and aloof. Cooper enthusiastically discounted that belief. "Looked like she was a cold dish with a man until you got her pants down," he once recalled. "Then she'd explode!" By this time, she was so desired that the young bride Jackie Kennedy enlisted Grace's help in "cheering" her husband up during his illness with Addison's disease. Legend has it that Grace pretended to be a "nurse" when visiting Jack Kennedy at his Georgetown home. After making *The Country Girl*, Crosby proposed to Grace but she turned him down.

During the summer of 1954, Grace's love life would take a dramatic turn. Grace and Cary Grant were on the French Riviera working on the Hitchcock movie *To Catch a Thief*. After she filmed the scene where she speeds along the Moyen Corniche to quickly get away from a tailing police car, she had time to look at the Mediterranean and the countryside along the coast. She asked the screenwriter, John Michael Hayes, "Whose gardens are those?" He told her they belonged to Prince Grimaldi (Prince Rainier). In March 1955, she received a call from Rupert Allan, *Look* magazine's West Coast editor, extending an invitation from the French government to attend the Cannes Film Festival in May. *The Country Girl* would be shown at the festival, and Prince Rainier would be attending. One of the twentieth centuries great romances was about to be born.

While she dated Prince Rainier, Grace continued to make movies. In 1956, she starred in the musical comedy *High Society*, which also starred Frank Sinatra and Crosby. The movie was well received and the success of the song "True Love" from the movie earned Grace a gold record. She was also voted the Golden Globe's World Film Favorite Actor, Female. This was her final acting performance before she became engaged to Prince Rainier. Forthright to the end, she explained her reason for leaving Hollywood: "I'll tell you one of the reasons I'm ready to leave. When I first came to Hollywood five years ago, my makeup call was at eight in the morning. On this movie it's been put back to seven-thirty. Every day I see Joan Crawford, who's been in makeup since five, and Loretta Young, who's been there since four in the morning. I'll be goddamned if I'm going to stay in a business where I have to get up earlier and earlier and it takes longer and longer for me to get in front of a camera."

Although the story seemed like a fairy tale, the real story was much more pragmatic. Prince Rainier needed a wife because if there was no heir to the throne, Monaco would again be part of France after his death and its citizens would have to pay French taxes. Grace was fertile, Catholic, and already Hollywood royalty. Equally practical, Grace thought it was time for her to select a man who would finally meet with her parents' approval. When Grace announced her engagement to Prince Rainier, a reporter called her father to ask him about the family's feelings about the engagement. Jack Kelly responded, "We're not impressed by royalty. We're impressed by the man. Marriage is not a game of musical chairs with us. We play for keeps."

In 1956, Grace married Prince Rainier Grimaldi of Monaco in what was dubbed "the Wedding of the Century" and became Her Serene Highness Princess Grace of Monaco. The wedding was highly publicized and articles featured pictures and descriptions of Grace's sublime dress as well as all the details about the wedding. The famous guests at the wedding included Aristotle Onassis, Gloria Swanson, and Ava Gardner. Before the marriage, she was required to take a fertility test and to sign an agreement to relinquish the children if there was a divorce. She was also required to renounce her U.S. citizenship. After she was married, she was forced to give up her successful acting career because of her royal status and according to most accounts, the life of a princess was not happily ever after. She missed the United States and her acting career. She was lonely and bored and eventually became depressed. However, she and Prince Rainier did have three children who gave her great joy: Caroline, Albert, and Stephanie.

Although she had left her movie career behind despite many offers to return to Hollywood, she was active in charity and cultural work and continued to receive publicity for her beauty, style, and talents. She became the president of the American Red Cross and continued to champion the cause of aid to underdeveloped nations. The Kelly bag, by Hermes, was named for her after she was photographed carrying one while stepping off a plane. It remains one of the most sought-after handbags in the world and boasts a waiting list of more than two years. In 1977, the gallery Faubourg St. Honore in Paris exhibited Grace's dried flower compositions. In 1978, Grace toured the northeastern United States with a program of poetry on "Birds, Beasts, and Flowers." Philadelphia honored Grace in the spring of 1982 with the Grace Kelly Film Festival.

In an ironic twist, Grace Kelly died in a car accident on a cliff road she had known so well since her first visit to the Riviera. The spot is said to be the same one where the picnic scene from *To Catch a Thief* was filmed in 1954—the spot where she first saw Prince Rainier's gardens. She apparently suffered a stroke and the car plunged down an embankment. She was just fifty-two years old and had a lifelong fear of driving.

After her death, Prince Rainier paid his wife the ultimate tribute by saying, "She is always in our hearts and in our thoughts."

37. SANDRA DAY O'CONNOR

B.1930
SUPREME COURT JUSTICE

Society as a whole benefits immeasurably from a climate in which all persons, regardless of race or gender, may have the opportunity to earn respect, responsibility, advancement and remuneration based on ability.
—Sandra Day O'Connor

The more education a woman has, the wider the gap between men's and women's earnings for the same work.
—Sandra Day O'Connor

The power I exert on the court depends on the power of my arguments, not on my gender.
—Sandra Day O'Connor

It is difficult to discern a serious threat to religious liberty from a room of silent, thoughtful schoolchildren.
—Sandra Day O'Connor

Thomas Jefferson and James Madison would be turning over in their graves right now, but let's hope that Abigail Adams would be pleased.
—Sandra Day O'Connor

The first female associate justice of the U.S. Supreme Court from 1981 to 2006, she is considered by many to be the most powerful woman in the United States. In 2004, *Forbes* magazine called her the fourth most powerful woman in the United States and the sixth most powerful in the world. With her case-by-case approach to jurisprudence and her relatively moderate political views, she was the crucial swing vote of the Court for many of her final years on the bench. Sandra Day O'Connor was a moderate conservative on an ideologically polarized Court and often cast the deciding vote in 5-4 decisions dealing with some of the most important and contentious issues of public debate. An advocate of women's rights throughout her career, she was a role model to feminists throughout the country, and in light of her successor John Roberts, her advocacy for reproductive rights remains a revelation.

Sandra Day O'Connor was born on March 26, 1930, in El Paso, Texas. Her parents, Harry and Ada Mae Wilkey Day, were both from Irish American families. The family owned the Lazy B Cattle Ranch, a 155,000-acre ranch in southeastern Arizona. Her parents inherited the ranch from grandfather Henry Clay Day, who bought the land and set up the ranch in the 1880s, when Arizona was still a territory. He had moved from Vermont and had planned to live in California and let his foreman manage the ranch. But he found that the foreman and others were stealing from him, so he was forced to live on the ranch. Sandra's father, who was the last of five children, lived on the ranch until he was in elementary school. Then his father moved the family back to Pasadena so that the children could go to school there. After high school, he planned to go to college in California but his father died suddenly. When Harry discovered that the foreman had left the ranch in serious financial trouble, he moved back to the ranch to manage it alone. He met Sandra's mother when he went to El Paso to buy cattle from Mae's father. They maintained a long-distance romance until they married in 1917 and settled at the Lazy B. Sandra said her father would often joke that he "went to buy some bulls from her father and she was part of the deal." They were married three years before they had Sandra.

The ranch was very isolated and still very rustic when Sandra's parents moved there, so life was difficult. There was no electricity or running water until she was seven. The family's nearest neighbors lived twenty-five miles away, so the family spent most of their time in isolation. Also, Sandra was an only child for many years; her younger brother and sister were not born until she was eight years old. To combat the loneliness, she became friends with many of the ranch's cowboys. She also had many pets, including dogs, horses, cats, and even a bobcat. She spent her time reading, helping with many ranch activities, and riding horses. When she was seven, she learned to drive and by the time she was eight, she could fire rifles and ride horses proficiently.

Sandra's mother, who was a college graduate and a sophisticated young woman, taught her to read when she was four. The ranch's isolation made it difficult to provide formal education and there were no adequate schools in the area, so her parents sent her to live with her grandmother in El Paso when she was five. She attended Radford School, a private school for girls, from kindergarten until she was thirteen. Sandra was apparently a gifted student; she was allowed to skip a grade and still maintained excellent grades. Although she went home for the summer, she missed her parents and the ranch and grew more and more homesick. After her sister Ann and her brother Alan were born, she begged to live at home and attend a local school. She returned to Arizona for a year when she was thirteen to attend school. The nearest school was a twenty-two-mile walk away, so she left home before daylight and returned after dark. The next year she was back at Radford. After another year at Radford, she transferred to Austin High School in El Paso, where she graduated when she was sixteen.

Because she lived with her grandmother for much of her childhood, Sandra attributes much of her later success to her grandmother's influence. Her grandmother instilled confidence in her by believing in her ability to succeed in any endeavor. Sandra later said that confidence inspired her to persevere and to refuse to admit defeat.

When she graduated, she was accepted at Stanford University, where she majored in economics. She chose economics because she intended to operate her own ranch or possibly the Lazy B Ranch. She was intrigued by law when her parents were involved in a legal dispute over her family's ranch. When she graduated with a bachelor's degree in economics in 1956, she decided to enroll at Stanford Law School. While in law school, she served on the *Stanford Law Review* and received membership in the Order of the Coif, a legal honor society. She also met her future husband, John Jay O'Connor, who was also a law student. Because she was a brilliant student, she was able to complete law school in two years rather than the usual three years. Sandra graduated third out of a class of 102. Coincidentally, William H. Rehnquist, who would become chief justice, was first in her class. She married John O'Connor soon after her graduation in 1952.

After she graduated, she had difficulty finding a job. None of the law firms in California would hire her and only one offered her a position as a legal secretary. Since she could not find a job with a firm, she went into public service. She became the deputy county attorney for San Mateo, California. John graduated from Stanford a year later, and he was drafted by the army into the Judge Advocate General (JAG) Corps. When he was sent to Frankfurt, Germany, for three years, Sandra was able to go with him. While in Germany, Sandra served as a civilian lawyer in the Quartermaster's Corps. During his service, they traveled in Europe extensively. They even lived in a Swiss chalet for several months. In 1957, the couple returned to the United States and decided to move to Phoenix, Arizona.

When they moved to Phoenix, she again had difficulty obtaining a position with any law firm. She and an associate decided to start their own firm. They were essentially job sharing and took any small cases that came their way. Within the next six years, Sandra and John had three sons: Scott, Jay, and Brian. The job-sharing arrangement worked well when her first son was born because she could be home for half a day with her son. After her second son was born, Sandra stopped working temporarily to take care of the children. She also volunteered for many charities and organizations, such as the Arizona State Hospital, the Arizona State Bar, the Salvation Army, and various local schools. She also became involved with the Arizona Republican Party.

After she was home five years as a full-time mother, she became an assistant state attorney general in Arizona from 1965 to 1969. This job launched her political career. The Arizona governor Jack Williams appointed O'Connor to occupy a vacant seat. She was elected to the state senate for two more terms and eventually became the first female majority leader in the United States. Her voting record as a legislator, which ranged from moderate to conservative, predicted her voting record as a judge. She favored limiting government spending, restoring the death penalty, and some selected feminist issues (e.g., she voted for the Equal Rights Amendment and for some revisions in legislation designed to protect women in a paternalistic manner). She also seemed to generally favor women's right to abortion, but her voting record was mixed. She voted to repeal Arizona's laws that essentially made abortion illegal. Later, she opposed a resolution seeking a constitutional ban on abortion, and she opposed an attempt to limit access to abortion. However, she voted to restrict state funds for poor women's abortions and also supported the right of hospital employees to refuse to perform abortions.

In 1974, Sandra ran for a judgeship on the Maricopa County Superior Court. While serving on the bench, she gained the reputation of being a fair but tough judge. During her tenure as a superior court judge, she remained politically active. She was an alternate delegate to the 1972 Republican National Convention and cochaired Richard Nixon's reelection committee in Arizona. In 1976, she backed Ronald Reagan when he opposed President Gerald Ford for the Republican nomination for president. In 1978, state Republican leaders urged her to consider a campaign for the governorship, but Sandra declined.

In 1979, the governor appointed Sandra to the Arizona Court of Appeals. In the beginning, she was regarded as a competent judge but undistinguished. She began to attract some attention when she attended a judicial conference in England with Chief Justice Warren Burger, and later she participated in a program on federalism and the state courts, in which she expressed her judicial philosophy. She wrote an article in 1981 for the *William and Mary Law Review* stating that if state courts had already given a matter full and fair treatment, then federal judges should refuse to intervene or hear appeals. This belief that federal and state judges were equally competent and that federal judges should not intervene would continue to be her belief throughout her career.

While she was serving as a judge, Reagan was elected president, and he promised to appoint the first woman to the Supreme Court. When Justice Potter Stewart retired in 1981, Reagan nominated Sandra. She was an ideal candidate because she had conservative credentials, interpreted the Constitution strictly, and was likely to gain widespread support. The confirmation hearings were not without controversy, however.

Feminists were excited about her because they thought she would be a justice who would support legalized abortion and other issues of the women's movement. Conservatives were upset because she was too liberal on a number of issues, but particularly on abortion. They were angry with Reagan because he did not nominate someone who was clearly anti-abortion. However, the Senate approved her nomination with ninety-one votes, in time for Sandra to join the other justices in deciding which cases they would hear during the 1981–1982 term.

After she was approved, the Court no longer used "Mister Justice" as the form of address, but instead adopted the gender-neutral "Justice." In the beginning of her term, she made it clear that she was a conservative. The public often associated her with Rehnquist, since they shared common roots and values. She voted with Rehnquist and Burger on many decisions. During her second year on the Supreme Court, feminists grew disenchanted with Sandra. While she voted to eliminate pension plans that did not offer women equity with men, she refused to allow the pension-plan decision to become retroactive. She also disappointed pro-choice advocates when she supported the minority opinion to uphold a series of local laws curbing women's access to abortion. Feminists observed that O'Connor voted much like a conservative male justice. It was difficult to attribute any aspect of her judicial record to her being female.

Over time, Sandra established her own unique position on the Court. Although she generally sided with the conservatives, she would often write a concurring opinion to attempt to narrow the scope of the majority's opinion. Her core legal philosophy was actually difficult to define. She approached each case as an individual case and always sought to arrive at a practical solution. In the classic case *Grutter v. Bollinger*, she wrote that the University of Michigan's law school could constitutionally employ a race-based affirmative action system so long as it considered each applicant individually rather than as a member of a group. She went on to say that the state's legitimate interest in using race as a factor for admission had gradually declined over the past twenty-five years as minority test scores improved. She thought that the Court should continue to monitor whether race was a legitimate reason for admission until it decided that it was no longer sufficient to merit racial distinctions. Like many of her other opinions, this gave the Court a great deal of flexibility and discretion in future cases.

Her views about state's rights caused her to vote with her conservative colleagues in a series of cases called the "Federalism Revolution," which gave back some of the power to states that the federal government had taken since the New Deal. Ironically, this meant that the Court was called on more to determine whether a particular federal practice was constitutional.

During her time on the Court, Justice O'Connor was regarded as a consummate compromiser. She also made it clear that the high court's role in American society was to interpret the law, not to legislate. On July 1, 2005, Associate Justice O'Connor announced her retirement from the Supreme Court after twenty-four years of service on the bench, much to the chagrin of many feminists and women's rights activists.

38. EDNA O'BRIEN

B.1932
AUTHOR

When anyone asks me about the Irish character, I say look at the trees. Maimed, stark and misshapen, but ferociously tenacious.

—Edna O'Brien

Perhaps more than any other female writer in modern literature, Edna O'Brien has laid bare the dichotomy of the Irish character. With her fierce sensuality, deft, supple prose, and lyrical voice, she has explored sex, feminism, love, and the female heart more adeptly than any author of her generation. Ironically, although she remains one of Ireland's finest writers, she also remains its most tortured. At the age of twenty-eight, she published *The Country Girls*, the novel that introduced two girls looking for romance and adventure in Dublin. While it took the world by storm, it was banned in Edna's own country for its "shocking" depiction of female sexuality. Like her literary hero James Joyce, Edna would be shunned by her own countrymen and be forced to leave Ireland to free her own voice. As she explains about her fellow writer, "James Joyce lived all his life away and wrote obsessively and gloriously about Ireland. Although he had left Ireland bodily, he had not left it psychically, no more than I would say I have. I don't rule out living some of the time in Ireland, but it would be in a remote place, where I would have silence and privacy. It's important when writing to feel free, answerable to no one. The minute you feel you are answerable, you're throttled. You can't do it."

Edna O'Brien was born in Tuamgraney, County Clare, in the west of

235

Ireland, on December 15, 1932. It was a strict upbringing that would influence some of her greatest short stories. Although little is known about
her parents, she often depicts a strict, somewhat joyless childhood in her
works. Later, in her novels of the *Country Girls* trilogy and the short story
collection *A Fanatic Heart*, she recalls a tyrannical, alcoholic father and a
kind but passive mother. In interviews, she describes her father's drinking binges, lasting two or three days, and his crushing depressions, which
often frightened her as a child. She has often commented that her parents
were opposed to any kind of literature. It was an opinion that would influence the rest of her work. As she recalls, "In a country so dedicated to
the banning of books, it is amazing and maybe relevant that literature is
still revered."

Nevertheless, Edna was a gifted student and won a scholarship to the
Convent of Mercy in Loughrea. To escape the stifling countryside, she
then moved to Dublin, where she lived with her best friend and worked
in a pharmacy while studying at the Pharmaceutical College at night. As
she recalls, "Dublin was where I veered towards and eventually I got
there, arriving by train, the suitcase reinforced with twine, the head full
of fancy; concerning of my destiny as being that of a heroine who, upon
being brought from Munster, faded into the city, for consumption has no
pity for blue eyes and brown hair." During her time in Dublin, she fell in
love with the works of James Joyce and Shakespeare, and began writing
pieces of her own that were published in the *Irish Press*. It is this time in
Dublin that would become the inspiration for her what many consider to
be her greatest work, the *Country Girls* trilogy.

A brilliant coming-of-age novel, *The Country Girls*, the first in the trilogy, traces the lifelong friendship of Baba Brennan and Cait Brady, two
convent girls seeking adventure, love, and excitement in Dublin. In the
novel, Cait escapes her repressive, backward town in the west of Ireland
and works in a chemist shop. She also meets and falls in love with a married man named Eugene Galliard, a filmmaker and writer of Czech descent. In 1954, Edna met and married the Czech-Irish writer Ernest
Gébler, who must have greatly inspired the character of Eugene in the
novel, in a "metamorphosis from child to bride." Her devoutly Catholic
parents were vehemently opposed to her marriage to Gébler, who was

also Jewish. The two had a fraught relationship, and Gébler was jealous of his wife's growing renown as a writer. The couple had two sons and divorced ten years later.

Edna published *The Country Girls*, the first novel by a female Irish author to depict women's sexuality openly and honestly in 1960. As she recalls, "The novel is autobiographical insofar as I was born and bred in the west of Ireland, educated at a convent, and was full of romantic yearnings, coupled with a sense of outrage." Because of its frankness, it was banned in Ireland. And just like her idol, James Joyce, she felt that to freely express her voice as a writer she had to leave her native country. And like Joyce, she wrote of nothing else.

In 1971, Edna returned to the Ireland of her childhood in *A Pagan Place*, her homage to James Joyce's *A Portrait of the Artist as a Young Man*. Like Joyce's Stephen Dedalus, Edna's protagonist must deal with her burgeoning sexuality, her artistic drive, and the oppressive Catholicism that surrounds her, as seen in the following passage:

> You tried to whistle. Only men should whistle. The Blessed Virgin blushed when women whistled and likewise when women crossed their legs. It intrigues you thinking of the Blessed Virgin having to blush so frequently. The bird that had the most lifelike whistle was the curlew.

The novel echoes Joyce's stream of consciousness style and sense of disillusionment, and remains one of Edna's darkest and most poignant works. In 1976, she published *Mother Ireland*, a sensual and unrelenting memoir of her Irish childhood, in which she writes, "To be on an island makes you realize that it's going to be harder to escape and that it will involve another birth, a further breach of waters." 1984, Edna wrote *A Fanatic Heart*, a short story collection that revisited her life in the convent. In it we see all the brutality, oppression, and sometimes joy that she experienced. The short story "The Doll" depicts the cruelty of the nuns and tells the story of one girl who is tortured by the sister who teaches her class. In "Sister Imelda" she recalls her love for a young nun who had just entered the convent. She also discloses some of the more bizarre aspects of convent life, where baths were considered "immoral" and the girls had to undress under their nightgowns in preservation of their modesty.

Throughout the '80s and '90s, Edna continued to write award-winning stories and plays about her native land. As she writes in her short story *A Scandalous Woman*, "I have always thought that ours was indeed a land of shame, a land of murder, and a land of strange, throttled, sacrificial women." In 1994, she continued to pursue the truly controversial when she published *House of Splendid Isolation*, which portrayed the relationship between a soldier in the IRA and the older woman he has kidnapped. In 1999, she paid the ultimate tribute to James Joyce when she wrote a short biography entitled *James Joyce* for Viking's Penguin Lives series. In this sensual and lyrical portrait of the artist, Edna uses stream of consciousness to depict the man in all of his glory and suffering.

In one of her most controversial novels, *Down by the River*, Edna depicted the true story of a fourteen-year-old rape victim attempting to travel to England to obtain an abortion. The 1992 case became a cause célèbre in Ireland and added fuel to the abortion debate. The story would also go on to influence another novel, the best-selling *Felicia's Journey* by William Trevor. *Down by the River* was widely acclaimed and only served to add to the controversy surrounding Edna's work in her native Ireland.

Edna now lives in New York City where she teaches writing at City College. With her unflinching eye for the troubles of women, she has influenced a whole new generation of female writers like Emer Mullins, Emma Donahue, and Nuala O'Faolain. She has received several awards, including a Kingsley Amis Award in 1962 and the Los Angeles Times Book Prize in 1990 for *Lantern Slides*. In 2006, she was named adjunct professor of English literature in University College, Dublin. In the ultimate tribute to her work, Frank Tuohy remarked, "The world of Nora Barnacle had to wait for the fiction of Edna O'Brien."

39. NELL MCCAFFERTY

B.1944
JOURNALIST, FEMINIST

Nell McCafferty is an original. She is one of those few lucky people who must be loved or hated, because she has a magnetic pull that polarizes energy.

—*Irish Press*

Once women sanction revolution, there's no stopping it.
—Nell McCafferty

In late 1960s America, the women's movement had already begun to gain steam. Thousands of women were taking to the streets demanding equal pay for equal work, sexual freedom, and respect in the workplace. In late 1960s Ireland, feminism had not even gotten off the ground. The only way a woman could obtain a prescription for the Pill was to claim to have an irregular menstrual cycle. Unwed mothers were still shunned by society and often sent to Magdalene laundries, brutal convents in which they were verbally, physically, and emotionally abused. Once a girl entered the laundry, she often never came out. Even feminist treatises like *The Second Sex* by Simone de Beauvoir were banned by the Irish government. As for equality in the workplace, women weren't even encouraged to stay in the workplace once they married and were often legally bound to resign once they became wives and mothers, particularly in professions like teaching and clerical duties. According to the Irish Constitution, "The state recognizes that by her life within the home, woman gives to the state a support without which the common good cannot be achieved. The state shall, therefore, endeavor to ensure that mothers shall not be obliged by economic necessity to engage in labour to the neglect of their duties at home." In some nationalist communities, women faced the barbaric prospect of being shaved, tarred, and feathered for fraternizing with British soldiers. Even in pubs, women were barred from ordering full pints of beer, as it was considered too "unladylike." But all of that was soon to change under the influence of one woman who came from a small, working-class town in Northern Ireland. For the past thirty years, Nell McCafferty has been called a harridan, a strident feminist, a foul-mouthed troublemaker, and an Irish Republican Army (IRA) sympathizer. More important, she has been called one of Ireland's most fearless journalists and its most important feminist.

Born Ellen McCafferty in Derry's nationalist Bogside in 1944, Nell hailed from a close-knit, loving family. Although her parents were both Catholic, her maternal grandmother was a Protestant and her maternal grandfather, Sergeant Duffy, was the one of the few Catholic members of the heavily Protestant Royal Ulster Constabulary (RUC). The fourth of six children, she recalls an almost idyllic childhood in which her brothers and sisters were well cared for, and although they were surrounded by crushing poverty in the Bogside, the McCafferty family was relatively well off. Nell's father, Hugh McCafferty, held a respectable clerical job and was the first to teach her about the magical power of words. While she was ill throughout her childhood with rheumatic fever, heart trouble, and chronic asthma, she kept herself entertained with the dozens of books that her father brought home for her. Ironically, Nell's mother, Lily, a stay-at-home mother, was the first to impart a yearning for women's liberation into her young daughter's life. As Nell later recalls, "We were educated and trained to be spinster teacher, spinster social worker, or if we were really lucky, a married woman." Lily showed Nell that the world held much more promise for a bright young woman. In her autobiography *Nell*, she remembers, "She never had her own job, and I know she would have liked to have her own money and not have to wait for my Dad to hand it over to her. . . . In 1968, when we were all reared, in a way she was redundant—but then civil rights happened and she became active in local politics and her house became a political salon and full-time refuge."

Nell was a dearly loved child, yet from the beginning, she recalls feeling like an outcast. *Feminism* was not the only word that didn't yet exist in 1950s' Ireland; the term *lesbian* was completely foreign to Nell, but from early childhood, she knew her love for women was a feeling that she could not control. It was also an insecurity that would haunt her for the rest of her life, even into her late sixties. She recalls having her first crush on a neighborhood girl at the age of eleven, a love that remained unrequited. After she turned to the only book she could find on the subject, *The Well of Loneliness* by Radclyffe Hall, she began to feel doomed to a life of loneliness and isolation, until she found a young woman who returned her affection. Maureen smoked, spoke Irish, and had a boyfriend. At the age of thirteen, Nell had experienced her first fulfilling sexual relationship, but her feelings of insecurity were not fully erased. When she confessed the encounter to a priest, he refused to absolve her unless she promised never to see the girl again. "I never went to confession again," Nell affirms.

While she was feeling sexually and socially ambivalent, Nell was excelling academically. She attended a Gaeltacht school, where she became proficient in Irish, and soon began taking night classes in Derry, where she met the young activist Eamon McCann, who would later become one of the most seminal figures in the Irish civil rights movement. In 1961, she won a scholarship to the prestigious Queen's University in Belfast and became the first in her family to attend college. After a faltering start, she began to excel academically and wrote a poem for the university's English Society that surpassed that of a third-year student Seamus Heaney, who would later become poet laureate. After graduating in 1964 with an arts degree and faced with the prospect of marrying or emigrating, Nell decided to stay on at Queen's. It was a wise choice—she began supporting John Hume, the Social Democrat Labour Party leader who would later help to broker the Good Friday Agreement, and her own political awareness began to develop. She also attended McCann's televised debate about the future of the north, where she began to fully understand the depth of Catholic discrimination in Northern Ireland.

After a year of traveling to Cannes, Greece, London, and Israel, Nell returned home in 1967 to find a very different Ireland. Derry had become a dire place, where most Catholic couples were living in slums and the wait list for housing was in the thousands. Unemployment in Belfast was now a staggering 25 percent. With McCann's encouragement, she joined the Londonderry Labour Party and soon began writing for its journal. The party's platform "One man, one vote one family, one house" called for full civil rights for all, including jobs and housing, and Nell began to aid families trapped in squalor by helping them move to "Squats" (empty housing that was being refused to Catholics) and joining marches for civil rights. For the first time, Nell witnessed the appalling discrimination all around her. The practice of gerrymandering, or confining the Catholic community to one area so that the Protestant majority might have more votes, was rampant. Catholics were refused housing in other areas, thereby leaving almost no available residences for Catholic families. In addition, businessmen in Derry were often given extra votes because they paid more taxes than homeowners. Coincidentally, most of these business owners were also Protestant. Furthermore, Northern Ireland soon saw the suspension of habeus corpus, internment without trial, and the call-up of an armed constabulary. The nationalist community was being crammed into tenements with no recourse.

Nell soon became an integral part of the seminal civil rights marches called the Long March and the Battle of the Bogside, along with her friend and civil rights icon Bernadette Devlin, and witnessed the civil rights movement transform from a peaceful to an armed campaign. As Nell saw British soldiers fire plastic bullets into crowds of unarmed Derry citizens and her fellow neighbors beaten to within inches of their lives by police, her inevitable role as a revolutionary soon became clear to her. She recalled later, "In effect, the non-violent movement for civil rights died the night the RUC came in to beat Catholics into their houses." She was soon throwing Molotov cocktails at armed tanks, right alongside her mother. Her role as a future journalist was also being defined as she began shadowing the famed correspondent Mary Holland and became the go-to reporter for reporters seeking the real story on the riots in Derry. "By then, many of the journalists who came to Derry were looking to talk to me, not least on the grounds that I gave the facts first, then my own interpretation of them." One of these journalists was Jimmy Breslin, who gave the best advice of her career: "Tell the friggin' story."

In 1970, Nell received her first big break when Fergus Pyle, the editor of the *Irish Times,* asked her to follow the Unionist leader Ian Paisley. Despite her nationalist leanings, she remained objective and was given a position that paid twenty pounds a week as a reporter with Ireland's most renowned newspaper. She moved to Dublin, where she was promptly assigned to the "Woman's Desk" to cover stories on babies, fashion, and plants. Her colleagues were Maeve Binchy (later a bestselling author) and the journalists Mary Maher and Mary Cummins. It was this small group of women who would start the first grassroots women's movement: the Irishwomen's Liberation Movement. Despite being a small group, the women drew up a list of major demands: equal pay, equality before the law, equal education, legal contraception, justice for deserted wives, and one family, one house. Because many of the women in the group were journalists, they decided to turn the women's pages over to the cause of women's liberation.

Nell made more headlines when she was assigned to cover the most disenfranchised section of Dublin society: the children's court. At that time, the age of criminal responsibility in Ireland was seven. If a child was caught throwing stones during a riot, or even stealing candy, he would be sent to reform school, where he would most likely be sexually and physically abused. "In 1970, the series I wrote about the mere fact of the imprisonment of these children in remote areas caused a sensation." She also covered Bernadette Devlin's release from jail (her friends McCann and Mary Holland scooped her on the story), and that same year *Hibernia* magazine named her as Journalist of the Year for the children's court series. Already a seasoned activist and journalist at the age of twenty-six, she began speaking on women's liberation all over the country. The talk show host Gay Byrne devoted an entire show to the burgeoning women's movement, and the Irish Women's Liberation meetings drew crowds in the thousands.

The next year, Nell organized the infamous Contraceptive Train from Belfast to Dublin, which was determined to bring illegal contraceptives into the Irish Republic. On May 22, 1971, forty-seven Irish women traveled by train, knowing that they needed a doctor's prescription for the Pill. Undeterred, they bought packets of aspirin in the guise of the Pill, condoms, and contraceptive jelly. When they arrived in Dublin, they were met by custom's agents who tried to arrest them. In response, they threw condoms, "birth control" pills, and jelly at the officers. What the protest lacked in numbers, it more than made up for in publicity. The Contraceptive Train made every front page in Ireland. Birth control was officially part of the nation's consciousness, and Nell began lecturing on contraception all over Ireland.

By the next year, the north had erupted with violence, and Nell once again found herself on the front lines. The introduction of internment, whereby the British army could round up Catholics and hold them without trial, had the nationalist community in a stranglehold. Teenagers, old men, and activists who were not even involved in the armed struggle were subjected to torture. That same year, thirteen innocent civilians were killed by British soldiers during Bloody Sunday. Nell witnessed the deaths of two of them and wrote a firsthand account of the tragedy for the *Starry Plough*, the newspaper of the Republican movement. She reported that:

Bloody Sunday was carried out with one objective. The British Army decided coldly and deliberately to shoot the risen people of the streets. We were shot with our backs turned, in some cases with our hands in the air as we went to rescue the wounded. We were killed on the barricades, in the courtyards . . . and a few died God knows where. For the least of these and the best of these, thirteen men were murdered last week. Let it be said of them with pride, they died on their feet and not on their knees. Stay free, brothers and sisters. There will be another day.

Her account was so moving that she was asked to testify on Bloody Sunday before the Subcommittee on Europe of the Committee on Foreign Affairs before Senator Edward Kennedy, along with Jimmy Breslin. Throughout the 1970s, Nell remained an impassioned advocate of civil rights and women's rights. When the Irish Women's Liberation Movement folded, she formed Irish Women United, which later helped pave the way for such revolutionary changes as state-financed birth control clinics, women's studies programs, divorce, and finally the Pill. In 1977, bored and uninspired with her job at the *Irish Times*, she left to write her novel. The next year, she suffered the loss of her beloved father and returned home to Derry to care for her family, but her reputation as a radical was never far behind her. When in 1979 she tried to reclaim her job at the *Irish Times*, she was refused on the grounds that she was too radical. As a result, Nell became even more outspoken, criticizing organized religion, which broke new ground in her country. In 1980, she took up the cause of IRA prisoners, particularly that of the Armagh Women, who were suffering unspeakable conditions in one of the worst jails in Ireland. She became an opinion columnist, where she championed the plight of the Irish female prisoners. That year, she published her first book, appropriately titled *The Armagh Women*. She also began writing for the *Irish Press* and *In Dublin* about the taboo subject of abortion, appeared regularly on the *Women's Programme* on Radio Telefis Eireann (RTE), and became the contributing editor of *Ms.* magazine. And her personal life was just as satisfying: she had finally met the love of her life, the TV producer Nuala O'Faolain, who later became the bestselling author of *Are You Somebody?* In 1984, Neil published two more books, a collection of her columns called *The Best of Nell* and *A Woman to Blame*, an exposé on the Kerry babies case, in which Joanne Hayes, a single mother in Kerry, was falsely accused of killing her children.

In 1987, she generated even more controversy when she announced her support for the IRA on a current affairs program. The next day, an IRA bombing in Enniskillen killed eleven Protestants. RTE banned her from its airwaves the day after that, and several of her fellow journalists shunned her, but universities and civic groups all over the country asked her to speak. She became the guest of politicians everywhere, including the U.S. ambassador to Ireland Jean Kennedy Smith. Soon, she was back on RTE, appearing on the show *Liveline*, and had published her book *Peggy Deery: A Derry Family at War*, the brilliant story of the only woman who was shot during Bloody Sunday. In 1995, she had split with O'Faolain, and was presented with an honorary doctorate by Straffordshire University. Over the next few years, Nell continued to cover major stories, from the World Cup to the 1994 IRA cease-fire. In 2003, she interviewed the infamous loyalist paramilitary leader Johnny Adair. The same year, she opened a new reproductive health care facility in Dublin.

Today, at the age of sixty-two, Nell McCafferty has left an incredible legacy. Women in Ireland are in charge of their own lives, sexually free, esteemed in the workplace, able to marry or not marry as they so choose, and finally able to divorce. Wives are no longer at the mercy of their husbands. In 1992, the birth control pill was finally legalized in the Republic of Ireland. In 1996, the last of the Magdalene laundries was closed. Family planning centers are accessible all over Ireland. And most important, Nell herself is free. In 2004, after the publication of her autobiography and before her beloved mother died, she told the world about her own sexuality.

40. MARY ROBINSON

B.1944

FIRST FEMALE PRESIDENT OF IRELAND

I was elected by the women of Ireland, who instead of rocking the cradle, rocked the system.

—Mary Robinson

I've always recognized the importance of addressing shortcomings and being outspoken, an awkward voice.

—Mary Robinson

In 1970, when Mary Robinson was a young senator and feminist in Ireland, she introduced a bill in the Irish government to legalize contraception. By American standards, she would have been doing nothing revolutionary. Millions of American women had already been introduced to the Pill. But in Ireland, she was committing what would amount to heresy. Religious leaders accused her of being antichurch and antifamily. As Nell McCafferty recalls, "Mary Robinson was being treated like a parliamentary leper, as she spoke the unspeakable." No one could foresee that it would take another twenty-two years for birth control to be legalized in Ireland, and another twenty years for Ireland to elect a female president. When Mary Robinson was elected, it marked a sea change in women's rights in Ireland and human rights all over the world. Robinson soon became an outspoken, compassionate champion of the poor, the oppressed, and the forgotten, particularly in third world countries. In the Ireland in which Mary Robinson was raised, it would have been unthinkable for a woman to become president. In the Ireland that came after

Mary Robinson, there have been two female presidents. As she so eloquently quipped at the Glamour Women of the Year Awards in 2005, "The young boys of Ireland now sit at their mother's knee and cry 'Mammy, why can't I be president?'" Not only is Mary Robinson recognized as being Ireland's first woman president but she is also recognized as being its most successful.

Mary Therese Bourke was born in Ballina, County Mayo, on May 21, 1944, into a family of professionals. Both of her parents were doctors and both sides of the family had heavy ties to Republican politics. One ancestor was a leading activist in the Mayo Land League and the Irish Republican Brotherhood. Mary's roots also stemmed from Anglo-Irish aristocracy, which gave her an awareness of both the Catholic and Protestant communities in Ireland. From an early age, Mary knew she wanted to affect change and stand up for those who could not stand up for themselves. Her grandfather was a lawyer who took on pro bono cases that no one else wanted to touch. As she recalls, "He spoke about law as important as a way of changing things, so from a very early stage I wanted to be a lawyer, to bring about change."

Determined to receive the best education possible, Mary attended Trinity College in Dublin in 1962, a daring move for a Catholic in 1960s Ireland. Trinity was a Protestant university, and Catholics were forbidden to attend without special permission from the church. Her academic brilliance won her a fellowship to Harvard Law School in 1967. In 1969, at the age of twenty-five, she was appointed the youngest Reid Professor of Constitutional Law at Trinity College, where she began to practice her passion for equal rights for women, particularly contraception, abortion, and divorce. That same year, she was elected to the Irish Senate, where she fought tirelessly for the rights of women in the workplace and in the home. In 1971, she challenged the Juries Act, which stated that only property owners could sit on juries. As most property owners happened to be men, this left out half of Ireland's population. Mary soon took on the Act when she began representing two women who had taken part in a demonstration for the legalization of birth control called the Contraceptive Train. The women asked how they could be tried by a jury of their peers when the jury consisted entirely of men. Mary challenged the act constitutionally and won. It was the first of many of her victories for the women of Ireland. The same year, she fought a personal battle of her own. She met and fell in love with Nicholas Robinson, a fellow lawyer who happened to be a Protestant. Although her parents were educated and had an Anglo-Irish background, they were furious at Mary's decision. They had already allowed her to attend a Protestant university, but marrying a Protestant was a different story. They refused to attend her wedding.

As Mary became more outspoken, she gained more enemies, particularly among her male peers. In the mid-1970s, she joined the Labour Party, believing that she would find more sympathy there. She was wrong: she found as much opposition to her first bill proposing to legalize contraceptives as she did when she was an independent candidate. She soon began receiving condoms in the mail from members of the Conservative Party in Ireland.

Not intimidated, she joined the Irish Women's Liberation Movement in 1971, which was calling for equal hiring practices for women and rights for deserted wives and unmarried mothers, and became the group's legal advisor. She also became the legal advisor for the Campaign for Homosexual Law Reform with the future Trinity College senator David Norris. Furthermore, she took on such unpopular issues as the effort to restore Dublin's historic Viking sites.

In 1985, Mary finally announced that she was through with the Labour Party when she was passed up for the attorney general position that she was guaranteed to receive (the post went to a less-qualified male candidate). Most important, she resigned in protest over the Anglo-Irish Agreement, which was conceived by the Irish prime minister Garret FitzGerald and the British prime minister Margaret Thatcher. The agreement stated that the majority of people in Ireland wanted no change in the status quo in Northern Ireland. Robinson disagreed with this view, believing that Unionists should also have a say in altering their government.

Because of her tremendous legal acumen and her ability to pass important, controversial legislation successfully, many of her core dreams had been realized: women had (limited) access to birth control, they could retain their jobs even after they married, and they could now serve on juries. In 1989, the Labour Party asked her to seek the Irish presidency. Seeing a way to further the agenda for all women, she accepted. No one thought she had a chance. Again, she proved everyone wrong. Although she was running against Noel Browne and Brian Lenihan, two formidable opponents, she used her public speaking skills, brilliance, and compassion and toured the country, captivating voters everywhere she went. Ironically, she received a big boost from Lenihan, whose campaign was about to collapse in scandal.

The final boon for Mary came when Pádraig Flynn launched a controversial personal attack on Mary's suitability as a wife and mother. The attack against her character, as well as her visits to women's centers and her background as a feminist, struck a chord in Ireland's women. Soon, female voters all over the country were behind her. Mary Robinson became the first woman in Ireland's history to win the presidency. In her victory speech, she reserved her most passionate thanks for "the women of Ireland—Mna na hÉireann."

Robinson was inaugurated as the seventh president of Ireland on December 3, 1990, at the age of forty-six. Her campaign slogan was "You have a voice and I will make it heard" and she more than made good on that promise. She became the most beloved president in Ireland's history. Although the Office of President had been a traditionally symbolic job, Mary made it her own, continuing to provide a voice to the voiceless. In 1992, she became the only head of state to visit war-torn Somalia, where she declared that she was "so outraged that this would be happening in the 1990s, that I'd be beside a woman and children, and the children would be dying in front of me." For her efforts in Somalia, she received the CARE Humanitarian Award. She took on the issue of what she called the "diaspora," the vast number of Irish emigrants and people of Irish descent. She also changed the face of Anglo-Irish relations and became the first Irish president to visit both the queen of England and Sinn Féin leader Gerry Adams. In her seven years, she brought more attention to civil war, famine, and international disasters than all her predecessors combined. And she signed two bills that forever changed Irish society and that she had worked her entire life to see realized: the full legalization of birth control in Ireland and the decriminalization of homosexuality.

Impressed by her deep commitment to human rights and her controversial, impassioned views, Secretary General Kofi Annan asked her to become the United Nations High Commissioner for Human Rights. Mary resigned as president a few weeks early to accept the post. When she resigned, her popularity in Ireland reached 93 percent, and when it was learned that Robinson was taking up the role of commissioner, *The Nation* ran the article, "Should This Woman Run the World?" The magazine praised her as the only leader who could effectively change the UN: "While her fellow law school graduates were laying the groundwork for lucrative law practices, Robinson was using her prominence—as a constitutional scholar, a senator and law professor at age 25—and blazing oratorical skills to help pry the wheels of the justice system off the backs of the country's least-served communities—the poor, the unemployed, single mothers, the itinerant population known as Travelers, and Ireland's present day emigrants, who still must leave their country to find work." Robinson was appointed to reenergize the UN's human rights agenda, which she did masterfully. During her term, she traveled to some sixty countries, calling attention to human rights atrocities in Zimbabwe, Columbia, and Cambodia. In 1998, she became the first commissioner to visit Tibet. During her term, she attacked the Irish system of permits for non-European Union immigrants as similar to "bonded labor." She was so effective that Annan asked her to stay on another year. She served out her post until 2002. And she endured more controversy. After the attacks on the United States on September 11, 2001, she implored the United States to uphold the rights of Afghan citizens. She also attacked the United States' apparent violation of the International High Court concerning the imprisonment of prisoners at Guantánamo Bay and its use of the death penalty. Although she left her post in 2002, she has remained a tireless campaigner for human rights. In 2002, she was awarded the Sydney Peace Prize for her outstanding work as UN High Commissioner for Human Rights. In May 2005, she was awarded the first "Outspoken" award from the International Gay and Lesbian Human Rights Commission and was chosen as one of several 2005 Women of the Year by *Glamour* magazine. She was named one of *Time* magazine's top 100 men and women in 2005 whose "power, talent or moral example is transforming the world." She is now based in New York, where she is the founder and director of the Ethical Globalization Initiative (EGI), which brings global norms and standards of human rights in established and developing nations. Dedicated to equitable trade practices, treatment and prevention of AIDS in Africa, and immigration policies, the EGI has garnered support from President Jimmy Carter and Desmond Tutu. At the age of sixty-two, Mary Robinson has become one of the world's great human rights leaders. As the president of Ireland, she became more well known than the country's first president, Eamon de Valera, who devoted his reign in office to keeping women in their place—in the home. Fortunately, Mary showed the world just how wrong her predecessor was.

41. BERNADETTE DEVLIN MCALISKEY

B.1947

ACTIVIST, POLITICIAN, REVOLUTIONARY

To gain that which is worth having, it may be necessary to lose everything else.

—Bernadette Devlin

Yesterday I dared to struggle. Today I dare to win.

—Bernadette Devlin

There is perhaps no other woman who has had more influence on the struggle for civil rights and the nationalist movement in Northern Ireland than Bernadette Devlin. If one were to ask any Irish or Irish American woman today to make a list of her heroes, it is more than likely that Bernadette would appear at the head of it. Yet from the beginning, this articulate young woman from a humble working-class background was an enigma even to those who admired her so deeply. To the mainly nationalist Catholic community, she was the fearless voice it had never dared to dream of. To the heavily Unionist Protestants, she was "Castro in a miniskirt." To Americans abroad, she was an eloquent, yet uninhibited Irish woman with a strong Northern Irish accent who often felt more empathy with the African American community than with Irish Americans. By the age of twenty-one, she was the youngest woman ever elected to the British parliament, a published author, a feminist, a socialist, and a young woman who took no prisoners, feared no man, and suffered no fools.

Josephine Bernadette Devlin McAliskey was born on April 23, 1947, in Cookstown, County Tyrone, to John James and Elizabeth Devlin. The young activist-to-be entered the world on the same day as the patron saint of England, St. George, which she later said, "I suspect this has some sort of ironic meaning." From the start, she received a thorough education in Irish history and politics that would stand her the rest of her life. The victim of anti-Irish discrimination while living abroad in England, John Devlin was himself a political suspect and taught young Bernadette about the atrocities of the British government. Although the Devlins were a staunchly Republican family, Bernadette's grandfather was a British soldier. As a child in the 1950s, Bernadette began to experience firsthand the war between the Protestants and Catholics, which was beginning to escalate to a fever pitch. Although Bernadette found the Protestants she grew up with to be generous and kind, she began to understand the suffering and unfair treatment of her own community at a very early age.

One of six children, Bernadette was raised in a working-class, close-knit, loving family. Although her father was forced to seek work in England because of rife unemployment in Northern Ireland, he was an attentive man who regaled all the Devlin children with Irish history and myth. Interestingly enough, he also kept an egalitarian house in which Bernadette's mother had an equal say, and he took on a lion's share of cooking and housework. It is more than likely that John's view of women as equals must have fueled his daughter's own feminist leanings. As a child, Bernadette also attended a "madly Republican" grammar school, where she learned the subtleties of political theory and debate that would later land her in some hot water. A few years later, when she was twelve, she engaged in her first political protest when she entered a local talent competition and chose to recite a line from a speech by the Irish revolutionary leader Robert Emmet. The whole town was in such a rage that young Bernadette had to have a policeman escort her home from school. It was her first—but certainly not her last—experience with the law.

In 1956, at the age of nine, Bernadette experienced the first undermining of her secure childhood. Her beloved father died of a heart attack while working in England. He was just forty-six years old, and he left behind a wife and six children who were now forced to fend for themselves and live off the welfare of the state. Bernadette was also suffering from asthma, which left her physically ill but mentally defiant. It was a strength she learned to develop and that enabled her to survive much more insurmountable obstacles later in life. When Bernadette began attending St. Patrick's Academy in Dungannon, she became fully indoctrinated in Irish history, culture, and politics. Her keen mind and superior debating skills set her apart from other students and she soon showed an early penchant for political debate with the other girls at St. Pat's. After graduating, she was accepted in to the prestigious Queen's University in Belfast in 1965, just two years before the civil rights movement began to swell. By the time she was a student, Bernadette was beginning to become attracted to socialism and its tenets like so many other activists in the Republican movement, despite her staunchly Catholic upbringing. She also changed her course of study from an honors Celtic degree to a concentration in psychology and joined the debating society, where she shined for her accomplished oration. During this same year, the minister of northern affairs in Northern Ireland banned all nationalist organizations at Queen's. In protest, Bernadette joined the university's Republican club.

Despite forging a notable college career, Bernadette suffered an incredible loss in 1967. Her mother, Elizabeth, died of cancer at the age of forty-six, the same age as Bernadette's father. Now, at the age of twenty, Bernadette was a full-time student, who was also trying to keep her brothers and sisters together through a time of overwhelming grief. She soon moved back to Cookstown to care for her family at night and then traveled to Belfast everyday to resume her life as a student.

In tribute to her parents, Bernadette pursued her love of Irish politics even more fervently. She became interested in the politics of James Connolly and Michael Collins and, most important, the concept of a truly united Ireland. In August 1968, she joined the Civil Rights Association's march from Coalisland to Dungannon. What began as a peaceful protest soon turned violent when police tried to reroute the march. Undeterred, Bernadette joined the next major march on October 5, which the minister of home affairs attempted to ban. Police beat protestors off the street and suddenly the civil rights movement in Northern Ireland was being broadcast all over the world. Seeing her fellow protestors in the brutal hands of the police suddenly gave Bernadette her life's direction. When she organized a march from Queen's University to Belfast City Hall, 2,000 people showed. Fueled by the growing support for the movement, she helped form the student-led civil rights political party called the People's Democracy. The party's philosophy included a call for "One man, One vote" (Bernadette later regretted that this wasn't changed to "One woman, One vote"), a fair drawing of electoral boundaries, the repeal of the Special Powers Act (in which a prisoner could be held for seventy-two hours without charge), and fair employment and housing. True to her socialist outlook, the People's Democracy had a faceless committee, but Bernadette soon became a prominent figure and drew the ire of the Reverend Ian Paisley, the Unionist leader who became her lifelong foe. Paisley made his career out of fiery, anti-Catholic, antipapal rhetoric and the People's Democracy became the perfect target. But Bernadette was not swayed. She organized a historic march from Belfast to Derry in 1969, which was modeled on the African American civil rights march from Selma to Montgomery that took place just four years before in the United States. "The Long March" as it was known was met with violent opposition from police and Paisley's supporters, who tried to stop the march. As usual, the police used an iron fist to keep protestors in line, but it was the event that put Bernadette on the map. As she later recalled, "Policemen always call me a stupid Bitch, and I deny that I'm stupid." She also famously called Derry "the capital city of injustice" and it became the phrase that captured the Irish imagination. Bernadette was officially a force with which to be reckoned.

In February 1969, Northern Ireland held a general election, and Bernadette ran in South Derry against James Dawson Chichester-Clark. She won 6,000 votes to his 9,000—a rather impressive showing against the man who later became the prime minister of Northern Ireland. When George Forrest, the member of Parliament (MP) for mid-Ulster died, the Republican Party approached her as someone who could help its cause. Although she was not a hard-line Republican, she had Republican sympathies and seriously considered the offer. She was still a student and just twenty-one years old. On April 2, 1969, Bernadette Devlin accepted the nomination. She had just fourteen days to campaign and she won by a majority of 4,211 votes. Her campaign slogan was "I will take my seat

and fight for your rights." Four days later, the British government deployed soldiers to Northern Ireland to quell the growing violence on the
streets. It was supposed to be a temporary measure; those British forces
still patrol the streets today.

When Bernadette arrived at Parliament, she was appalled by the old-
boys club it had become; and the British MPs were appalled by her
"brash" behavior. As she recalls, "It wasn't long before people discovered
the final horrors of letting an urchin into Parliament."

Nonetheless, she continued to fight the British prime minister Harold
Wilson on the Special Powers Act and became the flavor of the month at
a high price. "I wasn't just an MP, but a phenomenon," she declared in
her autobiography *The Price of My Soul*. Hounded by the press, patron-
ized by her much older (and much more male) counterparts, threatened
by Unionists including Paisley, who snidely called her the "International
Socialist Playgirl of the Year," Britain's youngest elected female MP
began to feel the cruel backlash of fame. She also began to feel resentment
from her own nationalist constituency, who felt that she was becoming
too staunchly Republican for their tastes. Although she remained an MP
until 1974, Bernadette began to realize that she could be of more use in
another capacity. "Parliament is all too slow and abstract for someone like
me. What I want is action, involvement."

Amazingly, she found time to write her autobiography *The Price of
My Soul*, and she returned to the streets to take up the cause for equal
housing in Northern Ireland and to begin collecting money in the United
States for the Irish civil rights movement. On August 12, 1969, Bernadette
joined the infamous Battle of the Bogside, during which protestors battled with British soldiers. The Unionist Orangemen were holding their
annual parade in Derry, and the Catholics decided to stay in their own
area, but the Orangemen had other ideas. They decided to lay siege to the
Bogside. Bernadette was on the front lines and was soon arrested and
charged with inciting a riot. She was sentenced to six months and served
four in Armagh Jail in 1970.

In 1971, she took up the cause again and began touring the United
States, giving lectures and raising money for the victims of sectarian violence in Northern Ireland. It was during this tour that she began to

empathize with the plight of black Americans. As she traveled through the United States, she began to realize that she did not share the same experience as the affluent, socially privileged Irish Americans who were clamoring to meet her. She recalls:

> I was not very long there until, like water, I found my own level. "My people"—the people who know about oppression, discrimination, prejudice, poverty and the frustration and despair that they produce—were not Irish Americans. They were black, Puerto Rican, Chicano. And those who were supposed to be "my people", the Irish Americans who know about English misrule and the Famine and supported the civil-rights movement at home, and knew that Partition and England were the cause of the problem, looked and sounded to me like Orangemen. They said exactly the same things about blacks that the loyalists said about us at home. In New York, I was given the key to the city by the mayor, an honour not to be sneezed at. I gave it to the Black Panthers.

She also refused to meet Chicago's Mayor Richard Daley in protest of his treatment of the students opposed to the Vietnam War. This viewpoint made her just as controversial on this side of the Atlantic as on the other, but no less admired.

In 1972, she was invited to speak at what became the most infamous event in recent Irish history: Bloody Sunday. Again, what began as a nonviolent protest against interment ended in bloodshed; thirteen innocent civilians were shot dead by British soldiers and twelve others were seriously wounded. One week later, Bernadette slapped British home secretary Reggie Maudling across the face in the House of Commons when he declared that the British soldiers had acted in self-defense. Although Bernadette had witnessed Bloody Sunday firsthand, she was denied the chance to speak in Parliament and was suspended from Westminster for six months. She later tried to reclaim the seat in 1974, but she lost to another nationalist candidate.

By the early 1970s, Bernadette's private life was no less controversial and this would ultimately affect her political career. In 1971, she became pregnant out of wedlock and gave birth to a daughter, Roisin. To this day, she refuses to name the father. The pregnancy offended the conservative sensibilities of a good many Catholics in her constituency, which later cost her votes. She later married Michael McAliskey on April 23, 1973, with whom she had two more children, Deirdre and Fintan.

In 1974, Bernadette began to galvanize her passion for politics and justice in Ireland. That year, she helped form the Irish Republican Socialist Party, a dramatic break from the official Sinn Féin, and served on the executive until 1975. Four years later, she stood as an independent candidate, in support of Bobby Sands and his fellow blanketmen who were on a hunger strike in Long Kesh Prison. She became a passionate supporter of prisoner's rights and the leading spokesperson for the "Smash H-Block Committee."

But all her renown was soon to cost her dearly once again. On January 11, 1981, three members of the Ulster Defense Association, a Protestant paramilitary group, stormed the home of Bernadette and Michael McAliskey in County Tyrone and shot four bullets into Michael's body; then they went for Bernadette. She had been lying over her son on the bedroom floor, protecting him. The gunman emptied his gun into her body—seven bullets entered her, including one that traveled from the back of her skull to her left leg. What is most shocking is that British intelligence had been warned of the attack and did not take any measures to prevent it. It kept her house under round-the-clock surveillance and sat just minutes away while Bernadette and her husband were left for dead. Against all odds, they both survived, and their attackers were arrested without incident. Unshaken and unsilenced, Bernadette continued to champion human rights in Northern Ireland and abroad and remained just as visible. In the early 1980s, she ran for election to the Dáil Éireann, the parliament of the Republic of Ireland. She failed to win, but continue to lecture on women's and civil rights all over the world.

By the mid-1990s, Bernadette Devlin was a bone fide icon and the most important female figure in the nationalist struggle. By the age of forty-nine, she had overcome prejudice, sexism, sectarianism, imprisonment, and attempted murder, but the British authorities were not done with her yet. They targeted her most precious asset: her daughter Roisin. On November 20, 1996, Roisin was arrested in Northern Ireland on an extradition warrant issued by the German government in connection with an Irish Republican Army mortar attack on a British army base in Germany. She was just twenty-five years old and five months pregnant, and even though she was not charged British authorities held her on remand for seven days. During her interment, she was threatened physically, as were members of her family. But Roisin remained every bit as strong as her mother. Despite her frail condition and the constant intimidation, she never confessed to a crime she didn't commit. She was presented with a prewritten statement admitting to her involvement in the mortar attack. As she recalls later, "I refused to sign." Roisin was later transferred to Holloway Prison in England, where she was subjected to daily strip searches and was denied fresh air, exercise, and proper medical treatment. She was also told that she would be forced to give birth while handcuffed to a bed. Roisin remained in poor health throughout her pregnancy, suffering from asthma, an eating disorder, and mental exhaustion. The world community responded with outrage. Immediately, human rights organizations like Amnesty International and Helsinki Watch decried Roisin's imprisonment and campaigns all over the world, including those in London and the United States, began to take up her cause. In May 1997, Roisin gave birth to Bernadette's first grandchild, Loinnir, in a prison hospital. By March 9, 1998, the public's outrage finally began to sway the British Home Office and Home Secretary Jack Straw announced that Roisin's extradition to Germany would be "unjust and oppressive." Roisin now lives in Northern Ireland with her family.

Although the British government had done the unthinkable when it targeted her daughter, Bernadette refused to disappear. In 2000, she remained an impassioned activist and spoke out against the Good Friday Agreement, despite opposition from Sinn Féin. In 2003, despite being welcomed warmly to the United States during previous trips, she was detained by immigration officials in Chicago on the grounds that she "poses a threat to the security of the United States." She was threatened and promptly sent directly back to Northern Ireland. There is a wicked irony in her detainment. Bernadette has gained icon status in the United States and her ill treatment by the U.S. government has only made her more revered. More than thirty-five years after she burst onto the world political scene as a college student, she remains one of its most electrifying figures.

42. CHRISTA MCAULIFFE

1948–1986
ASTRONAUT

I touch the future—I teach.

—Christa McAuliffe

What are we doing here? We're reaching for the stars.

—Christa McAuliffe

In 1986, a young teacher named Christa McAuliffe stepped from the classroom into history as part of a radical new approach by the National Aeronautics and Space Administration (NASA). By 1984, space shuttle flights had become ordinary occurrences to many Americans, and NASA wanted to rekindle the excitement that had once surrounded the space program. It thought that if an ordinary citizen were involved, a good "talker" who could communicate the excitement of travel in space, the public might once again become enthusiastic. President Ronald Reagan made the decision that the first ordinary American to travel on board a space shuttle would be "one of America's finest, a teacher." His search finally led to Christa McAuliffe, a social studies teacher from Concord High School in Concord, New Hampshire. She was supposed to be the first civilian in space, but she died with the rest of the six-member crew when *Challenger* exploded shortly after launch on January 28, 1986. Although the mission on the shuttle was one of the worst tragedies in the U.S. space program, Christa's tireless mission as a teacher continues.

Sharon Christa McAuliffe was born on September 2, 1948, in Boston, Massachusetts, to Edward and Grace Corrigan. She was the oldest of their five children. Before she was born, her father was completing his sophomore year at Boston College. Her parents had married after Ed returned from service in the navy and planned to wait to have children until Ed graduated. Despite their planning, Ed and Grace became parents on September 2, 1948. Christa's young parents could barely afford a one-room apartment, so she slept in a car bed while her parents slept on the couch. Their financial problems were compounded by Christa's illnesses. She was in the hospital on numerous occasions with asthmatic bronchitis and later infant diarrhea. She was so ill that her parents worried that she might die. Although a new antibiotic saved her life, the medical bills caused her parents to lose their apartment. Grace took Christa to her parents' house in Connecticut while Ed moved in with college friends. Soon after, a friend helped them secure low-income housing near Boston Harbor so that they could reunite as a family.

Despite her rocky beginning, Christa was a bright child who walked early, spoke in full sentences and conversed when she was one, and learned nursery rhymes when she was eighteen months old. She was always precocious mentally and physically. She was also an active child who took risks frequently. Her family remembers that when she was three, she rode her tricycle into the street and was apparently planning to take a trip. They caught her before she could get away. She was so active that her parents had difficulty finding babysitters for her. Ironically, she did have motion sickness as a child.

When Ed graduated, they moved back to their hometown, Waterbury, Connecticut, where Ed secured an accounting job. By then, their second child, Christopher, had arrived. Christa's beauty brought her to the attention of a modeling school and she appeared in a televised fashion show. But not long thereafter Ed took a job as an assistant comptroller at Jordan Marsh, a Boston department store, so the family moved to the Boston suburb of Framingham. While her mother taught nursery school, Christa started school. She made friends easily, was an excellent student, and participated in many extracurricular activities. When she was in second grade, her teacher talked to her parents about her tendency toward perfectionism. Her parents remember that she always pushed herself and was energetic and goal-oriented. She was involved in dance, voice and piano lessons, religion classes, and sports. When her mother started a

Brownie troop, she began her career in the Girl Scouts. She also took care of her younger brothers and sisters, Christopher, Steven, Betsy, and Lisa. As the first daughter, she had a very close relationship with her father. They played the piano and sang together and enjoyed a special bond. She recalled, "He had faith in me. He made me strong." In 1957, when she was nine, an event occurred that would profoundly affect her life: the Soviet Union launched *Sputnik*. The space race had begun.

Throughout her school years, the space race shaped the American psyche and influenced many U.S. decisions about education. Schools introduced more math and science, required more physical fitness, and set higher expectations. While Christa was affected by these changes, she was also personally interested in space exploration. When Alan Shepard took the first U.S. manned flight, she wrote her impressions in a notebook. She told a classmate that she would like to go into space some day despite the fact that women were not even considered for careers in space at that time. She listened to President John F. Kennedy's challenge to the United States to put a man on the Moon and she read his book, *Profiles in Courage*. As she watched all the television coverage of the space missions, she was inspired, particularly by the *Apollo* Moon landing program, and wrote years later on her astronaut application form that "I watched the Space Age being born, and I would like to participate."

In 1961, she entered Marian High School, a small Roman Catholic school in Framingham. While in high school, Christa met Steve McAuliffe. The way they met could be a scene from a movie. When Christa walked into her homeroom class, she saw a new boy in the class, Steve McAuliffe. As she entered, he asked another student who she was; the boy answered, "Christa Corrigan." Steve responded, "She's beautiful." Later, she told a friend that Steve was "the cutest boy" she had ever seen. For a while, they admired each other from afar, but finally friends introduced them and Steve asked her for a date. The couple was popular and active in extracurricular activities. She was involved in a wide range of clubs, performances, and sports, distinguishing herself as an all-star softball player. She still helped with her younger siblings and found time to babysit for numerous families. Although she was a student with average grades, she studied hard and made the National Honor Society. She graduated seventy-fifth in a class of 176, but teachers at the school recall that she was memorable in other ways. She was curious, kind, giving, and energetic. During their junior year, when they were sixteen, Christa told Steve that she would marry him if he asked. He asked and they were engaged. They agreed they would wait until after they graduated from college to marry.

When she graduated from high school, she was accepted at the University of Lowell and Framingham State College. Although her parents encouraged her to go away to school, she elected to stay home to attend Framingham State College. She told her parents to save their money to send the younger children to college. Steve received a scholarship to Virginia Military Institute (VMI), so he went south without her. Friends were correct in their predictions that the distance would not negatively affect their relationship. While Christa majored in U.S. history and secondary education, she also worked nights for a trucking company, continued babysitting, and still found time to participate in many activities. Her mother, who decided to go to college as well, also attended Framingham State College. They rode together to school each day. During college, Christa made regular trips to VMI to see Steve and often stopped in Washington on her way to tour the White House, museums, and other sites. She also became engaged in politics during the Vietnam War, protesting the war and advocating for civil rights. Christa and Steve both received their bachelor's degrees in 1970. That summer she and Steve were married, and then they moved to Washington, D.C., so Steve could attend Georgetown Law School.

When they arrived in Washington in late August, she could not find a full-time teaching job. She took a job as a full-time substitute for a U.S. history teacher at a junior high. The next year, she began full time at Thomas Johnson Junior High teaching U.S. history, social studies, and English. Johnson was one of the most difficult schools in Washington, D.C., but she was recognized for her ability to work with troubled students. The conditions were also difficult due to overcrowding, so she had to teach in a corner of the library. She made the best of the circumstances by employing some innovative teaching methods. She played the guitar and sang Pete Seeger and Woody Guthrie songs, designed games for her students to learn history, and took her students on numerous field trips to historical sites throughout Washington, D.C., and the surrounding area. In fact, the field trip became her favorite teaching tool. While Steve completed his law degree and she taught, she also completed a master's in education administration from Bowie State University in Maryland.

In 1976, Christa learned she was pregnant. She gave birth to Scott on September 11, 1976, at Andrews Air Force Base. When Steve completed his military service two years later, he was offered a position in the U.S. Justice Department. Christa reminded him that they had decided to live in New Hampshire and raise their family there. He tried to convince her to stay in Washington but when they went to visit New Hampshire, she was even more determined to live there. He agreed to apply for assistant to the state attorney general of New Hampshire and move if he was hired. When the state hired him, they moved to Concord, New Hampshire, in 1978. She did not begin a teaching job immediately but tutored a student who had been suspended from school for assault. The superintendent was so impressed with her work that he hired her for a full-time position at the junior high the next year. At the end of the year, she was laid off due to budget cuts, which worked out well since she was seven months pregnant. Their second child, Caroline, was born in 1979. The McAuliffes settled into an old, three-story house, but Christa quickly grew restless to return to the classroom.

In 1979, she began teaching English and social studies at Bow Memorial, then in 1982 she moved to Concord High School. At the high school, she taught law, economics, U.S. history, and a course she developed titled "The American Woman." In her history courses, she emphasized the impact of ordinary people on history, saying they were as important to history as kings, politicians, or generals. Christa was also actively involved in the community—church, a tennis club, the local playhouse, the YMCA, and Concord Hospital. In addition, she was a Girl Scout leader, a jogger, and a swimmer. Her students considered her an "inspirational human being, a marvelous teacher who made their lessons come alive." She continued using field trips as a teaching tool and was called the Field Trip Teacher. In fact, she later referred to her flight on the *Challenger* as the Ultimate Field Trip.

In 1984, she learned about NASA's efforts to locate an educator to fly on the shuttle. NASA officials thought if an ordinary person could communicate the excitement of travel in space, the public might be enthusiastic again, and President Reagan said that a teacher would fit the bill. When the opportunity came to apply to be the first teacher in space, everyone encouraged Christa to apply. Her friends said, "Go for it!" She completed the eleven-page application and hoped that she might be a finalist. After becoming a finalist, Christa did not think she would be chosen when she saw that some of the other teachers were doctors, authors, and scholars.

In June 1985, Christa and nine other teachers were invited to the White House. These ten teachers had been selected from a pool of 11,500 applicants. From those ten, only one would be an astronaut. Because President Reagan was hospitalized with cancer, Vice President Bush was going to greet the teachers and make the public announcement. Christa later commented that all the publicity and secrecy made her feel like a beauty pageant contestant waiting to hear, "And the winner is ... Miss New Hampshire." All the teachers were very nervous but also angry while they waited for the final decision. They were upset that they would not be told who was selected until the vice president announced it in front of the television cameras. Unwilling to be part of what felt like a publicity stunt, they took a pact that they would boycott the ceremony unless they were told in advance. NASA officials agreed to tell them on the condition that they would not leak the information to the press.

Finally, Ann Bradley, a NASA executive and chair of the selection committee, told them that Christa was the final choice. Christa was shocked by the news, partly because Bradley told her in such an offhand way. They had been talking about her husband's stint as a single parent since she had become involved in the NASA program. When Christa commented that her husband frequently served the children corn flakes, Bradley told her that her husband should stock up on corn flakes. When she understood what this comment meant, she realized she was the one. Soon after, Bradley told them that Barbara Morgan would be the alternate teacher in space, and she would provide Christa with support during the next months. Christa had not only forgotten to write an acceptance speech but also had forgotten to bring a brush or any makeup. So the other teachers loaned her what she needed to prepare for the televised announcement. She told the others, "Imagine me teaching from space, all over the world. Touching so many people's lives—that's a teacher's dream." When Vice President Bush announced which teacher had the "right stuff," she could not believe he was about to say her name. Finally, he said, "And the winner, the teacher who will be going into space, is Christa McAuliffe." She began her acceptance speech by saying, "It's not often a teacher is at a loss for words. I know my students wouldn't think so." Then she talked about the other nine teachers, commenting that only one body would go into space, but "there's gonna be ten souls I'm takin' with me."

All the publicity about Christa helped to increase public interest in the space program. After the announcement, she was constantly mobbed by reporters, but she handled the intense questioning with poise and humor. Even at NASA all the employees were so excited that they engulfed her when she entered the building. In addition, she became an inspiration to the teaching profession. She was pleased that the Teacher in Space Program highlighted the good work of all teachers. Regarding the space program, she said, "A lot of people thought it was over when we reached the Moon. They put space on the back burner. But people have a connection with teachers. Now that a teacher has been selected, they are starting to watch the launches again."

In September 1985, Christa began her training at NASA's facility in Houston. When she first arrived, she was worried that the other astronauts might think she was not qualified and just wanted to go along for the ride. She wanted to prove she could work just as hard as they could. But when they met, the other members of the crew treated her as part of the team. She was trained as a payload specialist. She studied emergency procedures for dealing with space accidents and emergency landings. She studied stacks of training manuals and endured a crash course to learn the intricacies of life in orbit. She learned how to deal with a crisis and experienced weightlessness in a space agency training jet. Christa trained for 114 hours, which was typical for shuttle guests. She told her son Scott she would take his stuffed frog, Fleegle, with her for good luck.

While aboard the shuttle, Christa was scheduled to teach two lessons from space. In the first lesson, she would introduce each flight member, explain their roles, show the cockpit, and explain how crew members live in microgravity. Her second lesson plan included an explanation of how the shuttle flew, why people explore space, and the technological advances created by the space program. In addition, she was supposed to tape six science demonstrations. These lessons were to be televised by the Public Broadcasting Service and broadcast to schoolchildren across the country. She also planned to keep a journal, inspired by the journals of the pioneer women who left their homes in search of a new frontier. Christa said, "That's our new frontier out there, and it's everybody's business to know about space." After the flight, the plan was for her to stay with the space agency until September, speaking to students and civic groups around the country about her experiences.

On January 28, 1986, her mission in space ended in tragedy. Just seventy-three seconds after liftoff, the space shuttle *Challenger* exploded, killing all seven astronauts aboard.

Christa is survived by her husband and her son and daughter. Grace Corrigan, Christa's mother, said in her book *A Journal for Christa*, "Christa lived. She never just sat back and existed. Christa always accomplished everything that she was capable of accomplishing. She extended her own limitations. She cared about her fellow human beings. She did the ordinary, but she did it well and unfailingly."

The Christa McAuliffe Planetarium was erected in Concord in her memory. The idea for a planetarium was chosen because it combined Christa's dream of going to space with her dedication to teaching. In 1990, the planetarium began its mission to educate, excite, and entertain learners of all ages in the sciences and humanities by actively engaging them in the exploration of astronomy and space science. Since then, thousands of children and adults have experienced the Ultimate Field Trip. The planetarium continues Christa's personal mission: "I touch the future, I teach."

43. MARY MCALEESE

B.1951

LAWYER, JOURNALIST, PRESIDENT OF IRELAND

We are a vibrant first-world country, but we have a humbling third-world memory.

—Mary McAleese, on her home country
of Ireland

Mary McAleese is a loose cannon and a very dangerous woman.
—Irish historian Conor Cruise O'Brien

In the Belfast of the 1950s and early 1960s, Catholic children came to believe that they could expect very little from life. The men in their families were twice as likely to be unemployed, and Catholic tenants found it virtually impossible to find housing in Protestant areas. If they did find housing, they were often burned out of their homes by loyalist paramilitaries. In addition, the Catholic vote was being heavily gerrymandered, and more votes were granted to business owners (who were mainly Protestant) than homeowners. The civil rights movement would not gain steam in Northern Ireland until the late 1960s. Much like African American children in the U.S. South, young Catholics in Northern Ireland came to believe that being second best was the best they could hope for. Women's rights in Ireland were even more abysmal. As a young girl born into anti-Catholic and antifemale discrimination, it is difficult to imagine that Mary McAleese could have ever foreseen the fate that would await her. In 1997, forty-six years after she was born into political turmoil and bigotry, she became the first person from Northern Ireland ever to be elected president of Ireland. She would also become the second female president and an acclaimed champion of women's rights throughout the world. Acclaimed as the people's president, she has overseen Ireland's greatest economic boom, the Celtic Tiger, and has worked tirelessly for peace in Northern Ireland.

Mary Patricia Leneghan was born on June 27, 1951, in Ardoyne, a small Catholic area within a heavily Protestant area of Belfast to Paddy and Mary Leneghan. As one of nine children, she witnessed the worst kind of anti-Catholic discrimination. Her deaf brother was beaten by Loyalists and her father's business, the Long Bar, was destroyed by Protestant gangs. Exhausted by sectarian violence and terrorized by witnessing their friends being attacked in the streets, the family moved outside of Belfast in County Antrim. In 1968, when gunfire sailed through the Leneghan home, her family was forced to leave the area entirely. Because of the injustice she witnessed, Mary decided to pursue a career in law. When she announced this to her parents, she faced a new kind of discrimination from the local priest. She recalls, "It was at home, in the presence of my parents and our parish priest. His response was immediate and emphatic: 'You can't—you have two terminal impediments. You are a woman and you have no relatives in the law.'" Mary's mother threw the priest out, convinced that her daughter was destined for a brilliant future. Her mother admonished her, advising, "You! Ignore him!" Always a bright student, Mary heeded her mother's advice and attended St. Dominic's High School on the Falls Road, with the goal of becoming a lawyer, despite the fact that only 10 percent of the nation's law students were female.

In 1969, Mary attended Queen's University in Belfast, where she graduated with honors in 1973. It was at Queen's that she became interested in family law, particularly as it pertained to women's rights. By 1974, she was called to serve on the Northern Ireland Bar and the next year she was appointed Reid Professor of Criminal Law at Trinity College—a position that fellow president Mary Robinson held just before her. During her tenure as Reid professor, she took an interest in prisoner's rights and reform. It was a passion that would pervade her life. Later, she became one of the leading figures in the cases of her fellow Irish citizens who had been unjustly imprisoned for Irish Republican Army crimes—in particular, the Guildford Four (whose story was later re-created in the movie *The Name of the Father*), the Birmingham Six, and the Maguire family.

In 1976, Mary's personal life also took a positive turn when she married Dr. Martin McAleese. It was a fascinating union as Martin was a Protestant who had grown up in east Belfast, the same people who had caused her such strife in her childhood. The couple were engaged shortly after they met at a school debate two years earlier, and Mary had broken off the engagement to pursue a relationship with the civil rights attorney Rory McShane, only to return to Martin.

Although she was now a married woman in Ireland, she continued to pursue her career with the same intensity. Again, along with her colleague Mary Robinson, she became a founding member and legal advisor for the Campaign for Homosexual Law Reform. She eventually left the post to become a journalist for Radio Telefis Eireann (RTE) in Dublin, where she faced discrimination akin to the prejudice she experienced in the north, but for very different reasons. As a reporter and presenter for *Today Tonight*, she felt the same anti–Northern Ireland sentiment that fellow journalist Nell McCafferty felt. She was "a Catholic, a Northerner, a nationalist and a woman—a quadruple deviant in the eyes of many influential people in RTE." Despite a fairly successful two-year career as a reporter and presenter, she became eager to return to practicing law. In 1981, she returned to the Trinity Reid professorship, and continued to work part time for RTE until 1985. In 1987, she returned to Queen's University to become the director of the Institute of Professional Legal Studies, which she helped reform into a leading department of the university. By this time, she was a major player in the Irish political scene. In 1984, she became part of the Catholic Episcopal Church's delegation to the New Ireland Forum, where she was critical of the Catholic Church's policies on women. She was also a favorite of Irish prime minister Charlie Haughey, but her credentials were not enough to get her elected. In 1987, she ran for the Dáil Éireann and lost. In 1994, she became the provice chancellor of Queen's University, the first woman to hold the position. Despite her ties to the Catholic Church, she remained constantly critical of its stand on child abuse by priests and on the ordination of women. Three years later, Mary became the Fianna Fáil candidate for the president of Ireland, much to the shock of many in the party. Her brilliance and community standing helped her cause, as did the fact that her only real opponent, Prime Minister Albert Reynolds, was facing opposition within the party.

While today she is one of Ireland's most beloved presidents, her campaign was one of the ugliest in Irish history. Because she was following the beloved Mary Robinson, and more important, because she was a nationalist Catholic from Belfast, journalists attacked her. The Unionist and reporter Eoghan Harris referred to her as a "tribal time bomb" (he now calls her "our nation's heart"). Others accused her of having ties with Sinn Féin, an accusation that was greatly fueled when the Sinn Féin president Gerry Adams endorsed her presidency. Despite the hostility she was feeling, Mary built her campaign on the premise of "Building Bridges." She earned 57 percent of the vote and beat three of her female opponents. On November 11, 1997, she was inaugurated as the eighth president of Ireland, the first time in history that a woman had succeeded another woman as an elected head of state anywhere in the world. As president, she has seen Ireland develop from a third world economic nation into one of the richest in the European Union. And she had kept her promise to build a deeper understanding between southern and Northern Ireland. In 1999, she published *Love in Chaos*, her plan for peace in Northern Ireland. Like Mary Robinson, she has made numerous trips to the north, proving that she is in no way the sectarian figure that the press accused her of being. In March 1998, she reached out to Northern Ireland's Protestants by announcing she would officially celebrate the Twelfth of July (a Protestant holiday) as well as St. Patrick's Day. In 2004, Mary McAleese boasted an approval rating of 80 percent and was reelected unopposed for her second term. In 2005, she was voted one of the 100 Most Powerful Women in the World by *Forbes* magazine. She will serve out her term until 2011.

44. EILEEN COLLINS

B.1956

FIRST WOMAN TO COMMAND A SPACE SHUTTLE

We want to explore. We're curious people. Look back over history, people have put their lives at stake to go out and explore . . . We believe in what we're doing. Now it's time to go.

—Eileen Collins

My dream, now, is that people will discover and invent new ways to fly higher, faster and farther and that someday humans will travel beyond our solar system.

—Eileen Collins

On July 22, 1999, Colonel Eileen Marie Collins became the first woman to command a space shuttle mission, the STS-93 *Columbia*. It was the fulfillment of a lifelong dream for her and would mark a milestone in U.S. history, but as Eileen Collins so eloquently stated, "Whether your commander is a man or woman doesn't really matter when it comes to getting your mission done."

Eileen Collins was born in Elmira, New York, on November 19, 1956, to James Collins (an Irish-American with roots in County Cork), a postal worker, and Rose Marie Collins. Eileen was one of four children, and the family was often short of money, but Eileen already displayed a rich imagination and a fascination with space. She recalls, "I can't give any specific moment when I decided what I wanted to do. When I was a child, there were no women astronauts and no women military pilots. But as I grew up and started learning more, the space program started becoming more visible. . . . As I got older, I started wondering why we didn't have women in these fields."

As a child, she read stories of Amelia Earhart and other women aviators. As her mother recalled in an interview, "Eileen's love of flying really started with *Star Trek*. She used to come straight home from school and watch it whenever she could." After attending St. Patrick's School through the eighth grade, followed by two years at Notre Dame High School and the last two at Elmira Free Academy, she enrolled at Corning Community College. Although her family could not afford college, Eileen was a diligent student and often worked odd jobs at the local pizza parlor and the church to earn extra money. She graduated with an Associates degree in science and math, then went on to earn a two-year scholarship to Syracuse University, where she earned a B.A. in mathematics and economics. Going on to Stanford, she earned a master's degree in operations research in 1986. Three years later she completed another master's in space systems management at Webster University.

In 1979, Eileen had become one of the first women to enroll in Air Force pilot training directly after college. She became a T-38 instructor pilot from 1979 to 1982. From 1983 to 1985, she was aircraft commander and instructor in C-141 cargo jets at Travis Air Force Base, then went on to become assistant professor of mathematics and a T-41 Air Force instructor at the U.S. Air Force Academy. Despite her hectic schedule, she also participated in Operation Urgent Fury, in which she helped evacuate medical students from Grenada after the U.S. invasion. In 1988, she married fellow pilot Pat Youngs. After graduating from the U.S Air Force Test Pilot School at Edwards Air Force Base in 1990, she was selected for NASA's astronaut program.

Eileen would also become the first women to pilot a space shuttle. She was also two months pregnant with her first child, Bridget. On February 2–11, 1995, on the first flight of the new joint Russian-American space program, mission STS-63 was launched with Eileen at the helm. She received the Harmon Trophy in recognition of her achievement.

On July 22–27, 1999, she became the first woman to command a shuttle mission for mission STS-93, which deployed the Chandra X-Ray Observatory, invented to capture phenomena such as exploding stars and black holes. As she famously announced during the mission, "Houston, we have a good deploy. Chandra is ready to open the eyes of X-ray astronomy to the world." Most recently, in 2005, Eileen commanded STS-114 *Discovery*, during which she was assigned to check flight safety and repair techniques.

Since becoming an astronaut, Eileen Collins has overseen four successful missions and has logged more than six thousand hours in thirty types of aircraft. In November 2005, she suffered personal tragedy when her mother Rose died. The next year in 2006, her father was tragically killed in a car accident. In January 2005, she retired from the Air Force as a colonel, and in May 2000, she announced her retirement from NASA, but her contribution endures. During her career, she received numerous honors, including the Defense Superior Service Medal, The French Legion of Honor, the Free Spirit Award, and the National Space Trophy.

45. CAROLINE KENNEDY

B.1957

ATTORNEY, AUTHOR

I have come to believe, more strongly than ever, that after people die, they really do live on through those who loved them.

—Caroline Kennedy

Caroline is embodying the finest traits of her parents.

—Senator Edward Kennedy

At the age of three, Caroline Kennedy was Camelot's princess and the world fell in love with her instantly. More than forty years later, she has proven herself to be the keeper of its flame and heiress to the Kennedy legacy of power, wealth, unfulfilled dreams, and terrible tragedy. With her parents and brother gone, she is the sole survivor of America's first family. During the 1960s, she and her little brother John Jr. were the two most famous children in America, but Caroline has remained a mystery. Bright, generous, and kind to a fault, she has managed to escape the scandal, drug abuse, and taint that has plagued many of the Kennedy grandchildren and has gone on to achieve remarkable accomplishments. As the *New York Observer* has commented, "With her personal grace and intelligence and her family's place in New Yorkers' hearts. Ms. Kennedy will command attention and respect."

Caroline Lee Kennedy was born on November 27, 1957, in New York, and her famous parents, John Fitzgerald Kennedy and Jacqueline Bouvier Kennedy, were elated. They had been trying to have a child for several years, but Jackie had a miscarriage and a stillborn child. Jackie later said Caroline's birth was "the happiest day in my life." One of Jack's friends commented, "Jack was more emotional about Caroline's birth than he was about anything else."

Caroline, like her grandmother, Rose Kennedy, was a first child and a first daughter. Her grandmother was the first child born to John F. Fitzgerald and Mary Josephine ("Josie") Hannon Fitzgerald. Her grandfather on the Fitzgerald side, called Johnny Fitz or Honey Fitz, was a famous politician. He served on the Boston Common Council, in the state senate, and in Congress and was the mayor of Boston. Her grandfather on the Kennedy side was Joe Kennedy, a wealthy businessman who was the force behind his sons' political careers. Her great-grandfather John Francis Kennedy came from Ireland during the Potato Famine and settled in the Boston tenements. Her mother, Jacqueline Bouvier, was the daughter of John ("Black Jack") Bouvier and Janet Lee Bouvier. Her mother's family was French, Scottish, and Irish, while her father's family was Irish and English. Jacqueline Kennedy was half-Irish, her mother being the granddaughter of four immigrants from County Cork, who came to New York during the 1840s' Potato Famine.

After Caroline was born, her nanny, Maud Shaw, soon became responsible for raising and feeding her, changing her diapers, and performing all the typical parental duties. Jack apparently tried feeding her a bottle once but became bored quickly and handed her back to Maud. Her parents never changed her diapers and rarely cared for her physically, but they loved her deeply. Friends commented that Caroline changed Jack profoundly. His connection with her helped him connect with others in a way that he had not been able to previously. As one friend said, "Until he had Caroline, he never really learned how to deal with people. It was fascinating to watch him grow in this capacity." Her birth also may have saved her parents' marriage. Jack's infidelity, frequent absences, and callousness had caused Jackie to consider divorce several times in their young marriage. When Caroline was born, she not only transformed Jack but she also changed Jackie. Jackie's self-esteem had suffered greatly during her marriage but having Caroline made her more confident. When she became a mother, she no longer lived in the shadow of her mother and her powerful mother-in-law.

Caroline was also a political asset in her father's quest for the presidency. Joe Kennedy had told Jack that if he wanted to make a serious bid for the presidency, he had to be married and have children. Some friends speculated that the primary reason that Jack wanted children was to further his political ambitions. Soon after Caroline was born, the media began vying for pictures of the baby. When Jack promised *Life* magazine photos and an exclusive story, Jackie adamantly refused to allow any pictures to be published. Eventually, she relented when Jack promised to spend more time with the family. In April 1958, the first photos of Caroline appeared in *Life*, including an engaging scene of Caroline playing peek-a-boo with her daddy. After that door was opened, Caroline was photographed with Jack and Jackie by many famous photographers, including Norman Rockwell and Jacques Lowe. Jack also wanted to take Caroline with him on as many public appearances as possible, but Jackie drew a firm line. As Lowe said, "He wanted to cart out Caroline as often as he could, but he would not defy Jackie when it came to their child."

During this time, Jack was still involved with many other women, including Marilyn Monroe. To try to keep a closer eye on her husband, Jackie began campaigning more with her husband. While her parents were off campaigning, Caroline stayed at home with Maud. Although her parents were fighting constantly, almost no one saw them argue, including Caroline. As Jackie became a more effective and popular campaigner, Caroline was left at home with Maud for longer and longer periods of time. Sadly, her first word was "good-bye." Her next words were "New Hampshire," "West Virginia," and "Wisconsin." She was obviously learning how to be a member of this political family.

In 1960, Jackie discovered that she was pregnant again. Not willing to take any chances with this baby, Jackie was adamant that she would not attend the Democratic National Convention and would not continue campaigning at her previous pace. She and Caroline stayed in Hyannis Port, Massachusetts, while Jack campaigned furiously for the nomination. In Hyannis Port, Grandmother Rose spent considerable time with her granddaughter. Although Rose had been a distant mother who managed her children rather than mothered them, she was a much more affectionate grandmother. Caroline was one of her favorites because she was a charming, intelligent child, and thanks to Jackie, she was much better behaved than the other grandchildren.

After Jack won the Democratic nomination, he spent several weeks with the family in Hyannis Port. This was the longest period Caroline spent with her parents since she was born. As she bonded with her father, he developed an even deeper affection for her and gave her a nickname that he called her for the rest of his life: "Buttons." In Hyannis Port, Caroline was often surrounded by her grandparents, aunts and uncles, and cousins. She was part of the frenetic activity that was ever present when the Kennedys gathered. After this hiatus, Jack began campaigning continually to win the presidential race. Jackie stayed in Hyannis Port with Caroline for at least three months, so they seldom saw him except on television or in magazines. When Caroline did see him on television, she ran to the set, pointed, and yelled, "Look, Daddy!"

Although Jackie was not on the campaign trail, she and Caroline appeared in numerous magazine layouts. Jackie's style was a publicized contrast to Pat Nixon's plain appearance, and the pictures of Caroline captivated America. Maud did not appear in any of the photos and Jackie actually told reporters that she had raised Caroline without a nanny. Jackie did accompany Jack on the final leg of the campaign in New York, and then moved on to Hyannis Port to wait for the results. The family stayed up late to watch the election results, but they didn't learn anything until the morning. That morning Caroline ran into the bathroom to tell her father that he had won. Although he already had been told, he pretended not to know and feigned surprise when she told him. When he asked if winning meant he would be president, she answered, "Yes, Miss Shaw told me to call you 'Mr. President' now." Later that day when Richard Nixon conceded, Jack scooped up Caroline and went out to talk to the reporters while Jackie walked along the beach alone.

When they moved back to their house in Georgetown, the media coverage was relentless. For the first time, Caroline heard reporters call her name and experienced the frenzy she had missed on the campaign trail. Caroline was an easygoing child who did not mind the chaos, but she did notice how it affected her more reticent mother. The chaos continued inside and outside of the house. Jack's staff virtually moved into the house during the transition between the election and the inauguration. When Jackie talked to Jack about how all the bedlam was upsetting her, he ignored her or snapped at her. Caroline was a very perceptive child who sensed the tension between her parents.

Possibly in response to Jackie's protestations, Jack began spending more time in Palm Beach with his advisers preparing for his presidency. Jackie's delivery date was growing closer, so she begged Jack to stay with her. He did not think it was necessary because Caroline had been born on her due date without complications. But one day Jackie began screaming because she was bleeding. When Caroline and Maud ran to Jackie, Caroline saw what was happening to her mother. She became frightened and ran back to her room. Maud stayed with Caroline while Jackie was rushed to the hospital for a caesarean section and her father was still in Palm Beach. John Fitzgerald Kennedy Jr. was born on November 25, 1960. His father did not arrive until after his son was born.

To make up for his absence during the baby's birth, Jack visited the hospital several times a day with Caroline. John Jr. had been born prematurely and was in an incubator for a week; his mother was recovering from her surgery. The media became even more captivated by Caroline, snapping photos of her with her father having fun while her mother and baby brother remained in the hospital. Caroline was thrilled by her brother's arrival. Her parents had told her he was a birthday present for her third birthday. So she thought the baby was hers and called him "my baby."

After John Jr. and Jackie came home, things took a turn for the worse. Jack insisted that Jackie go to the White House for a tour with Mamie Eisenhower while he took the baby to Palm Beach. Jackie went into a relapse that required her to stay in bed for several weeks. At the same time, John Jr. suffered from a respiratory inflammation that made his health decline to the point where he was near death. Fortunately, a Palm Beach pediatrician saved the baby's life. While her mother and baby brother rested, Caroline showed off for the cameras. At times, her father would have to escort her from the room when her mugging became too distracting.

When Jackie recovered, she went back to Georgetown alone to or-chestrate the move and the refurbishing of the White House. The first rooms she redecorated were the nursery for Caroline and the baby and a kindergarten for the children of White House employees. When the fam-ily moved into the White House after the inauguration, the children's toys were the first belongings to be unpacked. Jackie wanted the children to be raised in "more personal surroundings" and be cared for by their parents, not "nurses and Secret Service agents." She said, "It isn't fair to children in the limelight to leave them in the care of others and then ex-pect that they will turn out all right. They need their mother's affection and guidance and long periods of time alone with her." While they lived in the White House, Jackie tried to give the children a stable life with as much privacy as possible.

The family followed essentially the same routine during their time in the White House. Caroline and John Jr. spent time with their father every morning while he prepared for the day. Then Caroline went to school upstairs with the other children who attended school in the White House. Jackie took the baby for a walk and then later joined the children for lunch in the small family dining area she had created. Every day the whole family took naps in the afternoon. Then the president went back to the Oval Office to work while the children played in the play area out-side his office. In the evening, Jackie sat with the children during their dinner and talked to them about the events of the day. Later in the evening, Jack and Jackie had drinks and dinner with friends. Over time, the family acquired a huge number of pets, including dogs, guinea pigs, lambs, ducks, rabbits, birds, and a cat (the cat was given away because Jack was so allergic to it). Then Jackie decided both children needed ponies, Macaroni and Leprechaun, and had a stable built for them. Jackie kept her promise to make life for Caroline and John Jr. as structured and normal as possible while their father was president.

Caroline was continuing to show signs that she was highly intelligent. She could read when she was three years old and amazed everyone with her extensive vocabulary. Jackie commented, "Of course I shouldn't be surprised if she is precocious. She is Jack's daughter, after all." Caroline talked like an adult and would often let adults know that she did not want to be talked to like a child. She was very well behaved and even tempered. Even when most children would be upset by disappointments or limits, she accepted her parents' explanations with little complaint. She also tried to correct her brother's behavior and admonished him to "be a good boy." Jackie's taste in music, dance, and other cultural events also influenced Caroline. As she listened to classical music and watched ballet, she realized that her mother was the one who appreciated the arts while her father preferred cowboy movies and pop music. Like many gifted children, she was not only brilliant intellectually and academically but also socially perceptive and insightful.

Although Jackie was always concerned about the welfare and safety of her children, she did not want them to be overprotected or dependent on others. So she limited the role of the Secret Service and staff in their lives, forbidding them to do things for the children. She and Jack also allowed the children to take risks, including riding horses, swimming, and other athletic pursuits. Jackie made sure that they had the same experiences as other children. They colored eggs at Easter, went trick or treating, made hearts for Valentine's Day, and decorated the White House Christmas tree. Jack also played games with the children and often roughhoused with them in the way he had played with his siblings. However, Caroline and John were treated differently by their parents and grandparents. Caroline was expected to be much more well behaved and polite than her brother. The family tolerated John's rambunctious behavior, need for attention, and rebelliousness to the point that some thought John was the favorite. Maud was often irritated that John seemed to be the center of attention and to receive more affection than Caroline.

The family's remaining years in the White House were marked by highs and lows. From all appearances, it appeared that they continued to live in the magical world of Camelot. However, they endured political and global crises, including the Bay of Pigs. They also suffered family hardships, the worst of which was the death of Caroline's little brother, Patrick. Patrick was born with the same respiratory condition that had caused the death of another child and had plagued John when he was born. When he died, Caroline remained calm as usual, trusting that the angels would care for her little brother. Her mother was so distraught that she required a lengthy trip to recover.

November 1963 brought the tragedy that would alter their lives completely when John F. Kennedy was assassinated in Dallas. Her mother endured the horror of the shooting, the hospital, and his death and then had to return to the White House to tell her children. In the end, the family decided that Maud should tell them. Caroline was desolate but she coped as well as could be expected. She wrote a poignant letter to her father: "Daddy, We are going to miss you. Daddy, I love you very much, Caroline." During the funeral, when Jackie finally broke down, Caroline took her hand and said, "You'll be all right, Mommy. Don't cry. I'll take care of you." Then Jackie asked John to say good-bye to his father. While Caroline comforted her mother, John saluted his father's coffin. This was the heartbreaking scene that millions of people would remember forever.

Because Caroline was older and so bright, she absorbed all the events and emotions during and after her father's funeral. Friends noticed a change in her demeanor that persisted for a long time after her father's death. The carefree, happy child became serious and tense. Many said she seemed to age before their eyes. When they moved out of the White House to a new home in Washington, Jackie tried to make the home as comfortable as possible. However, Jackie was so grief-stricken and depressed that she cried constantly. While John was kept busy and was generally oblivious to his mother's pain, Caroline was keenly aware of her mother's grief. Many times she tried to comfort her mother, but at other times she realized that she could not console her mother and left her alone. She told the nuns at her school, "My mommy cries all of the time." The Kennedy family, particularly Bobby, struggled through their own grief to care for Jackie and the children. As Bobby became their surrogate father, he and Caroline developed a very close bond that continued throughout her childhood.

Jackie's sister Lee finally convinced Jackie to move to New York to escape the madness of Washington. Jackie bought an apartment in Manhattan and enrolled Caroline in the Convent of the Sacred Heart where Pat Kennedy Lawford's daughters were students. Caroline developed a close relationship with the Lawford girls, which Maud described as being more like sisters than cousins. Nevertheless, Caroline had a difficult time adjusting to life in New York. She missed her friends in Washington and she had difficulty making new friends at first. When Jackie asked why she was not invited to a party, it became clear that the parents were hesitant to presume that they could invite the famous little girl. After that, Caroline was invited to all the events and made new friends easily. Jackie's friends tried to keep her occupied and spent time with her children. When Bobby was elected senator in New York state, the children saw him even more frequently than they had when they lived in New York. In fact, Bobby spent so much time with Jackie and the children many suspected that his relationship with Jackie had become romantic. Caroline was happy to see the affection between her mother and Bobby.

Just as Caroline's life seemed to be returning to a more normal, happy state, Jackie fired Maud, the nanny who had been like a mother to her. In the following months, Jackie fired Secret Service agents, drivers, piano teachers, cooks, and other staff. It seemed that Jackie was worried if the staff became too close to the children or if they seemed to have any connection to the press. As soon as Caroline became accustomed to someone, her mother fired the person, which Caroline found bewildering and scary. Jackie had also become very active in the New York social scene, so she was not home much of the time. That, combined with the dismissal of staff that Caroline liked, made her more anxious. Concerned that Caroline was becoming too withdrawn, Jackie took the children on trips with her and spent more time with them. Caroline continued to do well in school and her social life was as typical as possible given her station in life.

In 1968, life in the United States became tumultuous again. Martin Luther King Jr. was assassinated, and race riots plagued many cities. Then Bobby announced his intent to run for president. Jackie and Caroline were worried about Bobby's safety, and Jackie predicted that what happened to her husband would happen to Bobby. Tragically, she was correct. Bobby was assassinated during the California campaign. Caroline lost her beloved uncle and adopted father. Jackie and Caroline were both traumatized by Bobby's death. It was as if they were reliving Jack's death and the grief was crushing. After the funeral, Jackie decided that the solution was to get her children out of the United States. She had begun an affair with Aristotle Onassis earlier but had kept the relationship a secret because Bobby had asked her to hide it until after the election. In an effort to protect her children, Jackie decided to marry Onassis. Ari tried to win over Caroline and John and succeeded in winning their affection, but Caroline was shocked by her mother's announcement that she would marry him. Caroline was only ten years old and had endured an incredible amount of tragedy and change in her young life.

Although Caroline was not happy about the marriage, life with Onassis did have its perks. The children were accustomed to affluence, but their stepfather offered a whole new level of privilege. They traveled to exotic locations on his yacht and enjoyed a lavish lifestyle. Onassis often stayed in Europe while Jackie and the children lived in New York. When he did spend time with the family, he spent most of it with John. Jackie and Onassis decided that John needed a strong father figure, forgetting that Caroline needed a father just as much, if not more than John. Caroline relied on her uncle Teddy in the way she had relied on Bobby. Over the next few years, Jackie's marriage to Onassis became increasingly volatile and deteriorated.

During these years, Caroline attended several schools, Brearley in New York and Concord Academy in Concord, Massachusetts. After she graduated from Concord, she went on to Radcliffe College at Harvard. She seemed more relaxed with herself when she was at school and away from her mother's powerful presence. She remained a good student but became more of a typical teenager who engaged in some pranks and rebelled. She always had to deal with classmates who were jealous of her or who were afraid to approach her, but she made friends in every school. She dated casually until her mother introduced her to Tom Carney from Doubleday. She soon fell in love with Carney and he said he wanted to marry her. After a while, he grew tired of dating a girl in college, wanted to get married, and decided that Caroline was too young for him. After she graduated from Radcliffe, Caroline was devastated when she learned that he planned to marry someone else. To bury her sorrow, she took a job as a production assistant at the Metropolitan Museum of Art's Television and Film division. This was where she met and began dating Ed Schlossberg.

While she was dating Ed, she attended law school at Columbia University. She still saw her mother several times a week and she saw her brother or talked to him every day. John and Jackie were fighting because John wanted to become an actor and Caroline sympathized with his need to be his own person. Regardless, Jackie and John remained close until the day she died.

In 1986, Caroline married Ed in a wedding that captured the public's imagination and boasted a celebrity-studded guest list. While she was completing her law degree, she discovered that she was pregnant. In 1988, she graduated from law school, then prepared for the birth of the baby while she studied for the bar exam. On June 25, she gave birth to Rose. She and Ed had two more children: Tatiana and John. Jackie was a doting grandmother who enjoyed her time with her grandchildren. In 1993, tragedy struck again when Jackie learned that she had non-Hodgkin's lymphoma, an aggressive form of cancer. The family kept it a secret for a while as Jackie's condition continued to deteriorate. She died in 1994, leaving John and Caroline to grieve.

Although she missed her mother, Caroline was busy with her family and the many social obligations that now fell to her. She also supported her brother through his relationship with Darryl Hannah and his launch of the magazine *George*. She was happy when John married Carolyn Bessette but worried when the marriage became rocky. She also worried when John began flying lessons. Again, her fears about the safety of a Kennedy man would be prophetic. In 1999, John was killed in a plane crash when he flew to Hyannis Port to attend the wedding of his cousin, Rory Kennedy. Now Caroline was completely alone.

Despite her personal tragedies, Caroline has proven herself to be the keeper of her father's flame. She has written two books with the coauthor Ellen Alderman, *In Our Defense: The Bill of Rights in Action*, which became a best seller, and *The Right to Privacy*. She has also served on numerous boards and committees, and after September 11, 2001, she became the head fund-raiser for the New York City School System. She also paid the ultimate tribute to her mother by editing *The Best Loved Poems of Jacqueline Kennedy* for Hyperion Books. In tribute to her father, she conceived the "Profile in Courage" Award, which honors commitment and excellence in leadership. In 2000, she was the keynote speaker at the Democratic National Convention, where she was regaled with the sounds of a euphoric delegation chanting, "Caroline, Caroline!" As usual, the quiet Kennedy welcomed the show of affection with grace and style. Caroline Kennedy Schlossberg lives in New York City with her husband and three children.

46. MAIRÉAD FARRELL

1957–1988
FEMINIST, MILITARY LEADER, REPUBLICAN ICON

Everyone tells me I'm a feminist. All I know is that I'm just as good as others . . . and that especially means men. . . . I am oppressed as a woman, and I'm also oppressed as an Irish person. Everybody in this country is oppressed, and yet we can only end our oppression as women if we end the oppression of our nation as a whole. But I don't think that that alone is enough. This isn't the first time that women have been seen as secondary. But women today have been through so much that they won't just let things be.

— Mairéad Farrell

Do not stand at my grave and weep,
I am not there I do not sleep,
Do not stand at my grave and cry,
When Ireland lives I do not die.

—From "The Ballad of Mairéad Farrell" by
Chris Byrnes

In May 1981, a young man from Belfast, Northern Ireland, named Bobby Sands died in Long Kesh Prison at the age of twenty-seven. Two months before, in March, he and his fellow prisoners embarked on a hunger strike to gain political status for all Republican prisoners in Northern Ireland. Nine young men were to follow Sands—and eventually die—in this fight for what would become known as the "Five Demands in Northern Ireland": the right not to wear a prison uniform; the right not to do prison work; the right to free association with other prisoners; the right to one visit, one letter, and one package per week; and the right to organize their own educational and recreational pursuits. Just a few months later, on October 3, the British government granted Sands's demands. After his death, Sands became the most recognized and admired figure in the Irish nationalist struggle. Images of this red-haired, smiling young man graced posters and murals all over Ireland—and in several U.S. cities. But during those final months of Sands's life, just miles away, a twenty-three-year-old female prisoner was leading a hunger strike for political status in Armagh Jail in County Armagh, Northern Ireland. Her name was Mairéad Farrell, and just seven years after Sands's death, she would take her place beside him as the most important Republican icon of the last fifty years.

Mairéad Farrell was born in Belfast on August 3, 1957, and grew up on the Catholic Falls Road, the only girl in a family of six children. From an early age, Mairéad was entrenched in politics. "Living in Belfast was a political education in itself. My own family [had] a Republican background, but living on the Falls Road, I saw internment, I saw the British soldiers. . . . At that time women were involved and I was very young when I became involved in the Republican movement."

Mairéad's own family was politically aware, although not stridently Republican—her parents voted for the moderately nationalist political party (the Social Democrat and Labour Party), not the more militant Sinn Féin, and her grandfather was imprisoned in the 1920s for refusing to follow orders from the British Black and Tans. A well-educated Catholic school girl, Mairéad had very little connection to the Irish Republican Army (IRA) during her upbringing—the nationalist group in which she later became the most important female figure—unlike many of her fellow nationalists.

To understand Mairéad's growing passion for the nationalist cause, it is essential to understand the city that surrounded her during her childhood. By 1968, when Mairéad was just eleven years old, Belfast (and the rest of British-ruled Northern Ireland) was rife with discrimination. Catholics were twice as likely to be unemployed as Protestants and Catholic families who lived in Protestant areas were being burned out of their homes and as a result were finding it increasingly difficult to find decent housing. All these factors were the catalyst for a growing civil rights movement in Northern Ireland—and increasing unrest between Belfast's Catholic and Protestant populations A year later, the city was teeming with British soldiers who were sent there to "keep the peace" between the two communities. While it was supposed to be a temporary measure, the troops are still patrolling the streets. The nationalist community found itself under increasing surveillance and discovered its civil rights eroding even further. By 1971, the British government had introduced internment, the practice of imprisonment without trial, and illegal strip searches in exclusively Catholic homes. Now, young Catholic men found themselves being carted off to jail cells with no recourse, and young Catholic women were now responsible for caring for their own households. By 1972, when Mairéad was fifteen years old, Belfast was a powder keg and the civil rights movement in Northern Ireland had gained momentum. And in January of that year came the event that would define the course of the nationalist movement forever—and the course of young Mairéad's life. On January 30, in Derry, Northern Ireland, civil rights marchers gathered in a peaceful protest against internment. The British army began firing into the crowd, shooting twenty-seven people and killing thirteen. While several officers claimed that they were defending themselves against armed suspected IRA members, a later inquiry and testimony from residents and journalists found the protestors to be unarmed. Bloody Sunday was an earth-shattering event that prompted many young Catholics to join the IRA, including Mairéad. Although she was a gifted student and studying hard for her A levels, the Irish equivalent of college-prep courses, her passion for the cause subsumed her desire for a formal education. Four years later, in 1976, at the age of eighteen, she graduated from school and joined the IRA.

That same year, Mairéad was arrested and convicted for her part in the IRA's growing bombing campaign in response to the British government's removal of the political status for IRA prisoners. After attempting an attack on the Conway Hotel in Belfast, she was charged with causing three explosions and being a member of the IRA and sentenced to fourteen and half years in prison. As was the custom with all political prisoners, she refused to recognize the nonjury or Diplock court and found herself, just a few months before her nineteenth birthday, imprisoned in Armagh Jail, one of the worst prisons in Ireland.

Mairéad began raising hell almost as soon as she set foot in Armagh. Because she was arrested after the removal of political status, Mairéad was the first woman prisoner to be denied the rights that were afforded the prisoners who came before her. She was allowed to associate with other Republican prisoners for no more than a few minutes during the week and denied access to weekly visits from her family. In response, Mairéad began a no-work protest and was soon joined by her fellow Republican inmates. Buoyed by the support of the other women, Mairéad began to put her keen mind and convent education to work and organized Irish-language lessons and political education classes. She soon became the commanding officer of all female prisoners of war, a role that would become critical in the coming years. Conditions in Armagh were already appalling. This nineteenth-century building had not been updated since it was built, so it lacked even the most basic amenities, and the food was inedible, but the growing tensions over political status made life in the dilapidated building even more unbearable. In 1978, male guards locked the women prisoners in their cells for weeks without access to the exercise yards or bathrooms. The women were forced to use chamber pots, which they were not allowed to empty, so they had to throw the contents out the window, and sanitary conditions were reaching a crisis. They were now being locked in their cells for the entire day, with the exception of one hour, and were confined to cells no bigger than closets. By February 1980, the women of Armagh had had enough and the "Dirty Protest" was born.

Under Mairéad's command, the women refused to empty their chamber pots and refused to bathe. Because their cell windows were boarded up by the guards to prevent them from dumping their pots outside, the women were forced to put their waste on the prison walls. The cells soon became a breeding ground for disease and germs, and even the strongest women had to summon their will to endure the protest, which lasted more than a year. But the women of Armagh became legendary in their resolve, and by the time the male prisoners in Long Kesh called their first hunger strike in December 1980, the women were ready. Three female prisoners—Mairéad Farrell, Mary Doyle, and Mairéad Nugent—began their own strike, refusing all food and taking only water. The strike lasted eighteen days and ended when the British government made overtures to meet the prisoners' demands. It was a promise the British government was soon to break and it paved the way for a second hunger strike in March 1981, during which ten young men starved themselves to death and Mairéad watched in agony as her fellow inmates died one by one, but she remained dedicated to the fight for political status. "I am a volunteer of the Irish Republican Army and a political prisoner in Armagh jail. I am prepared to fight to the death, if necessary, to win the recognition that I am a political prisoner and not a criminal."

After the death of her brothers in arms and the reinstatement of the hard-won special category status for Irish political prisoners, Mairéad saw her own role redefined and began to examine her role as a female member of the nationalist struggle. As she recalls in Anne Crilly's seminal 1988 documentary *Mother Ireland*, many of the men in the movement "looked at us as the 'girls in Armagh' and 'we shouldn't really be in there—let the men do it.' Women are supposed to be looked after, taken care of. Women aren't supposed to be politically active. But we wanted political status as much as the men." In 1982, she found herself taking on a new struggle that affected her both as a woman and as a nationalist when women prisoners became the victims of brutal and humiliating strip searches at the hands of male guards. Again, it was Mairéad who fought back hard, and it was a fight she continued even after she was released from prison. She also refocused her energies on her education—she began studying political science and economics at Open University, a system introduced by British prime minister Harold Wilson in which prisoners could enroll in university classes and pursue a degree while still serving their time. Once again, her superior intellect and determination paid off when she was accepted into Belfast's prestigious Queen's University before her release in 1986 at the age of twenty-nine. By the time she left Armagh, Mairéad had served ten years—more than a third of her life—in jail.

Determined to make the most of her freedom, Mairéad continued to fight for the rights of female prisoners in Ireland, joining the strip searching campaign and speaking on their behalf all over the country. And she continued to fight for the freedom of her country.

More bound to the cause of Irish freedom than ever before, Mairéad resumed her service with the IRA just months after her release. By this time, Mairéad was either a full-fledged Republican heroine or a "terrorist"—depending on who was labeling her. Her voice and image were banned on British airwaves. Any documentary that featured an interview with her was automatically barred. Ironically, just two years later, after her untimely and violent death, Mairéad's image appeared everywhere and came to define the very symbol of Irish Republicanism.

In March 1988, Mairéad and two IRA volunteers Danny McCann, who was also Mairéad's boyfriend, and Sean Savage traveled to Gibraltar. British intelligence claimed to have a tip that the team was masterminding a bombing on the rock and in turn it planned an ambush. By the time Mairéad and her fellow volunteers reached Gibraltar, the British army was waiting for them, guns at the ready. They raised their arms in surrender, but the soldiers started shooting, pumping all three with enough bullets to kill them several times over. They shot Mairéad eight times, leaving her dead at the age of thirty-one. It was seven years later, in 1995, that the European Court of Human Rights ruled that Mairéad, Danny, and Sean were illegally assassinated in violation of the European Convention on Human Rights.

Ironically, Mairéad joined the Republican movement because of Bloody Sunday, a milestone that called thousands of young people to take up arms in the name of freedom and justice, and in turn her death became another milestone that gained sympathy for the nationalist cause. After the death of the "Gibraltar Three," as they became known, Mairéad's face came to grace posters, murals, and newspapers all over the world, just like that of Bobby Sands before her. Her plight helped energize the nationalist cause more than any other event since the hunger strikes of 1981. To this day, Mairéad remains the highest ranking woman in the IRA, and to young women across Ireland, she remains a symbol of feminism. Tragically, Mairéad did not live to see many of the drastic changes that occurred in Northern Ireland after her death—particularly the release of all political prisoners under the Good Friday Agreement that was completed a little more than a decade after her death. As she so poignantly observed before her death, "You have to be realistic, you realize that ultimately you're either going to be dead or end up in jail."

In her death, she is an icon, but in her life she was an intelligent, beautiful, educated, and extremely articulate young woman who literally changed the face of the Republican movement. Before this pretty, petite, and soft-spoken young woman joined the ranks, most viewed nationalism as a back-alley, working-class movement. With her middle-class background, Mairéad broke the stereotype and encouraged a whole new generation of Irish women—and men—to rethink the relationship between civil rights, nationalist rights, and women's rights, just like Maud Gonne and Countess Markievicz had done more than a half-century before.

47. VERONICA GUERIN

1959–1996
JOURNALIST

I am simply doing my job. . . . I am letting the public know how this society operates.
> —Veronica Guerin, shortly before she was assassinated for exposing Dublin's drug lords

That's what it takes to be a hero, a little gem of innocence inside you that makes you want to believe that there still exists a right and wrong, that decency will somehow triumph in the end.
> —Lise Hand, describing the late Irish journalist Veronica Guerin

If one were to wander the streets of north Dublin in the late 1980s and early 1990s, one would hardly recognize it from the bustling, cosmopolitan city we see today. Heroin-addicted teenagers lingered in doorways, and children could be seen picking up used needles on the city's streets and playgrounds. More than 15,000 people were estimated to have been using heroin daily, and methadone clinics reported admitting addicts as young as fourteen years old. Poverty and unemployment, coupled with the epidemic heroin problem, made the streets of Dublin treacherous. In areas of north Dublin, such as Ballymun and Coolock, the city's heroin problem had the entire community in a stranglehold. And because there were no stringent laws in Ireland to punish the drug dealers and no witness protection programs, Dublin's drug lords ran the streets with impunity. They were rarely arrested and if they were, they used violence and intimidation to threaten witnesses, so that they were rarely if ever convicted. Also, because of Ireland's strict libel laws, journalists found exposing these criminals to be virtually impossible without the threat of a lawsuit. The man who rose to the top of the drug underworld was the gangster named John Gilligan. Ironically, Gilligan was also a respected member of the community and "businessman" who had managed to escape the clutches of authorities for years, despite a criminal record that dated back to 1967. But in 1994, a fearless young journalist came on the scene and vowed to take on Gilligan's crew—exposing Dublin's corrupt underworld forever. Veronica Guerin was true to her word; she did forever change Ireland's criminal laws and managed to ensure the incarceration of Dublin's most feared criminals. It was a mission that ultimately cost her her life.

Veronica Guerin was born in 1959, one of five children, in the middle-class community of Artane, County Dublin, to Christopher and Bernadette Guerin. Even as a child, she was gregarious, athletic, and fearless, traits that came to full fruition during her early days as a journalist. According to her mother, she was interested in helping her fellow man from an early age. Bernadette said, "From the time Veronica was a child, Veronica cared about people. If she saw that there was a niche where she could help in some way, yeah, the crusader took over." Always a bright child, she attended Holy Faith Convent, where she displayed a growing passion for football and politics. Her passion led her to work for Fianna Fáil, Ireland's most prominent political party, where she captured the attention of Charlie Haughey, who later became Ireland's taoiseach (prime minister) and who was so impressed by her that he appointed her to several prominent posts within the party and employed her as a political researcher. After a brief stint in politics, Veronica started her own public relations business and then worked briefly as an accountant before starting a career in journalism.

Veronica took her first reporter's job at Ireland's *Sunday Business Post* and then went on to become an investigative reporter for the *Sunday Independent* in 1994. Even though she was a relative newcomer to journalism, she took on stories that even veteran reporters would have envied. She began to make a name for herself by relentlessly pursuing an interview with Bishop Eamon Casey, the defrocked priest who caused a scandal in the United States and Ireland by admitting that he fathered a child by an American woman. When she began writing stories on Martin Cahill, the man known as "the General" and Dublin's most renowned criminal boss who had been gunned down that year, Veronica gained nationwide renown and acquired a passion for seedy Dublin's gangland. Ironically, these articles centered on possible suspects in Cahill's murder (one of these suspects was John Gilligan, who later masterminded Veronica's murder).

It was during this same year, in 1994, that she began to cultivate a relationship with Dublin con artist John Traynor. Handsome, slick, and intelligent, Traynor had been suspected of working with Gilligan for years. Veronica called him "the Coach" and though he was her primary source, he was also playing both sides of the fence. By this time, Veronica had started to become interested in Gilligan when Traynor began supplying her with invaluable information about his immense wealth from a colossal drug empire that was supplying communities with hash, ecstasy, and heroin. The *Sunday World* newspaper had already run a story about Gilligan, without naming him, that implicated him in the country's largest drug ring, which only fueled Veronica's desire to catch him. While Traynor was feeding Veronica information, he was also feeding information about her right back to Gilligan. However, with Traynor's help, Veronica began publishing award-winning stories on Dublin's most dangerous underground figures, using only pseudonyms. But while she was acquiring fame and recognition, she was also putting herself in grave danger. In October 1994, she received the first of several death threats when bullets sailed through her house in Dublin. Undeterred, she feverishly pursued Dublin's criminals in print, culminating in a shocking story in the *Sunday Independent* that ran on January 29, 1995, which detailed the machinations of a man called "the Monk," a Dublin criminal who had pulled off a million-dollar heist right under the noses of Dublin's police force, the Gardai. The next day, a masked man knocked on her front door while her husband, Graham, and five-year-old son, Cahal, were out and pumped a bullet into her thigh. The bullet just missed a major artery and Veronica was hospitalized. From her hospital bed, she declared, "I vow that the eyes of justice, the eyes of this journalist will not be shut again . . . no hand can deter me from my battle for truth." The man believed to be guilty of the crime was Traynor.

According to *Evil Empire: The Irish Mob and the Assassination of Veronica Guerin* by Paul Williams, "After weeks of investigation, the police nominated the man that they still believed ordered the attack, John Traynor. The Coach had organized the shooting to show that that he had the 'bottle' to hit a reporter, who he claimed had annoyed him." It is doubtful whether Veronica knew this at the time, but she continued to play a dangerous game with him, especially as her passion to implicate Gilligan grew. Traynor warned her to leave the Gilligan story alone, and she in turn had threatened to expose him as well. Still undeterred, Veronica sent a letter to Gilligan requesting an interview. When the letter went unanswered, she drove to his sprawling house farm in Kildare and asked to speak with him. He began punching her in the face and threatened to kill her—a chilling warning. He dragged her to the car and continued to beat her. The next day he called her and threatened to rape and kill her son. She reported the incident to the police, who provided her with twenty-four-hour protection, but the damage was done. Veronica Guerin was now on John Gilligan's radar, and he intended to get rid of her. Several days later, when the *Sunday Independent* threatened to run a story on Gilligan's savage attack on their reporter, he offered Veronica several hundred thousand pounds to drop the matter; she refused and continued to press charges. Facing a potential six-month prison sentence, Gilligan vowed that he would see Veronica Guerin dead before he went back to prison again. It was a promise that he kept.

On June 26, 1996, after beating a traffic ticket in a Dublin court, Veronica Guerin was murdered on the Naas Road in Dublin when two men on a motorcycle fired six bullets into her car while she was stopped at a traffic light. She was just thirty-seven years old and the mother of a six-year-old boy. Her death shocked the world—it was the first murder of a journalist in the Irish Free State and her fellow reporters saw it as an attack on democracy and free speech. The Irish parliament marked her death with a moment of silence and supporters from all over the world sent condolences to Veronica's family. The next day the *Irish Independent* ran a story indicating that it knew exactly who was responsible for

Veronica's murder. Still, Gilligan proclaimed his innocence, and it took three years for an investigation team to put him away.

In 1998 and 1999, the crack Lucan investigation team hired to investigate Veronica's murder conducted over 150 arrests in conjunction with her murder, which resulted in the conviction of Paul Ward, one of Gilligan's gang and the man believed to have pulled the trigger, who was sentenced to life, and Brian Meehan, who was believed to have been the driver of the motorcycle. He was sentenced to life as well. Gilligan was also convicted but never sentenced of murder charges, but is currently serving a thirty-year sentence for trafficking by the Special Criminal Court. Her main informer and "ally," John Traynor is currently on the run—he was last seen in Portugal and is still fighting extradition back to Ireland on drug charges.

There is a bitter irony to Veronica Guerin's life. While after her assassination she became one of the world's most beloved and respected journalists, and her name became synonymous with journalistic integrity, during her career she often incurred the contempt of her fellow journalists. She was seen as a cowboy, untrained, and a fly-by-night, in their opinion. While much of this can be attributed to professional jealousy, it is important to note that Veronica earned her dues in the eyes of both her fellow journalists and the world, but only in death. Her legacy is now larger than ever. Because of her fearless investigation and untimely death, Ireland has completely reformed the way it deals with drug dealers and criminals. Because of her death in 1996, the Republic of Ireland altered its constitution to allow for the seizure of funds tied to criminal activities. The Criminal Assets Bureau was formed in the same year to seize the money and property of suspected criminals, and the gang that had Dublin police in a stranglehold for decades was finally destroyed. The state also set up a witness protection program that for the first time prevented intimidation by dangerous criminals. Since Veronica's murder, Dublin's crime rate has dropped 15 percent and the drug lords have all been forced out of the city.

Her compassion and tenacity also continue to capture the public's imagination. There have been two movies inspired by Veronica's life, *When the Sky Falls*, starring Joan Allen and directed by Jim Sheridan

(Veronica was the consultant on the movie before her death), and most recently *Veronica Guerin*, starring Cate Blanchett, which opened in 2003 to critical acclaim. In 2000, Taoiseach Bertie Ahern dedicated a memorial to her at Dublin Castle. Because of her tenacity, journalism in Ireland has taken on a new face. Reporters are no longer at the mercy of gangsters; the reverse is now true. Because of her hunger for the truth, she has inspired a whole new generation of journalists. Since her death ten years ago, more than 200 journalists worldwide have been killed in their pursuit of justice.

48. ROSEMARY NELSON

1959–1999

LAWYER

I believe that my role as a lawyer in defending the rights of my clients is vital. The test of a new society in Northern Ireland will be to the extent to which it can recognize and respect that role, and enable me to discharge it without improper interference. I look forward to that day.

—Rosemary Nelson

As one of the most internationally respected human rights lawyers in the world, Rosemary Nelson was raised in one of the most sectarian communities in Northern Ireland. But her commitment to justice rendered her blind to her clients' religious affiliations. She represented all members of her community—both Protestant and Catholic—and took on some of the most high-profile cases in Ireland. However, her dedication to legal equality led to her premature death. On March 15, 1999, Rosemary Nelson was killed when a bomb ripped through her car. She was sitting outside her daughter's school, and she was just forty years old.

Rosemary Magee Nelson was born in 1959 in Lurgan, County Armagh, Northern Ireland. During a childhood marked by the struggle for civil rights, she had undergone surgery to remove a birthmark that left one side of her face paralyzed, the skin unnaturally stretched, one eye pulled down. She spent the next twenty years of her life in and out of hospitals, undergoing painful skin grafts. The fifth daughter in a family of seven, she was always a cheerful, bright child, in spite of her disfigurement. Her academic success at Tannaghmore Primary School and later St. Michael's Grammar School helped her to gain acceptance to Queen's University in Belfast.

After graduating from Queen's in 1980, she worked in two law firms and then set up an advice and legal center dedicated to helping the disenfranchised, mainly senior citizens, women, and the homeless. She became the first woman to open a law practice in Lurgan in 1989, and soon began hiring other female lawyers. Because she was in the center of one of the more volatile areas in Northern Ireland, Rosemary soon began taking on some of the most controversial paramilitary cases in the country. She represented the Lurgan Republican Colin Duffy during the period when two sets of charges against him collapsed in circumstances that proved acutely embarrassing for the then Royal Ulster Constabulary (RUC). Rosemary was already well known in the Lurgan area, and when the Drumcree marching dispute began in neighboring Portadown, she was contacted by the Garvaghy Road residents spokesman Breandan Mac Cionnaith, who had grown up near her family in Lurgan. Rosemary also represented the family of Portadown Catholic Robert Hamill, who was killed in a brutal sectarian attack that echoed the racist murder of the black teenager Stephen Lawrence in London. While she was attaining national prominence with these cases, she always remained dedicated to the members of her community. Her clients were arrested under emergency laws and held in specially designed holding centers and were often interviewed without access to an attorney.

As one of a small number of lawyers brave enough to take up such sensitive cases, she was frequently the target of harassment, death threats, and intimidation. On a number of occasions, her life had been threatened by members of the RUC, primarily through her clients. In his 1998 report, Param Cumaraswamy, the UN Special Rapporteur on the Independence of Judges and Lawyers, paid special attention to these death threats and, in a televised interview, suggested that Rosemary's life could be in particular danger. Cumaraswamy's report made numerous specific recommendations to the United Kingdom government concerning police threats against lawyers—none of which, a year later, the government had implemented. At the time of Rosemary's death, Cumaraswamy was in the process of updating his report to reflect recent developments.

In September 1998, Rosemary was invited to testify before the U.S. Congress, at the House International Relations Committee's investigation into the human rights situation in Northern Ireland. In her testimony, she explained she had received "several death threats against myself and members of my family. I have also received threatening telephone calls and letters. Although I have tried to ignore these threats inevitably I have had to take account of the possible consequences for my family and for my staff."

On the tenth anniversary of her law practice, a bomb was placed under Rosemary's car. At approximately 12:40 P.M. on March 15, 1999, the bomb exploded as the forty-year-old mother of three braked in front of her daughter's school. The bomb tore her legs off and ripped through her abdomen. Sarah, her eight-year-old daughter, was on lunch break in her school yard, less than fifty yards away. Rosemary's sister, a teacher at the same school, spoke with Rosemary as firefighters tried to cut through the metal to save her. At 3:10 P.M., Rosemary was pronounced dead. She left behind three children, Gavin, Christopher, and Sarah, and a community without legal representation. In the aftermath of her murder, two controversies have arisen that have dominated the investigation of this killing. The first concerns allegations that members of the RUC had routinely intimidated and issued death threats against Rosemary. This in turn has fueled the second controversy. According to local people, the bombing took place against the backdrop of unprecedented security activity in the weeks and days leading up to the murder in the area surrounding the Nelson home. As a result, there is widespread suspicion of any inquiry carried out by the RUC, which in turn has led to demands for an independent investigation and inquiry.

49. MARY BROSNAHAN
SULLIVAN

B.1961
HOMELESS ADVOCATE, SOCIAL REFORMER

If compassion were an industry in New York, Ms. Brosnahan would be its chief executive officer.

—*New York Observer*

I think that when you look at the lives of Jesus or St. Francis or any of the people that have inspired so many by themselves finding a peacefulness, but knowing that homeless people need something to put over their heads every night—that's what draws me back.

—Mary Brosnahan Sullivan

The Giuliani plan is a return to the poorhouses of 100 years ago. Let's remember people used to chop wood and crack stone all day for shelter. That's what Giuliani is taking us back to.

—Mary Brosnahan Sullivan

During the mid- to late 1980s, when homelessness was epidemic in the United States, nowhere was it more painfully evident than on the streets of New York City. Because of President Ronald Reagan's social and economic policies and his decision to cut funds for mental health facilities, the mentally ill, disenfranchised, working homeless, and single mothers all lingered on the sidewalks of Manhattan, in search of shelter and food. Not only did these people lack even the most basic human necessities, they lacked a voice—an advocate who spoke for them when the government refused to listen. But in 1984, a young woman named Mary

Brosnahan moved to New York City and brought with her a sense of compassion and social justice that finally brought the problem of homelessness to the forefront—and finally convinced the policymakers that those without addresses and phone numbers were just as human as those privileged enough to have them. When she arrived twenty-two years ago, she was a pretty, petite young press advance worker for the Michael Dukakis presidential campaign who was living in the East Village. Just a few years later, she would become known as "the media's Madonna for the homeless," and the strong, fearless social advocate who took on Rudolph Giuliani, the city's iron-fisted mayor, and won.

Born in 1961 into a staunchly democratic, Irish Catholic family in Denver, Colorado, Mary was raised with a sense of "pervasive Irishness" early on, remembering her "Dan Barry-esque" childhood fondly. Her maternal grandparents moved from Andersontown, a famously nationalist section of Belfast, to Chicago, and her paternal grandparents hailed from Brosna, County Kerry. She explains, "We were almost all Irish except for one American Indian." Mary was instilled with a sense of social passion as early as she can remember, especially by her father, an outspoken "yellow dog Democrat." She recalls, "I remember when I was little, when the Vietnam War was raging, they had a casualty count every night on the evening news. I was five or six, and watching this and I said to my father, 'I just had to watch because I thought we were winning.' And he said 'No! This war is horrible. This is an unconstitutional war.' Similarly, her mother, who had been raised on Chicago's South Side, imparted to her daughter a strong sense of racial equality, telling her, "You've never seen racists like the ones I grew up with."

After moving with her family back to Chicago, and then onto Dearborn, Michigan, when she was eleven, Mary embarked on a life-changing adventure that forever altered the way she saw the world. At the age of sixteen, Mary traveled to visit an aunt in Belfast. She found herself transported from a sheltered environment to the war-torn streets of Belfast and saw oppression firsthand. After six weeks surrounded by British soldiers and checkpoints, she discovered that many of the Irish Catholics she saw there were unemployed and just as poor as the African Americans that her mother had grown up with on Chicago's South Side. "I discovered then that it wasn't about religion, it was about economic opportunity." This epiphany later paved the way for her work with people of all races, especially when she began working with the Coalition for the Homeless. "Irish immigrants when they came here were treated like dirt. And now you, when you look outside our reception office and you may not see the Kelly family or the O'Brien family, but you will see the Davis family and the Sanchez family. The struggle goes on, and that's why it's so important to remember the famine and what we came out of."

Impassioned by her trip to Belfast, Mary graduated magna cum laude from Notre Dame University in 1983 and moved to New York City. She immediately joined a number of political campaigns and in 1988 she embarked on a job that she calls "life affirming." She joined Governor Michael Dukakis's presidential campaign as a press aide and traveled the country, meeting constituents from all walks of life and socioeconomic backgrounds and had the opportunity to connect with the disenfranchised and reconnect with America. It was a position that also honed her media and public speaking skills—tools that became invaluable when she began the most important journey of both her professional and political life. After Dukakis's defeat, Mary returned to New York and to her $400-a-month apartment on the Lower East Side. Ironically, it was Mary's new home that served as the catalyst for her work with New Yorkers who found it impossible to find homes of their own. Every morning, when she left her apartment on Second Avenue between Fifth and Sixth Streets, she passed by Cooper Union: "There were dozens of guys living in this square. Some were pulling on their work boots and washing up in the fire hydrant, and some were completely encrusted in dirt and on the verge of becoming invisible and I thought 'This is out of control. This is completely out of control.'" Conflicted about the best way to stop the suffering she saw on her doorstep every morning, Mary sought counsel from her boyfriend at the time, who suggested that she join the Coalition for the Homeless, an organization that was dedicated to helping New York's forgotten indigent community. Since 1980, the coalition had been feeding and temporarily housing thousands of the city's forgotten. Mary joined in 1989, and six months later, she became its director. Two years after that, she became its executive director and put homelessness on both the city's and country's political agenda when she vehemently opposed Mayor Giuliani's new Dickensian approach to housing and human services.

When Rudolph Giuliani was running for office, New Yorkers were becoming increasingly weary of the city's burgeoning homeless population, and the new mayor was beginning to see homelessness as what Mary calls his "Willie Horton" issue—the one issue that could make or break his campaign. After his victory, he made it a priority to "get tough" on homelessness. Unfortunately, what that really meant was getting tough on the homeless themselves. His solution involved arresting, not housing, the homeless to get them off the streets. And it was at one of Giuliani's press conferences that Mary decided to get tough with the new mayor. She and other members of the coalition confronted him on his attempt to characterize the city's entire dispossessed population as a cadre of murderers and rapists. But when the mayor in turn tried to have Mary arrested, he was met with some formidable opposition. "The police who arrested me were all Irish!" she recalls. "And I think they talked the mayor out of it." It was "an affirming moment for me," she says. "I think that there's a moment in every person's life when you think this is it and whatever happens happens. And from that moment the gloves were on ice." The next day, supporters from Rosie O'Donnell to the *New York Times* agreed with the coalition's position on the homeless problem.

Undaunted by the mayor's rather excessive show of force and encouraged by the public outpouring of support (a poll revealed that more than 85 percent of New York City agreed with her), she continued to battle Giuliani daily on behalf of the homeless throughout the 1990s, particularly in 1999, when she challenged his new policy of demanding that every homeless person must work in exchange for shelter. This new announcement from the administration was in direct opposition to New York City's 1981 Callahan Consent Decree, which guarantees a shelter bed to every homeless person. Infuriated, Mary shot back, "Where's the logic here? We're going to round them up and bring them to a shelter, and if they refuse to work, they're going to be thrown back on the streets?" In 2001, Mary's personal life underwent a dramatic change when she met and married her soul mate, John Sullivan, the former deputy director of Pathways to Housing, an organization that helps the mentally ill find housing, and the current executive director of Friendship House, a group that helps homeless AIDS victims. They met when Mary was on Pathways' board of directors and the marriage has been a source of strength for both partners, particularly because they are both involved in the same kind of work. "It's incredibly supportive, because you both understand that homeless people can be very funny people and have great senses of humor and the miracles that can happen." The couple now has a new baby son, Quinn.

In the fifteen years that Mary has worked with the coalition, the organization has increased its budget from $1 million to $10 million and its staff from thirteen to seventy-two employees. The organization has served more than 2 million meals to the hungry and helps more than 3,000 people a day though rental programs, a summer camp for homeless children, and job training programs. In 2001, Mary was named one of Irish America's Top 100 Irish Americans and the following year she received the Thomas A. Dooley Award from Notre Dame University for her "outstanding service to humankind." Although she remains humble about her accomplishments, she is most proud of the group that she has been able to organize at the organization: "We have an amazing group of people that are here for people. I'm just happy we've been able to convey the simple truth about the homeless—that they long for the same sense of community as we all do."

Despite the reelection of a new mayor, Mary continues to fight just as hard for New Yorkers who can't fight for themselves. She continues to challenge Mayor Michael Bloomberg's policies concerning the city's poor and abandoned, which she calls, "More clever but every bit as challenging." She adds that just as recently as January 2004, "we had psychiatric patients and pregnant women sleeping on the streets in sub-zero temperatures. There were echoes of the famine here." She is also currently heading a $20 million campaign to renovate the coalition's building and to open a new job training program and a daycare. It is clear that her passion and persistence are just as fervent as when she took on Giuliani in the 1990s. Today, Mayor Giuliani has gone away, but the homeless have not. And as long as there are those who are in pain, in need, or in despair, they will have a tireless champion in Mary Brosnahan.

50. SINÉAD O'CONNOR

B.1966

SINGER, POLITICAL ACTIVIST

Don't let the bastards get you down.

> —Kris Kristofferson to Sinéad O'Connor
> at Bobfest

I'm not down.

> —Sinéad O'Connor to Kris Kristofferson

These are dangerous days / To say what you feel is to make your own grave.

> —From "Black Boys on Mopeds," lyrics
> by Sinéad O'Connor

In the fall of 1987, a twenty-two-year-old single mother from Dublin, Ireland, burst onto the U.S. music scene with such ferocity and splendor that she would forever change the way that the world saw female artists—particularly Irish female artists. From the beginning, Sinéad O'Connor was a mix of paradoxes: a classic beauty who sported a tattoo on her shaved head and wore clunky Doc Martens; a young feminist exploding with sexual energy who also extolled the virtues and joys of motherhood in her lyrics; a Catholic girl who defied the Church yet named her first album after a reference to Psalm 81 and quoted scripture in her songs; an Irish colleen who forever shattered the stereotype of the "Irish girl" singer; a vocalist with a range that went from angelic to banshee-like in a matter of a few notes; and a supremely gifted young woman troubled by demons that continue to affect her career. But no matter what the image is that she conveys, one thing is clear: this defiant, petite, and strong-willed woman will be remembered as one of the most seminal artists of the last twenty-five years—paving the way for the courageous young female singer-songwriters who come after her.

Sinéad Marie-Bernadette O'Connor was born in Glenageary, County Dublin, Ireland, on December 8, 1966, to John, a lawyer, and Mary O'Connor. One of four children, she later revealed that she suffered terrible abuse at the hands of her mother—a trauma that haunted her life and music. Her mother's depression and alcoholism shattered the O'Connor household and as the oldest child, Sinéad was at the receiving end of most of her mother's frustrations. Finally, her parents were divorced when Sinéad was eight, but the die had been cast, and her troubled childhood would never release its hold on her life. By all accounts, Sinéad seems to have been hit hardest by their traumatic childhood out of all her siblings. Her younger brother, Joe, became a renowned playwright and novelist in his own right and has remained remarkably silent about the domestic strife in the O'Connor household.

During her teen years, Sinéad began to act out, managing to be expelled from Catholic school and eventually getting arrested for shoplifting in 1981, all at the age of fifteen. She was shipped off to reform school later that year, and it began to seem as though Sinéad was headed down a hopeless path of self-destruction. Ironically, it would be only a year later before she was discovered singing at a wedding by Paul Byrne, the drummer for an Irish band called In Tua Nua and the man who would out her on a short path to stardom. After cowriting her first single "Take My Hand" with Paul, Sinéad left school to pursue her career and became a name on the Dublin music scene. She began studying voice at the Dublin College of Music and supplemented her income by working as a "Kiss-o-Gram Girl"—a singing telegram gig where she was able to show off both her wiles and vocal ability.

The next year she moved to London, was promptly signed on by Ensign Records, and was discovered by the Edge, the masterful guitarist for another Irish musical force, U2. The Edge was so impressed by her voice that he asked her to sing the lead song on his new project, the soundtrack to the movie *The Captive*. The evocative and passionate tune "Heroin" was the perfect platform for Sinéad's glorious sound. At once tender and wailing, her vocals are the highlight of the album and were a significant introduction to the talent that was to emerge just a few months later. But while Sinéad's career was on the rise, her personal life was being shaken to the hilt. Her fraught relationship with her mother came to an end in 1985, when she was killed in a car accident. Even though her mother was gone, the pain was not, and the opportunity for healing had been taken away from Sinéad. Two years later, at the tender age of twenty-one, Sinéad released her debut record with Ensign Records, a fierce and enigmatic masterpiece called *The Lion and the Cobra*. She dedicated it to her mother.

Destined to become the most lauded album of 1987, *The Lion and the Cobra* was an album she produced herself after being told that her original recordings sounded "too Celtic." The songs ranged from the defiant "Mandinka" (which reached #17 on the UK charts) with lyrics like "I don't know no shame / I feel no pain" to the downright sexy "I Want Your (Hands on Me)" (a track that would climb the college charts across the United States). Sinéad refused to compromise with record executives on the sound and vision of the record and she won. Suddenly, critics across the water had taken notice of this petite, woman-child singer and they loved what they heard. It was not the first time Sinéad would have to defy orders from the record company. During the recording of *The Lion and the Cobra*, Sinéad discovered that she was pregnant with her first child, Jake, by John Reynolds, her drummer. When record executives suggested that a baby would destroy her budding career, she knocked them between the eyes with a compelling argument: one of her contemporary male artists on the same record label was expecting a child with his girlfriend at the same time and no one asked him to give up his baby. The case was closed and by 1987 Sinéad had a newborn son and a hit record to celebrate.

During the late 1980s and through 1990, it seemed that nothing could harness Sinéad's rise, even though she continued to be an artist who refused to compromise and to keep her mouth shut. She performed at the Grammys in 1988 and received a nomination for Best Female Vocalist— she lost to another feminine tower of power, Tina Turner. In March 1990, she released *I Do Not Want What I Haven't Got*, the follow-up to *Lion*. It was this also-self-produced album that catapulted Sinéad from stardom to superstardom. With songs rife with themes like motherhood, particularly her own relationship with her mother in "I Am Stretched on Your Grave," miscarriage in "Three Babies," and racism in the poignant "Black Boys on Mopeds" in which she maintains "England's not the mythical land of Madame George and roses / It's the home of police who kill black boys on Mopeds," Sinéad proved once again that she was not just another pretty girl with a pretty voice. The first single "Nothing Compares 2 U" was her cover version of the Prince song and she made it entirely her own. Her spare, elegiac, and impassioned interpretation gave the lyrics a life of their own and the single shot to #1 in seventeen countries, including the United States. But it was the video that contributed to the singer's profile and image as an artist with which to be reckoned. Remarkable in its simplicity, the video for "Nothing Compares 2 U" features a pale, subtly made up Sinéad looking directly into the camera and singing, and by the end of the three-minute video, tears begin to role down her face. It remains one of the most stripped-down and most powerful music videos in rock history. Later that same year, Sinéad won three MTV video awards, including Best Video of the Year. It was also in 1990 that she made her first newsworthy decision when she refused to perform after "The Star Spangled Banner" was played at the Garden State Arts Center in New Jersey. After the incident, she received more press when Frank Sinatra famously and not so eloquently offered to "kick her ass"—a comment that Sinéad took in stride. She joked soon after that she was just flattered to have her name "running through his head."

By 1991, Sinéad had achieved bona fide mainstream status. *People* magazine chose her as one of its 50 Most Beautiful People in the World. She made regular appearances on the American television circuit and continued to speak her mind through it all. She won a Grammy for the album *I Do Not Want What I Haven't Got* and refused to accept it—an unprecedented act in the music world. When she was scheduled to appear as the musical guest on *Saturday Night Live* (*SNL*) and discovered that the guest host was the female-bashing comedian Andrew Dice Clay, she joined the *SNL* cast member Nora Dunn in refusing to perform in protest of his material. The next year she released *Am I Not Your Girl*, the accomplished collection of pop and jazz American standards like "Black Coffee," "Success Has Made a Failure of Our Home," and a gorgeous version of the Irish traditional classic "Scarlet Ribbons." While the material might have seemed strange to some of Sinéad's young audience, it cemented her reputation as one of the most powerful and unique female vocalists of her time. Now, it seemed that there was no stopping Sinéad— until one fateful night in October 1992.

After her aborted scheduled appearance on *SNL* the year before, Sinéad finally appeared as the musical guest on October 3, 1992. After performing a stark a capella version of Bob Marley's "War," Sinéad made the move that would come to define—and eventually threaten to destroy—her career. She stared directly into the camera, declaring "fight the true evil." She then produced a picture of Pope John II and tore it in half. The audience went silent, and NBC's switchboard rang off the hook with over a thousand irate phone calls. The next day, that image was plastered on the front pages of newspapers across the country, and Catholic leaders defiled her. Sinéad was left reeling and it seemed that there was no escaping the ire of the American audience. Soon afterward, she explained her intentions: she had torn up the picture as a statement against child abuse, particularly against what she believed was the proliferation of child abuse by the Catholic Church. Because the pope was the leader of the church, she held him responsible for much of this abuse. She had a valid argument, but it was one that fell on deaf ears. Ironically, a decade later the Catholic Church was plagued by scandal and charged with many of the abuses that Sinéad tried to bring to the forefront. However, it was not what she said but how she said it that sparked such an incendiary reaction.

Two weeks later, on October 16, Sinéad was scheduled to perform at Bobfest, a star-studded tribute to the legend Bob Dylan on his fiftieth birthday to be held at New York's Madison Square Garden. One would have believed that the politically aware and socially progressive Dylan fans would have shown Sinéad some sympathy, but nothing could have been further from the truth. After performances by Stevie Wonder and John Cougar Mellencamp, Lou Reed, Johnny Cash, and June Carter Cash, Sinéad took the stage. Immediately, the Garden erupted into an angry roar that continued even after she began the first bars of her song. She had planned to sing the Dylan classic "I Believe in You" but stopped the band and launched into a scathing version of Marley's "War," the song she sang only two weeks before on *SNL*. She finished and walked off stage—her life and career irrevocably altered.

Over the next decade, Sinéad tried to regain her footing, both personally and professionally. In 1994, she released the critically acclaimed CD *Universal Mother*, but it never garnered the commercial success of her previous albums. She soon announced that she would no longer speak to the press and focused on her family. In 1997, she gave birth to her daughter, Roisin, a child she had with the journalist John Waters, with whom she would later become embroiled in a bitter custody battle. That same year, she made an inspired appearance as an edgy Virgin Mary in Neil Jordan's acclaimed movie *The Butcher Boy*, in which she utters the film's most memorable line, "Ah, for fuck's sake, Francie." But through it all, she continued to make impassioned music. In 1997, she released the EP *Gospel Oak*, which was so well reviewed that it seemed to help her overcome some of the bad press she received more than five years before. In 2000, she released *Faith and Courage*, her first-full length album in six years. Two years later, she unveiled the produced *Sean-Nos Nua*, a CD of captivating Celtic-inspired tracks that she wrote and performed with celebrated Irish musicians Donal Lunny and Christy Moore. Also by this time, she seemed to have found domestic peace. She married Nick Sommerlad, a British journalist, in August 2001. Yet, despite the accomplished music and her relatively serene new life, Sinéad never seemed fully able to overcome her own image—reports of her becoming a Tridentine priest and announcing her homosexuality have colored the public's perception of this influential artist and have continued to garner most of the press coverage. Frustrated by her inability to move her music, not her antics, to the forefront, Sinéad announced her retirement from the music business in April 2003. In 2004, she and her husband welcomed a new son, Shane. Although she seems to have found personal fulfillment, she continues to battle the press, and in 2004 she took out an ad in the *Irish Examiner* declaring, "I have been the whipping post of Ireland's media for

20 years. And what have I done to deserve these lashings? I have not behaved the way a woman is supposed to behave."

Today, many people will remember Sinéad's controversial stands and erratic behavior, but in the end her legacy will be so much more. Despite all the drama, she is ranked a phenomenal #35 on VH1's 100 Greatest Women of Rock 'n' Roll. Before Sinéad came into the music world, Mary Black and Delores Keane represented the gold standard for the Irish female singer, women with pure voices who sang beautiful but innocuous songs with little or no mention of social issues or controversial subjects. Sinéad helped to knock this stereotype on its ear. Her glorious voice, strength of character, defiant beauty, and fervent lyrics forever changed the role of women in music, particularly in rock, and paved the way for talented and take-no-prisoner performers such as Courtney Love, Liz Phair, Alanis Morrissette, Fiona Apple, Delores O'Riordan, Lauryn Hill (another single twenty-two-year old mother who took the music world by storm with her own dazzling beauty and fierce lyrics), and P. J. Harvey. Without Sinéad, there most likely would never have been a Lilith Fair, and there most certainly never would have been a "Chicks with Attitude" tour. Today, it is women who rock the world and dominate the *Billboard* charts, and they have Sinéad O'Connor to thank for it.

Bibliography

Books

Anderson, Christopher. *Sweet Caroline: Last Child of Camelot.* New York: HarperCollins, 2003.

Bradford, Sarah. *America's Queen: The Life of Jacqueline Kennedy Onassis.* New York: Viking, 2000.

Cardozo, Nancy. *Maud Gonne.* New York: New Amsterdam Press, 1989.

Cash, Jean. *Flannery O'Connor: A Life.* Knoxville: University of Tennessee Press, 2002.

Chilton, John. *Billie's Blues.* New York: Stein and Day, 1975.

Clarke, Donald. *Wishing on the Moon: The Life and Times of Billie Holiday.* New York: Viking Press, 1994.

Coles, Robert. *Dorothy Day: A Radical Devotion.* Reading, MA: Addison-Wesley, 1987.

De Blacam, Hugh. *The Saints of Ireland.* Milwaukee: Bruce, 1942.

Devlin, Bernadette. *The Price of My Soul.* New York: Alfred A. Knopf, 1969.

Douglas, Emily Taft. *Margaret Sanger: Pioneer of the Future.* New York: Holt, Rinehart and Winston, 1970.

Eisenhower, Julie Nixon. *Pat Nixon: The Untold Story.* New York: Simon and Schuster, 1986.

Ellman, Richard. *Selected Letters of James Joyce.* New York: Viking, 1957.

Gelderm, Carol. *Mary McCarthy: A Life.* New York: St. Martin's Press, 1988.

Gonne, Maud MacBride. *A Servant of the Queen: The Autobiography of Maud Gonne*. Chicago: University of Chicago Press, 1938.

Goodwin, Doris Kearns. *The Fitzgeralds and the Kennedys*. New York: Simon and Schuster, 1987.

Hayes, Helen, and Dody Sandford. *On Reflection: An Autobiography*. New York: M. Evans, 1968.

Huber, Peter. *Sandra Day O'Connor*. New York: Chelsea House, 1990.

Jacobs, Diane. *Her Own Woman: The Life of Mary Wollstonecraft*. New York: Citadel, 2003.

Keogh, Daire, and Nicholas Furlong. *The Women of 1798*. Dublin, Ireland: Four Courts Press, 1998.

Kliment, Bud. *Billie Holiday*. New York: Chelsea House, 1990.

Maddox, Brenda. *Nora: A Biography of Nora Joyce*. New York: Fawcett Columbine, 1988.

Marlow, Joyce. *The Uncrowned Queen of Ireland: The Life of Kitty O'Shea*. New York: E. P. Dutton, 1975.

Marreco, Anne. *The Rebel Countess: The Life and Times of Countess Markiewicz*. London: Phoenix Press, 1967.

McAleese, Mary. *Love in Chaos: Spiritual Growth and the Search for Peace in Northern Ireland*. New York: Continuum, 1997.

McCafferty, Nell. *Nell*. Dublin: Penguin Ireland, 2004.

McCallum, John. *That Kelly Family*. New York: A. S. Barnes, 1957.

McCarthy, Mary. *How I Grew*. New York: Harcourt Brace Jovanovich, 1987.

———. *Memories of a Catholic School Girl*. New York: Harcourt Brace Jovanovich, 1957.

McCoole, Sinead. *Guns and Chiffon: Women Revolutionaries and Kilmainham Jail, 1916–1923*. Dublin: Duchas (Government of Ireland), 1997.

McCourt, John. *The Years of Bloom: James Joyce in Trieste, 1904–1920*. Dublin: Lilliput Press, 2000.

Norman, Diane. *Terrible Beauty: A Life of Constance Markiewicz*. London: Hodder and Staughton, 1987.

O'Brien, Edna. *The Country Girls Trilogy*. New York: Plume, 1960.

O'Hara, Maureen, and John Nicoletti. *'Tis Herself: A Memoir*. New York: Simon and Schuster, 2004.

O'Shea, Katharine. *Charles Stewart Parnell: His Love Story and Political Life*. London: Cassell, 1914.

Pyron, Darden Asbury. *Southern Daughter: The Life of Margaret Mitchell*. New York: Oxford Press, 1991.

Steel, Edward M. *The Speeches and Writings of Mother Jones*. Pittsburgh: University of Pittsburgh Press, 1998.

Torn, Elliot J. *Mother Jones*. New York: Hill and Wang, 2001.

Ward, Margaret. *Maud Gonne: Ireland's Joan of Arc*. London: Pandora Press, 1990.

———. *Unmanageable Revolutionaries: Women and Irish Nationalism*. London: Pluto Press, 1989.

Wellman, Judith. *The Road to Seneca Falls: Elizabeth Cady Stanton and the First Women's Rights Convention*. Chicago: University of Illinois Press, 2004.

Williams, Paul. *Evil Empire: The Irish Mob and the Assassination of Journalist Veronica Guerin*. New York: Forge, 2003.

Videos

Daughters of the Troubles, Marcia Rock, New York, NY, 1996. Derry Video Productions

Mother Ireland, Anne Crilly, 1988. Derry, Ireland, Derry Film and Video.

Index

About the Author

Gina Sigillito has studied Celtic mythology, art, philosophy, and Christianity since 1990 at a variety of schools, including the Irish Arts Center, Ireland House at New York University, and Trinity College, Dublin. She attended Columbia University and Fordham University in New York City and holds a Bachelor of Arts in English and Journalism. She has lectured in New York City on women in Irish history at a number of venues including New York's City Hall, Fordham University, the Irish Arts Center, and Hunter College, and has traveled extensively throughout Ireland. She is the coeditor with Patricia King and Sile Deady of *The Wisdom of the Celts*. She currently works for a major publisher in New York City and is a member of the Authors Guild.